Managing Complexity in the Public Services

Complexity theory has grown in importance over the last decade and its development has enabled a universal method of practice which proposes a pragmatic and humanistic management practice.

The application of complexity theory highlights the importance of the development of an organization's culture and communication, it enables them to be dynamic whilst maintaining coherence and stability. It places the workers, their values and mission at the heart of the organization's practices, recognizing that information technology may provide a framework for complex communication and knowledge use but cannot replace highly developed professional negotiations and cooperation.

This new edition of *Managing Complexity in the Public Services* argues that the complexity of the public service world limits the usefulness of classical and rational scientific management approaches like the new public managerialism (NPM). As a result overly rigid approaches to performance management and strategic management can be highly dysfunctional in the public context.

Managing Complexity in the Public Services takes further the articulation of a method of management practice that can cope with the stark realities of the complex and unpredictable public policy world. It includes a number of management practices developed in action research that will be of great use to both academics and practitioners and helps detail how complexity theory can be applied in practice. The result is a new value based practice for the post crisis public service world.

Philip Haynes is Professor of Public Policy and Head of the School of Applied Social Science at the University of Brighton, UK. He is the author of *Public Policy Beyond the Financial Crisis: An International Comparative Study* (Routledge, 2012) and has published extensively in journals such as *Public Management Review*, *International Journal of Public Administration* and *Social Policy and Administration*.

Managing Complexity in the Public Services

Second edition

Philip Haynes

Routledge
Taylor & Francis Group

LONDON AND NEW YORK

Second edition published 2015
by Routledge
2 Park Square, Milton Park, Abingdon, Oxon OX14 4RN

and by Routledge
711 Third Avenue, New York, NY 10017

Routledge is an imprint of the Taylor & Francis Group, an informa business

British Library Cataloguing in Publication Data
A catalogue record for this book is available from the British Library

Library of Congress Cataloging in Publication Data
Haynes, Philip.
  Managing complexity in the public services / Philip Haynes. – Second Edition.
    pages cm
  Summary: "Complexity theory has grown in importance over the last decade and its development has enabled a universal method of practice which proposes a pragmatic and humanistic management practice. The application of complexity theory highlights the importance of the development of an organizations culture and communication, it enables them to be dynamic whilst maintaining coherence and stability. It places the workers, their values and mission at the heart of the organizations practices, recognising that information technology may provide a framework for complex communication and knowledge use but cannot replace highly developed professional negotiations and cooperation. This new edition of Managing Complexity in the Public Services argues that the complexity of the public service world limits the usefulness of classical and rational scientific management approaches like the New Public Managerialism (NPM). As a result overly rigid approaches to performance management and strategic management can be highly dysfunctional in the public context. Managing Complexity in the Public Services takes further the articulation of a method of management practice that can cope with the stark realities of the complex and unpredictable public policy world. It develops a number of management practices developed in action research that will be of high use to both academics and practitioners and helps detail how complexity theory can be applied in practice The result is a new value based practice for the post crisis public service world"– Provided by publisher.
  Includes bibliographical references and index.
  1. Public administration. 2. Complexity (Philosophy) I. Title.
  JF1351.H396 2015
  351–dc23
            2014031765

ISBN: 978-0-415-73925-2 (hbk)
ISBN: 978-0-415-73926-9 (pbk)
ISBN: 978-1-315-81677-7 (ebk)

Typeset in Bembo
by Taylor & Francis Books

Printed and bound in Great Britain by
TJ International Ltd, Padstow, Cornwall

Contents

List of illustrations

Figures

Tables

Box

Acknowledgements

Many public service practitioners both managers and professionals have contributed to the theory and practice in this book. This influence has come via collaboration with practitioners both inside and outside the Higher Education environment, including multi-agency collaborations, consultancy and courses delivered at the University of Brighton.

In particular, I would like to thank the staff and students of the Masters in Public Administration (MPA) at the University, and the course leader, Mary Darking.

My time spent as a manager at the University of Brighton has been immensely rewarding and challenging. I would like to thank those who have served on the School management team with me and provided valuable support while sharing management responsibility for The School of Applied Social Science: Dawn Stephen, Julia Stroud, Mark Bhatti, Katherine Johnson, Flis Henwood, Helen Basterra, Rebecca Farmer, Peter Squires, Mark Erickson, David Bott, Marian Barnes, Susannah Davidson, Rebecca Mitchell and Sally Jones. My thanks also for the management support and development provided by David Taylor and Stuart Laing. The University of Brighton Community University Partnership Programme (CUPP) is a highly innovative project and I have benefited much from contributions and ideas from its leader Dave Wolff, and from his other staff, and the numerous community based partners they collaborate with, especially Paul Bramwell.

Many organizations and networks have influenced me. My thanks in particular to colleagues at: The International Research Society for Public Management (IRSPM), the International Conference on Public Policy, the Social Policy Association (SPA), Brighton and Hove Council, East Sussex County Council, The Public Governance Institute at University of Leuven, The Department of Public Administration at the Erasmus University of Rotterdam, the University of York online public policy and management program, and The Department of Social Policy and Social Work at Chi Nan University, Puli, Taiwan.

My thanks to all academic and practitioner members of the UK ESRC project entitled *Systems and Complex Systems Approaches in Public Policy and Practice: A Knowledge Exchange between Academics and Practitioners* (RES-192-22-0083) especially my colleagues, Jim Price, Chris Warren Adams and John Patience of the Nehemiah project, London. I also learnt much from the research of Carla Ricaurte Quijano, now at FIMCBOR, Escuela Superior Politécnica del Litoral. The ESRC provided funding for this Knowledge Exchange.

In the last year it has also been good to take part in the UK ESRC network entitled Complexity and Method in the Social Sciences: An Interdisciplinary Approach, led by Emma Uprichard, David Byrne and Brian Castellani. My thanks to them for their leadership and organization.

Many individual academics have influenced my evolving work in the last decade. A few theorists and authors have had a particular impact on ideas: David Byrne, Michael Hill, Christopher Pollitt, Robert Geyer, Paul Cairney, and the late Donella Meadows.

My thanks to the editorial staff at Routledge for their support of this second edition, especially to David Varley. When the structure and shape of this new edition was first discussed, David provided the necessary balance of enthusiasm and critical reflection.

Finally, my thanks to my family for their encouragement and support, especially to my wife Jane and son Jonathan for their advice and insights into the public and non-government sectors and their resulting influences on my own writings and editing. Jane has provided a lot of support with the final preparations of this manuscript. My daughters Mary and Lizzie have reminded me exactly what it is like to be an undergraduate student trying to learn from academic scholars.

Abbreviations

APS	Australian Public Service
CAS	Complex Adaptive System
DES	Department of Education and Skills (UK)
EI	Emotional Intelligence
ESRC	Economic and Social Research Council (UK)
GIS	Geographical Information Systems
HRM	Human Resource Management
IMF	International Monetary Fund
IT	Information Technology
MBO	Management by Objectives
NAO	National Audit Office (UK)
NGO	Non-Governmental Organization
NPM	New Public Management
OECD	Organisation of Economic Co-operation and Development
OGC	Office of Government Commerce (UK)
PAR	Programme Analysis and Review
PFI	Private Finance Initiatives
PPBS	Planning, Programming, and Budgeting System (USA)
PPP	Public Private Partnerships
PRA	Participatory Rural Appraisal
PSBR	Public Sector Borrowing Requirement
QE	Quantitative Easing
VBM	Values Based Management

Introduction

Since the writing of the first edition that was published in 2003 much has happened both in the application of complexity theory to applied social science and in the developing deconstruction and criticism of New Public Management practice.

Complexity theory is no longer an eccentric theoretical approach when taken outside of the natural sciences and is beginning to become a mainstream theoretical approach in the social sciences. This theoretical progress and journey is neatly evaluated and summarized in Byrne and Callaghan's (2013) seminal text that reviews the "state of the art" in complexity theory and its application. They rightly note the growth in the last ten years of text and citations about complexity and the social sciences.

One key influence on the writing of this second edition was the 2011 UK ESRC funded *Knowledge Exchange: Systems and Complex Systems; Policy and Practice*. This project brought together academics and practitioners to explore the application of complexity theory to public policy and practice. Indeed, trying to ascertain the most logical and practical way to apply theory to practice has remained at the core of my own work. Donella Meadows (2009) and Snowden and Boone's (2007) writing had key influences on what was achieved in the ESRC project with a resulting management toolkit published and made available via open access. What follows in this book is an attempt to revisit the earlier text of the first edition, but also to fully revise and edit in the light of the learning from the ESRC project and its implementation.

Inevitably, my personal journey with complexity theory has been entangled with how my own management practice has developed. Since the writing of the first edition, my own career has progressed from Principal Lecturer, to Deputy Head of School and then in 2007 I became Head of a Social Science University School. Alongside giving me increased management responsibilities, my University very much continued to encourage me as a researcher, promoting me to a Reader in 2005 and then to a full Professorship in 2008. I experienced for myself the storms and tides of public management, in a political context of increased privatization and marketization in UK higher education. The University School I manage includes the subject domains of Sociology, Politics, Public Policy, Social Policy, Criminology, Psychology, Social Work, Psychotherapy and Counselling, Social Work and Substance Misuse Interventions. Over 80 staff are employed in this activity and in a typical year, we would expect to have about 1,200 students enrolled. The creativity and industriousness of professional and support staff never ceases to inspire me, in particular given the difficult political and social context. Against all the odds, research and scholarship has increased in quality and outputs. We have a culture that encourages the holistic integration of research and teaching and this leads to much theoretical research being applied in the real world.

Management in public environments is challenging because of its unpredictability. Senior managers and leaders, including politicians, often communicate clear and concise directions based on relatively simple logics that they believe explain cause and effect. In the case of politicians, these simplistic assumptions are explicitly founded on a value-based ideology.

Take the example of austerity policies since the financial crisis. The ideological value base is that individuals should exist, wherever possible, without an interfering state because embedded in human nature is a tendency to avoid personal responsibility that will have a collective effect of increasing the size of the state. The economic result, the advocates of austerity argue, is a bankrupt economy where the state always spends more supporting those who are dependent on a subsidy than it can collect from the taxes of the hard working and responsible. Such a simple ideology is a denial of so much more. For example, the importance of sovereign money, the ownership of the monetary system by sovereign and state, and government's strong ability to intervene in the interaction of a money economy and with so many aspects of human economic behavior. Despite the financial crisis, most governments and their public policy have continued in recent years to underwrite the values of the market and a money system that feeds consumerism and wealth inequalities, often at the expense of other public values and collective possibilities. Public Service Management has evolved in this political climate.

We have seen in countries like the UK, USA, Spain and Greece, some managed withdrawal of activities from the public sphere. Managers have to focus on prioritizing the most essential services and finding some local criteria under guidance from politicians to justify the rationalism of priorities. Over-provision and inefficient provision are frequently said to be the cause of any managerial problem. Complexity theory demonstrates that such simplistic theories of the public sphere do not work. Managers experience contradictions, tensions and failures in implementing these simplistic ideas of cause and effect. A much more powerful alternative is that the complexity of human systems lends itself to the potential for great and extraordinary collective endeavors and that politicians and managers have the possibilities to improve the human experience and to look for ways of adding value to public and collective activities and how they are experienced.

A reason for dissonance in the post-crisis austerity management practice is the entanglement of physical, psychological and social variables. To use a theoretical analysis from the social sciences: this is the indeterminate dynamic of agency and structure. In short, if we impose a structural and hierarchical solution from above onto communities and individuals, it will never work in exactly the way we intended. The interaction of the community and individuals with the structural solution imposed creates a highly dynamic, not static process, and this has "many" potential outcomes rather than a few. One possibility is outright rejection of what the policy dictates. Another is passive acceptance of it. These are the most unlikely outcomes. Much more likely is that the communities and individuals interact with the policy to modify its impact and to try to ensure their survival, to maximize their benefits, and to give themselves a more advantageous future within the new policy environment.

Many organizations involved in public services deal with highly complex operating environments. The relationship between activities and outputs defies simple causation. For example, a drug intervention does not have a constant positive effect on all the patients to whom it is prescribed. Add in measures of the longer term outcomes that come after immediate outputs, and the ability to understand cause and effect becomes even more difficult to isolate. If a drug is immediately successful in suppressing pain and symptoms, can it be shown to provide the outcome of a cure in an underlying condition over the longer term? It is argued that complex systems are better understood as highly entangled interactions of physical, psychological, and social variables. As a result, understanding patterns of interactions across these systems becomes a better method for management intervention than trying to understand something by reducing it to a simple hypothesis of x causes y. Observing patterns can help avoid inappropriate simplifications. Managers need good holistic understandings of the systems they work in. They cannot reach such understanding using quantitative indicators alone, but also need the qualitative insights of others involved in the system, in particular the perceptions of professional staff and service users. Such a holistic approach was popular with the readers and practitioners who used and applied the first edition of this book and I am grateful for all the feedback and ideas they have provided since. Each has helped contribute to the reshaping of this second edition. A key aim of this edition has been to internationalize the material much more, with far less emphasis on the peculiarities of the UK context. Where UK case examples are still used these are in the context of applying concepts, practices and criticisms that are generalizable across the globe.

In addition to a complete updating of each chapter, this second edition has reordered the topics in some of the chapters.

Chapter 1 revisits post "new public managerialism" and concludes that, given the complex operating environment, managers need more than ever a clear statement of public values and a strong sense of how to work with professionals and other staff on achieving those values.

Chapter 2 substantially updates the background theoretical material on complexity science and its resulting application in applied social science and public service management practice. Two notable additions are the sections on networks and anti-fragility. Each of the subsequent chapters then illuminates further the implications of complexity for specific areas of practice: strategy, performance, information and managing people.

Chapter 3 considers the dominant practice of strategic management in public services and deconstructs the strategic discourse of trying to argue for a fixed path into the future. It therefore focuses on understanding that there are potentially multiple futures and strategic interventions that can partially determine which future really happens. Public strategies should be dynamic and interactive forms of communication that require that strategies are always evolving and being reconstituted as the external environment changes and the internal organization has to similarly adapt to understand external dynamics and act appropriately.

In Chapter 4, the focus is on the continuing practice of performance management and use of performance targets, a practice that has returned in many countries with a renewed and sim-plistic vigor because of the politics of austerity. The severe limitations of a traditional managerial approach to performance are criticised and an alternative approach to assessing systems performance is discussed. The aim is to make better judgments about how to intervene in systems by improving interactions that add value, rather than depending on isolated performance indicators in dislocated parts of the system.

Complexity theory implies that human communication (as the primary forum of system interaction) is at the core of understanding and managing a complex public service system. For this reason, Chapter 5 focuses on information management and the ongoing dilemmas of the best use of digital technology in practice. It also addresses the relationship of information technology with knowledge management. Technology needs to enhance the creative adaptability of human communication rather than dictate to it.

Finally, Chapter 6 examines the most important of all public service management issues, managing people. Given that the people engaged in public services are required to operate in challenging, changing and complex systems, this chapter gets to the core of how best to involve employees. It explores how to maintain motivation, improve decision-making and communication, and manage the constant ebb and flow of stability and instability that all organizations face by using methods of "change management". It ends by proposing a new values centred approach that does not assume that market values must be placed above all others.

I hope that you enjoy the second edition of this book and that it helps to move further forward the aspiration to apply complexity theory to the difficult task of managing and improving public services.

Philip Haynes
Brighton, UK
Twitter @profpdh

1 Management, professions and the public service context

Introduction

This first chapter examines the definition of management and how managerialism became increasingly used in the public sector in the last 40 years. Managerial approaches superseded more passive administrative practices. The relevance of a model of general management to the public service environment is explored in the context of the changing political and economic climate of the early twenty-first century. This leads to an evaluation of the term new public management (NPM) and some of the key literature that has been written about this phenomenon. It is argued that the general management model now used in public services and developed from imported ideas in business and the private sector is of limited relevance to the public services of the twenty-first century. A key aspect of this argument is the need to understand better the major tensions in public service work, such as the contradictions between professional and managerial agendas and the differing strengths and weaknesses of public, private and non-governmental provision. The chapter finishes by proposing an alternative approach to public service management that is able to embrace the complexity of the social and public world and appreciates both the similarities and differences between the public, private and non-governmental sectors. This alternative approach to public management puts public values and public service at the core of its practice and attempts to understand the complexity of modern societies and how best to intervene in the public interest.

What is management?

Classical definitions of general management can be divided between those that put the emphasis on the role of the individual as a manager (and the general part that the manager plays in the coordination of an organization) as contrasted with those definitions that focus on work outputs, and the related activities and tasks that managers perform to achieve these outputs. There is considerable overlap between these two approaches. In the past it has been argued that the public sector was more role focused and the private sector more task focused (Handy 1990), but this has changed in recent decades, given the arrival of a business management culture in public services. Concurrent with these changes in the public services, the business sector has evolved so that it has become more involved in human services and the creation of knowledge and ideas, rather than focusing primarily on manufacturing production. This makes the output task focus of business less clear at a time when public services are increasingly being asked to focus on outputs.

Henry Mintzberg (1973), one of the best known management writers, proposed in his book *The Nature of Managerial Work* that the management role comprised of three main areas of work: interpersonal skills, information processing and decision-making. Mintzberg suggested that managers need good interpersonal skills because other workers look up to them as figures of authority. They need to be good leaders, but also diplomatic. Diplomacy is important when liaising across the various departments and divisions of a large organization, or between horizontal networks of collaborating organizations, because in such situations managers cannot assume authority and respect. Such diplomacy requires personal integrity, good negotiation skills and characteristics of patience and tolerance.

Managers also need to be able to process information, to monitor qualitative and quantitative data, to disseminate important points to others and to act as a spokesperson or advocate of key information. This implies the need to be a presenter, teacher and researcher in some situations. It also requires the ability to be confident with financial data and budgets.

Finally, and perhaps most important of all, Mintzberg recognized that managers must make decisions. These decisions can be in different contexts: to resolve and handle conflict, to innovate and move forward in new directions, to allocate limited resources where they will be most effective, and to progress further negotiations with other parties.

The practice of management therefore requires a wide scope of aptitudes and the judgment of knowing what skills and actions to prioritize in a given context and situation. This indicates a blend of skills being applied with confidence and sensitivity. It requires a multi-tasked approach and someone with a range of abilities, rather than one specialist proficiency. The personal confidence and human skills of the manager are of the uttermost importance. They must supervise and communicate with a diverse range of individuals in order to match staff needs and aspirations with the survival, performance and improvement of the organization. The focus on the collective aspirations of the host organization is vital because the manager is not a psychotherapist or counsellor who can put the needs of an individual employee uniquely above the combined needs of the public service organization and those who require its services.

Mintzberg's classic study places emphasis on the role of the manager and the personal qualities and skills that the person has to enable them to perform the role. Although this approach has received recognition in public services, the dominant narrative of public service management in the last 40 years has focused on the management task, that is, what public managers need to do, rather than the personal qualities needed to do the work. However, increasing interest in the role of leadership in public services, rather than a dominant focus on management activities, has been one attempt to redress that imbalance towards the interpersonal and relational approach.

The task-based approach is illustrated by a large American study carried out by Luthans, Hodgetts and Rosenkrantz (1988). The research examined what tasks managers undertook and how much time they spent on key activities. They found the key tasks being performed included: managing information, paper based record keeping, planning, decision taking, controlling work processes, communicating with external contacts, networking and engaging in organizational politics, motivating and encouraging, disciplining and sanctioning, recruitment and training. It is immediately clear that some of these tasks are dependent upon personal skills and the personal resourcefulness of the individual. It is also apparent that managers undertake a wide range of tasks, whereas the Mintzberg study put the emphasis on the wide range of roles.

Luthans *et al.* went on to examine and judge how effective managers were at getting tasks done. They found that those who were effective at resolving tasks were not always the ones to be promoted. It was argued that the managers who were promoted to senior positions were more likely to be the individuals, who put networking and organizational politics high on their personal agenda, and this made them well known in the organization and they knew what the key political and personal agendas were. This implied that how the individual adapted and evolved to the personal role of being a manager was more important to their career development than being too focused on individual tasks and getting things done.

The task-based approach has led to a desire to define core management competencies. These are judged on evidence recorded in practice. Examples are: an ability to present financial figures, and the ability to chair a meeting and facilitate time-managed discussion and decision taking. There is clearly an overlap between task and role. The correct understanding of the role of being a meeting chair is a vital component in securing effective and clear decisions at meetings. There is some concern that the competency-based approach to management has produced "identikit managers", who are inflexible in difficult and unusual situations. A more personalized and individualistic ability to be creative and flexible in the face of changing situations is needed. Whiddet and Kandola (2000: 30), two organizational psychologists, conclude: "recruitment and performance management processes that rely purely on competencies are flawed."

Management is about role and task, about competencies and skills. It is also about creative individual judgment. Public service managers are people who have to take a lead and coordinate in complex environments. They will find strong similarities in the daily situations that they face, but no two situations will be identical and each challenge should be approached with a combination of prior knowledge, experience, sensitivity and individual creativity.

Management practice and public services

In the 1970s, governments in developed countries like the USA, Australia and UK began to attempt to introduce some business thinking into the public sector. This was driven by a concern that the federal, state, central and local governments were too concerned with the administrative detail of their organization and their public role, rather than a task focus of getting things done and service outputs provided. Programme Analysis and Review (PAR) was one such method applied in government (Campbell 1993: 315). Attempts to use such rationalistic tools found resistance in government administrative organizations which were not always supportive, and ideas like PAR failed to make a clear impact.

For the remainder of the twentieth century there were attempts to get public services to focus more on the tasks and outputs achieved, rather than on the complexities of administrative process, and public service ethos. Politicians, practitioners and academics looked to the private sector for ideas about what methods could be used to achieve a change of direction and a more task orientated approach. This agenda is still alive in the new millennium following the financial crisis of 2007–08 and the popularity with governments of so-called "austerity" policies. These policies apply large-scale cuts to government expenditure and assert that government debt was a major element of the crisis. They are accompanied by a narrative that public sector organizations are somehow uniformly more inefficient and ineffective than private businesses and therefore that public services still have much to learn from the business and market environment.

Many writers and academics have challenged this assessment of the causes and consequences of the international financial crisis (Haynes 2012). It is true that the majority of OECD (Organisation for Economic Co-operation and Development) nations saw their government debt levels increase after the crisis occurred, but household debt and corporate debt levels are also high in many OECD countries and these should be more of an economic and social concern than government debt. Therefore, the financial crisis was caused by the relaxation of credit, and lack of regulation of credit, the misappropriation of credit, and resulting severe debts across many sectors. This implies the solution is not the demise of government expenditure and debt in isolation from other parts of the economy, but rather a fundamental re-evaluation of international banking and finance, credit lending and debt management (Ryan-Collins *et al.* 2012). Similarly, this book questions the assumption that private business is uniformly better managed than public organizations. The two sectors are diverse, increasingly overlap, and the reality is that there are examples of badly managed organizations in both sectors. Likewise, the book questions whether the management of production in the private sector is similar to activities of coordination and leadership in the public sphere (Osborne *et al.* 2014).

Is management different in the public sector?

One study (Conway 1993) sought to understand the relevance of the general management model described by Mintzberg and Luthans to the modern public service environment. This found that local government social services managers in the UK were different. They spent a higher proportion of their time handling paper work and communicating information to their staff. Very little time was spent making key decisions or planning for future activities. A large amount of time was spent supervising pressurized professional staff, with front line decisions being made, after consultation, by those specialist staff. There was less of a focus on task-based activities, and more of a need to undertake a professional support role, so that professionals were positively engaged in their difficult and complex working environment. This type of study suggests that the attempt to make the public sector and its services more task focused is far from straightforward. An immediate tension and difference is that the public service environment often has indeterminate tasks, or abstract tasks, where a single and measurable outcome is not readily available. In these situations, highly trained professionals attempt to define and deliver front line tasks so they are relevant to the context of individual differences. No two police beats or school classes are the same. Nevertheless, the same argument about indeterminate outcomes can increasingly be made about the private sector given the growth of the service sector and knowledge based industries in OECD countries.

A familiar approach to this sort of debate cites bipolar examples. For example, a comparison of a manufacturing plant with the work of a school to educate children. The manufacturing plant must increase the efficiency and profitability of production, to produce more, at the same quality, for less input. It must then sell all its products quickly, to maximize its cash flow and profits. Sales figures will automatically be one key source of output data.

A school must educate children, but there is debate about what a good education is. Should it include a complex range of subjects that reflect the diversity of the modern world? Should it allow choice of what is studied—to encourage the diversity of children with a diverse culture? Alternatively, should education concentrate on only core skills that are needed most in society, for example reading, writing and mathematics? The personal communication skills of children, their ability to form appropriate relationships and to understand social relations and moral obligations to others, are also important developmental tasks. Schools should assist parents in developing these interpersonal skills in their children. The ability of children to enjoy and participate in sport, music and art is also important. Many governments and school services will believe that the education system also has a duty to promote cultural aspirations and social skills.

The manufacturing plant is deliberately producing standardized outputs where the market needs to be assured of a common standard if there is to be widespread trust in the brand. A school will not want to produce standardized children, but children who have adequate core skills and the ability to respond in flexible and creative ways to wherever their future life takes them. The school will want to encourage different children to find their own specialist skills, in areas like sport, music and art. Educating is a different role to manufacturing. There are a few similarities between the manufacturing plant and the school, but there are many differences.

What is new public management?

New public management (NPM) has been defined by a number of writers in differing ways (Pollitt 1990; Hood 1991; Osborne and Gaebler 1992) but a point of congruence in the definitions is the implementation of management ideas from the business and private sector into the public services. Governments never explicitly articulated NPM as an ideological or political program to implement management into public organizations, it is rather better understood as an academic critique of the public management reforms of the last 40 years. In the second edition of his leading textbook *Public Management and Administration*, Hughes (1998: Ch.1) commented that NPM was based on a belief in the primacy of economics, the usefulness of private management methods, and a desire to reduce bureaucracy. In the more recent 2012 edition, Hughes articulates the growing sense of divide between the academic and practitioner communities about these long-standing management reforms and their influences. The constant evolving of management reforms and changes, and their reinvention and re-specification, have resulted in a more unstable culture in public services, but this instability is also the experience in private business organizations. Concurrent to this overall change in culture and an increase in operational instability, academics have continued to try to theorize and synthesize the causes and consequences of contemporary developments, with the result that there is much criticism of the macro results. This may explain why in many OECD countries in the last two decades public agencies have increasingly looked to management consultancies for advice on how to solve specific strategic and operational challenges, rather than turning to the academic community who prefer to put these challenges into a macro and grand theoretical context. Academics have located micro managerial practice in the context of political economy. Similarly, in his recent overview of 40 years of public management reform, Pollitt (2013) argues there has not been enough high quality, academic led, evaluation of the changes to practice.

Much of this managerial change agenda became mainstream in the years dominated by the political leadership of Ronald Reagan in the USA and Margaret Thatcher in the UK, in the early 1980s; it continued under subsequent administrations, despite apparent changes in the dominant political party, although with some changes of emphasis. Reforms spread to many other countries, although Hood (1995) and Pollitt and Bouckaert (2004) note important aspects of variety and country diversity, and that the similarities are limited. If one tries to link NPM with an historical definition of importing business practice and language into the public services, NPM had its first roots in government projects pre-Thatcher and Reagan, for example, the PAR approach in the USA. Pal (2012) has researched the role of the international Organisation of Economic Co-operation and Development in public managerial reforms and concluded that while the OECD helped to articulate a shared implementation of market liberalism and market-based models of efficiency, it challenged a fundamentalist market doctrine when some reforms failed. In this way, it also contributed to more recent developments of network based governance approaches to public administration that were linked to sound institutional principles and public values. Overall, other international organizations, like the International Monetary Fund (IMF) and World Bank also had a tendency to respond to dominant western political discourse, especially as espoused in the USA, rather than presenting a bipolar account, or a radical alternative.

Despite commonalities in the critique of NPM developed in the academic literature, there are also important diversities in the extent to which writers position the changes as fundamentally driven by a political ideology associated with pro-market liberalism and a deregulation of markets, and the dismantling of the collectivist aspirations of the capitalist state. The writers who argue that NPM was a key feature of a liberalized and globalized political economy note how the dominant values and language used in public services changed toward markets, consumers and choice (Clarke and Newman 1997; Walsh 1995). To these writers, managerialism in public services is part of a global project to make markets and consumerism pervasive in all aspects of social life. Other academics take a more pragmatic and applied approach and emphasize the evolution of change in the public service practice, with a move from administration and professional bureaucracy to a more managerial and market based system (Hughes 1998, 2012).

Accounts that argue strongly that NPM and its values are an obvious and prescriptive answer to the challenges and problems of the public sector are rare. Perhaps the best known account that makes this argument is Osborne and Gaebler's (1992) best-selling American book *Reinventing Government*. This account did not emerge in North America until the early 1990s, after Ronald Reagan's period in office, and at the start of Bill Clinton's Democratic Administration. This is evidence of the long reach of ideological changes and the time they take to pervade complex and diverse societies. Market and financial global deregulation was a major international political feature of the 1980s, leading to increased flows of financial credit and capital around the globe (Haynes 2012). These changes drove the pervasiveness of market values over other social values across the world, continuing as it did for the next 40 years. This deregulation set the scene for the catastrophic failure of global financial markets in 2007. It underpinned the rise of a market based managerial culture in public services.

The overriding theme of public management reforms as argued by the theory of NPM is a normative assumption that management and organization science as applied in private business organizations will have generalized lessons for government, public services, and NGOs. This is despite the fundamental differences in democratic public sector organizations when compared with private business, and Non-Governmental Organizations (NGOs), in terms of their mission, ownership and organizational objectives. Radnor *et al.* (2014: 407) note that "the fatal flaw of public management theory over the last decade and beyond has been to consistently draw upon generic management theory derived from manufacturing and product-dominant experience."

Walsh (1995) noted the dominance of "marketisation" in this managerial process, where the values of the market place, especially a belief in the value of supply side competition, became dominant—even when the full-scale privatization of supply was not possible. Pollitt's (2013) review of public management reforms, over a period of 40 years in the UK (using documentary evidence from government reform proposals) concluded on the main continuities. These were: an illusiveness of impacts, a lack of evidence driving reforms, a desire for better horizontal coordination in public policy administration, and change was believed by politicians to be most needed in administrative structures and processes. Pollitt concluded that, of the five different political governments in the UK in the 40 year time period:

> all encouraged large scale contracting out and the widespread use of purchaser/provider splits and market-type mechanisms. They have all developed extensive systems of

performance measurement and target setting (despite intermittent promises to reduce the burden of measurement).

(Pollitt 2013: 918)

It is important that a number of authors have taken an approach to the reforms that is less critical in totality (for example, Hughes 1998, 2012). Such an approach seeks to understand the evolution of managerialism into public life as rather inevitable, given the disillusionment with certain characteristics of state organizations, namely the dysfunctions of state monopoly bureaucracy and professionalism, as exposed by public choice theory (Tullock 1976; Self 1993).

The two main historical criticisms of public policy and administration raised by the public choice literature can be summarized as failures of state bureaucracy, and failures of pluralist representative democracy.

The theory criticized the inability of state bureaucracy to create economic and efficient policy outputs. This was because of distortions in the policy and administrative process. These distortions were that state officials and professionals moved resources into activities that they chose for their own "provider interest" rather than maximizing outputs that were in the public interest. In addition, public choice theory criticized the inability of the political leaders of western pluralistic democratic political systems to provide a coherent strategic management of policy. This was largely due to complex political collations of interests that were renegotiated regularly. Such politics of change and compromise were not financially efficient or economically rational.

Public management reforms sought to proactively deal with these two fundamental criticisms, using management techniques derived from private industry. Perhaps the best known example is classical performance management, as discussed in Chapter 4.

Hughes (1998, 2012) describes these changes in the machinery of government, as the move from "policy administration" to "policy management". He defines policy administration as the relatively passive activity of serving the needs of government through a standardized bureaucratic machinery, while public management practice has established a more proactive and action based approach to the public services. At the core of this change is a manager who is empowered to take more responsibility over their specific element of the public service domain:

The administrative paradigm is in its terminal stages and is unlikely to be revived. Administration, as a system of production, has outlived its usefulness. There is a new paradigm of public management which puts forward a different relationship between governments, the public service and the public.

(Hughes 1998: 261)

Far more important in the longer run than the idea of a single management programme was the more gradual acceptance that the work of public servants was now about management in the sense of personal responsibility for achievement of results.

(Hughes 2012: 7)

Having considered the long standing and evolving academic critique of increased managerialism in the public services over the last 40 years, and related this directly to the accounts and experiences of practitioners, the author concludes the following as an overview of the strengths and weakness of the changes.

The main strengths of the public management reforms can be described as:

- The focus on outputs and outcomes of policy;
- The devolved system of financial accountability to help focus resource allocation and decision-making;
- Increased levels of accountability in the policy process;
- The opportunity for a more confident and authoritative directive for public agencies;
- The introduction of more realistic (strategic) short and medium term planning in the public sector; and
- More overlap between public, private and non-governmental sectors, allowing better partnership between sectors to achieve public outputs.

The main weaknesses of public management reforms can be described as:

- An over rigid adherence to artificial market boundaries;
- Some inappropriate and ineffective use of marketization and privatization;
- Loss of power, status and confidence for professional workers;
- Facility for politicians to avoid responsibility and blame the managerial system;
- Working practices are imported from the private sector without adequate reflection on their appropriateness for the public and non-governmental sector;
- Accountability can become unclear and fragmented, due to numerous levels and stake-holders; and
- A lack of attention to public values and human rights, and the interpersonal skills that managers need to mirror these commitments.

Clarke and Newman offer one of the most critical accounts of NPM and they conclude:

> Where champions of the managerial state have celebrated its dynamism, our analysis leads us to a different view. What we see is the unstable oscillations of a form of state that cannot reconcile the social contradictions and conflicts of contemporary Britain within a managerial calculus.
>
> (Clarke and Newman 1997: 159)

Many people working in the public sector share this cynicism, yet many would not want to return to the pre-managerial system with its core characteristics of centralized bureaucratic and administrative standardization. What then is the way forward? In this book, it is argued that growing emphasis placed by some writers on public values (Alford and Hughes 2008; Alford and O'Flynn 2009; Meynhardt 2009; Talbot 2009; Benington and Moore 2011) is a substantial advance in the debate. More recently, Osborne et al. (2014) castigate the return of versions of NPM after the financial crisis in the age of austerity and argue persuasively for a new management practice that is based firmly on the realities of public service. They suggest that a realistic model that can have consonance with public service will be: relational and process based, service focused, culture and value driven, co-productive (including participation with the public and service users), and in part transformed by digital technology.

In addition to this, the literature offered by complexity theorists that seeks to revolutionize how politicians and public service managers conceptualize the public policy system, and the problems and challenges it faces, is also vital. The key argument and contribution that this second edition of *Managing Complexity in the Public Services* makes is that these expositions of public values and social complexity need to be understood and applied together into a new combined synthesis. This also requires a pragmatic element that identifies what this means for those practicing in the public sector: those designing and implementing public policies and managing operational services.

The public value tensions in contemporary public services

The emergence of market managerialism in public services has led to some key tensions in designing and delivering services and these have been experienced often by the managers and professionals working to implement public policy (Dunleavy and Hood 1994). It is exactly these kinds of evolving tensions and instabilities that complexity theory requires us to understand. To see these tensions as a list of polemics is erroneous. Although presented below as bipolar, these tensions are not always in conflict. The degree of conflict is time and space dependent, it varies from one context to another and depends on the type of the public service examples being analyzed. These tensions are dynamic not static:

1   The tension of centralization and decentralization;
2   The tension between public, civil and private ownership and the use of privatization or marketization to coordinate services;
3   The tension between managerial control and professional discretion and the approaches to standardization and personalization; and
4   The tension of political accountability with market (consumer) accountability and the attempt to separate macro political strategies from micro managerial operations.

How these tensions are resolved can be either destructive or creatively constructive, depending on the context.

Centralization and decentralization

There is a paradox about the decentralization of public services into market structures, this in a world that is increasingly centralized and global at a financial level. Centralization and decentralization have to evolve together to counteract each other's extremes. How to interpret and act on the coexistence of centralization and decentralization is one of the defining tensions in public policy. New managerialism has tended to devolve responsibility in public services to the local level, for example with the mechanism of devolved budgets, so that local operational managers have to consider budgetary responsibility. If a central or higher element retains direct control of other aspects of operational delivery this local management can feel like responsibility without power. Politicians at the center of government may also use this system to minimize the political impact on themselves when difficult decisions, such as reducing expenditure, are required. After the financial crisis of 2007–08 in the USA and UK, local services were often targeted for the most severe reductions in expenditure, forcing locally based politicians and managers to reduce their services and deal with the consequences. The counterbalance is that there may be opportunities for local services and their managers to use creative forms of self organization to either form defensive actions to conserve and protect their local services, or alternatively to work with the community to form highly innovative and alternative approaches. Examples of defensive actions would be legal action against the center state, raising new local revenues, or local trade unions that take collective action against centrally imposed change. These responses aim to demonstrate to the public that some of the responsibility for what is happening results from the central state's behavior. Examples of innovative responses would be to encourage NGOs to take over services, as they may have more legal and revenue flexibility and more direct empowerment from local people and service users. The dynamic of self-organization is a key theoretical theme in complexity theory and one that is returned to in the next chapter.

Public, civil and private ownership and the use of privatization or marketization to coordinate services

The weaknesses of NPM are associated with differences between the private and public sector. In this section, the chapter explores the contradictions between public and private and asks how in the complex policy environment managers can make sense of the apparent contradictions.

Fixed service boundaries have long been recognized as a potential problem in the public sector. This has been referred to as the "silo" perspective, whereby workers and managers remain in their own organization and only very occasionally begin to appreciate the world outside their own organization (and profession) and how other perspectives see them. A rigid approach to managerialism and internal markets can reinforce this view, preventing collaboration. Diplomatic leadership and negotiation skills are central in the public services of the twenty-first century. Such skills allow collaborative services to build on the basis of shared values. Competition may have some part to play in raising standards, but paradoxically collaboration is needed to motivate and assist all in achieving the raising of standards.

It can be argued that the move towards more persistent financial and market disciplines went too far in the 1980s and 1990s. Rather than breaking down unhelpful barriers, public managerialism accompanied with the marketization of public services were in danger of further reinforcing service boundaries and cutting back the development of the multi-agency perspective. This was because marketization introduced devolved cost centers and the economic separation of purchasers and providers that replicated the demand and supply side of a market place. Boundary definition evolved from traditional departments to market based structures, but the devolution of financial responsibility did not encourage flexible boundaries and responsibilities. The opposite happened. Devolved units looked to clarify their own responsibilities and costs.

Devolved costing and financial responsibility can be important, but so too is coordination between the numerous, fragmented devolved units. The key becomes creating the right contextual dynamic between market ideas and inter-agency organization and multi-professional practice. For example, a major university introduced a system of devolved budgeting to individual academic schools based on a funding allocation for each student place on each unit of study. It found that paradoxically it needed a central management system that helped schools not to become over competitive. Central resources had to enable schools to see the opportunities of collaborative ventures. Some central incentives and projects were created to prevent dysfunctional fragmentation. On a much bigger scale, the breaking up of the UK railways into competing train providers faced similar issues of disintegration. How could services best share the responsibility for track and stations?

Market systems can lead to perverse incentives and displacements. This is most likely when the underlying social problem is too complex and multi-dimensional for a simple market structure to deal with issues satisfactorily. In these situations, a clearly focused targeted approach in one agency can lead to problems in other parts of the public sector. If public services start to operate with devolved budgets and then as separate provider services in isolation from other services, they may narrow their understanding of social problems as they attempt to build a stable core business. For example, hospitals may reject complex patients who do not have a clear diagnosis, seeing them as expensive and too high risk. Schools may try to reject children with challenging special needs if there is no adequate funding attached. Marketization does not resolve complex social problems by itself; rather market driven managerialism can shift organizational and professional boundaries into new market based structures that demonstrate limitations and rigidity. Previous administrative structures, as experienced before the market managerial changes of the last 40 years, were argued to block horizontal cooperation due to professional and specialist protective interests. This created a reluctance to move away from monopolistic administrative bureaucracy in order to be innovative with horizontal cooperation. The old monopolistic bureaucracies were argued to be risk averse. Nevertheless, there is no clear evidence that market structures incentivize horizontal cooperation any better, unless they can introduce horizontal incentives towards cooperation. Bouckaert, Peters and Verhoest (2010) document the considerable challenges for policy coordination when new managerialism results in the fragmentation associated with specialization and differentiation. Mazzucato (2011) has argued, through the concept of the "Entrepreneurial State", for the important role of government and the public sector in facilitating and helping to coordinate innovation in the market.

The post managerial reflection in recent years has seen a widening debate about the ineffective use of privatization and marketization. While the privatization of utilities has met wide international approval due to its ability to introduce needed investment, there have been difficulties with making judgments about appropriate price controls in such a limited and highly regulated marketplace. Such essential services also gave too much guaranteed profit to the marketplace and big investors.

The privatization of the railways hit the buffers in the UK with the collapse of the private infrastructure company, Railtrack, after a national crisis over health and safety. The Cullen Inquiry (2001) stated that there was no long-term evidence from time series data that health and safety had deteriorated since privatization. Nevertheless, Railtrack who had to increase their investment to deal with these pressures, found that it was unable to balance the financial outputs of share dividends and adequate investment with income received from government grants and shares sold. In its last year of operation, its share price collapsed. It declared losses of £500 million and was unable to raise the £3 billion income needed from investors and banks. The key attraction of privatizing the railways was to raise considerable investment from private investors on the premise that attractive dividends would be returned. Because investors had lost faith in the ability of the government and Railtrack's relationship to function, the government had to look for a new approach. The post Railtrack policy has established a new not for profit company, Network Rail. This body does not pay dividends, but has access to raising investment in the form of guaranteed bonds in the City of London. In summary, it is less subject to short-term market disciplines and pressures and less at risk of losing market confidence.

The balance of private and public ownership and organization and how they should be collaborating with each other is subject to lively debate and mixed evidence (Walker *et al.* 2013). The fear is that privatization offers attractive methods to government ministers for reducing the public debt and borrowing requirement, thus giving the appearance of a strong market based national economy, while in the longer term the use of private capital for public services leaves the public sector with expensive leasing costs picked up as fixed annual costs. Total privatizations result in the annual pressures to pay dividends to secure continuing investment.

Private suppliers are in a powerful position to lever up costs and cut quality once they secure a public contract as the last thing the government wants is for the contract to fail in the media. For many decades, government contracts with defence suppliers, where there is long-term research and development and high levels of complexity and uncertainty and a lack of real on-going competition, have suffered from this type of spiralling cost. Major capital projects are only subject to substantial competitive pressures at the point of bidding for an initial contract. After an agreement is reached, the government and the winner of the contract are locked into a relationship with each other that is difficult to subject to continuing competition. Collaboration, trust and a mutual sharing of interests become more important. Adversarial approaches to such long-term contracts may only result in lawyers benefiting from legal expenses, and are unlikely to achieve efficiencies for the taxpayer.

Privatization and marketization are solutions for public services in some circumstances and the judgment about when this is the case has become increasingly difficult to make. Marketization can include government contracts with NGOs for service provision. Here the NGO has a defined public mission and does not have to make a profit for owners and share holders. One of the key aspects at the heart of privatization tensions is public confidence in the government–market relationship and the public perception of a positive and trusting relationship occurring between the government and a private supplier (Commission on Public Private Partnerships 2001). If the public perceives a lack of trust between the government and the market then confidence is low and risks of failure become much higher. As is shown in the next chapter, the importance of feedback between individuals and social groups is a central concept in complexity theory.

For many managers operating in the private sector, there is an inevitability about the financial world of borrowing, banking and contracting. This is not so for all managers in the public sphere where block grants can be obtained from regional, national and continental government, and offer real possibilities for meeting most financial requirements. In other cases, a mix of public-private money can be negotiated (or may be required). In the management of private business, much risk is financial. A loan repayment or share value might not be satisfied by profits returned. In the public sector, the converse is true. The key risk is to the public good. Profits extracted from a government contract may not deliver adequate value to the public in the service provided. For a private business, a supply contract with a public body is a near guarantee of payment from future revenue public funding, reducing the risk exponentially for the lender. The operating business carries minimal risk that the government will go bankrupt and default on the contract. The risks are to the "public good". The public contract might be abused and used to extract additional profits that are not based on competitive advantage, or an inadequate financial return is put back into the public service. Think of the large, long-term contracts with government departments for computer systems over the years where projects have failed to meet expectations and costs have spiralled (see Chapter 5). The government does not want to pull out of the contract because of political loss of credibility and the fear that all previous expenditure will be lost. Often there is no pragmatic competition to turn to after the initial contract is signed.

The public manager is not primarily concerned with profit, but with the end benefit to the public. This difference is fundamental, although it is more obscured in the modern policy world that includes private and non-governmental organizations. For example, there may well be sections of the public sector today that are essentially discreet production services, operating very similarly to businesses, with the need to generate a financial surplus to requirement. This can have similar consequences to the profit motive in private business. Private companies delivering for the government are under pressure to demonstrate benefits to the public and society, in addition to their primary job of generating profits for their shareholders, and so should be more aware of public values.

Markets give government some flexibility and allow some new approaches, but bring with them new boundaries and risks also. The coordination and regulation of market policy is as important today as it has ever been. The provision of balancing feedback to the market through policy regulation is a critical factor in market success. Non-governmental organizations, which offer clear public values and are not tied to the need to make a profit for their shareholders (but which nevertheless will need to make a small surplus and balance their accounts) offer the contemporary public policy environment considerable "value aware" and "value adding" advantages.

Managerial control and professional discretion and the approach to standardization and personalization

Consider the evolution of two multi-disciplinary community mental health teams, in similar policy environments. One found that the tension between managerial control and professional discretion was solved by having a strong professional team identity and a loose link to operational management. User services developed rapidly and there was more creativity and innovation than standardization. The other team opted for a strong link with health management and standardization based on health bureaucracy and waiting lists. Small differences in the interpretation of central government guidance at the beginning of the process led to local services interpreting the policy tensions in different ways and over time, the services evolved rather differently. Both were able to provide reasonable levels of service. The service that experienced greater managerial health service controls had a higher number of older and long term drug users with chronic and multiple problems who traditionally took a lot of time across a range of public services including criminal justice and accident and emergency. The other service with the softer management approach, did less of this targeted management of the most challenging cases, but did better at intervening with younger and more chaotic substance misusers. These differences were relatively small and there were strong common features about the work and interventions both teams did. They were certainly able to learn from each other and to adjust their service delivery as they moved forward.

The sociological account of professions attributes the power, enhanced earnings and social status of professionals to their long periods of training and their resulting claim to possess a technical knowledge base. This knowledge is linked to complex skills and reflective individual judgments, so that it can be argued that it is applied usefully to the public good. Clarke and Newman (1997: 6) comment: "professionalism stresses the indeterminacy of the social world as necessitating the intervention of expert judgement."

The ability of professions to enhance further their earnings and social status in comparison with other professional groups is related to the extent of their claim to populate a unique area of technical knowledge. It will also relate to their ability to restrict the use of that knowledge base by others, the strength and lobbying of their own professional association, and their ability to prevent direct government bureaucracy and regulation from encroaching on their working domain. Self-regulation, therefore, often forms an attractive element to powerful professional bodies, because it enables them to retain some distance from direct government organization and control. Nevertheless, in the modern state, some dialogue with government is inevitable, and skills of negotiation to reach collaborative agreement about the scope of social practice become critical.

Part of the new managerial revolution in the public sector has been connected to a political attempt to curb professional power. Public choice theorists saw professional power in the public services as too strong, and distorting the development of public services away from meeting public needs to enhancing professional status and rewards. It was argued that social workers focused on ill-defined specialist counselling and community work skills, rather than assessing and meeting the basic material needs of their clients (Brewer and Lait 1980). Teachers became preoccupied with experiential and philosophical approaches to learning that neglected core skills and competences for their pupils (Woodhead 2002). The medical professional sought the rewards of scientific pioneering advances, rather than improvements based on good preventative public health advice and the effective practice of routine medical screening.

In addition to professionals being criticized by the language and concepts of the public choice theorists, they were also criticized by the ideological "left". Marxists criticized them for being dominated by middle class values and professional concerns that neglected the real needs of the working classes (Corrigan and Leonard 1978). Illich (1973) talked of a professional mystique that reversed the outcome of public services and delivered social control for the capitalist state, thus teachers prevented children from being educated by containing children, but succeeded in teaching them useful employment related skills, doctors contributed to ill health by avoiding public health responsibilities and focusing on the individual. Professionalism became linked to the idea of social closure and restricting ordinary people's access and rights to life improvements and a better quality of life.

Clarke and Newman (1997) argued that managerialism becomes an ideological method for deconstructing the power and prestige of professions and calling them to account. Professionals were increasingly called to the accountability of market values, based on competition and consumerism, rather than a wider public accountability based on democracy and participation. New managerialism failed to take account of the democratic base of public services and their accountability to political representatives. Democracy added a dimension that the business based managerial discourse could not easily understand.

Exworthy and Halford (1999) documented the inability of managerialism to solve the challenges of professional power and professional accountability. In many situations, the new managerialism recruited its managers from a professional base, ensuring that new managers, such as budget holding head teachers had as much commitment to their professional body as they did to the new managerial vision.

Professionals have been battered by the storm of new managerialism. There are few clear insights into how they have been called to account as a result in ways that are more positive for the public. There has been some de-skilling and a drive to build an evidence base and core competencies. Woodhead (2002) implied that schoolteachers had too many theories and practices to choose from, with a lack of scientific evidence to support a diverse and experimental approach; he argued they should stick to a few sound principles that ensure children get core skills. Teachers, however, have to use their experience and personal skills to get the best out of all children in difficult circumstances; their flexibility and creativity is a vital aspect of their job.

In some countries, an increased use of low paid support staff without professional qualifications has accompanied the growth of managerialism. Deprofessionalization has been accompanied by a de-skilling of labor. This has made professionalism focus on more elite skills and competencies, rather than making it more accountable. Professionals are sometimes less willing to act in creative and imaginative ways to deal with user diversity, because of the fear that they will be called to account for actions that do not reflect dominant management standardizations. Some schools have become reluctant to take on extracurricular activities and organize children's educational holidays. Professional initiative and innovation can be more difficult because of increased managerialism, unless managers can acknowledge and reward such value-adding practices on the periphery of core business.

Hughes (1998) has implied that the clock cannot be turned back to a golden age of public bureaucracy and administration. Most would agree with him and dispute that there ever was a golden age. Where does this leave new managerialism?

The reality of the introduction of new managerialism into public services was that the boundaries between managerial and professional roles were blurred. In particular, an increasing number of professionals found themselves undertaking managerial roles and tasks, but with them being still very much in touch with their professional body and experience. There was not a clear separation of managers and professionals. Although some managers have been recruited into public services from business and come with a business background, many have evolved their path into management from a professional base. Many front line managers—head teachers, social work team leaders, and social housing managers—have strong and continuing ties with their professional roots. Their management practice is informed by their professional allegiance. These people are what Exworthy and Halford (1999) call "managerial professionals". Such people have a key role in the buffer zone between managerial philosophy and professional culture. Front line managerial professionals have to interpret the managerial demands and new language used by politicians and senior strategic managers, and then facilitate change from their professional colleagues. It is the most senior managers at the apex of large organizations who are under direct pressure from politicians to deliver on performance targets. Middle managers and front line managerial professionals have to "make sense" of the business sector models that are increasingly applied to their work. To survive this process they have to select which managerial models are most appropriate and demonstrate that they are at least implicitly meeting the senior management agenda, even if they are not explicitly engaging with it. Kakabadse (1982) has documented the difficulties of this role in local government social services departments and he described the tension as creatively negotiating between a role and task culture. He argued senior managers focus on tasks needed to deliver outputs, while those lower down an organization are more likely to appreciate the importance of a worker retaining a holistic professional role. Here the individual professional who has taken a managerial role experiences the creative or destructive organization tension and this has implications for their identity (Causer and Exworthy 1999).

Some tensions are difficult to resolve. Witness for example the counsellor who refuses to accept targets for her counselling activities, arguing that personal change cannot be easily managed and predicted, but is dependent on numerous contingencies, and that psychotherapeutic approaches are likely to take years to lead to a better quality of life. Strategic managers will find it hard to continue funding such a project if they cannot understand its short-term quantitative outputs in comparison with other service interventions.

Table 1.1 summarizes the key tensions between senior managers and professionals and examines the management of these conflicts by "managerial professions".

The tensions between managerial and professional ways of thinking are related to the fundamental differences between the business and public sector environments. The public service environment is often more complex than the business environment, it does not lend itself easily to market accountability and price based allocation. The public service environment is characterized by its intricate systems and complex accountabilities. The importing of managerial ideas from business into the public service environment is therefore fraught with difficulties. It is challenging for managers to continue to understand complex individual differences and personal needs while relating this to the allocation of resources against performance targets.

Nevertheless, there will be situations where managerial models are of value and can be used satisfactorily to improve public services. The key is likely to be contextual and

Table 1.1 The differences between managers and professionals

	Senior managers	*Managerial professionals*	*Professionals*
Activity focus	Output effectiveness	Efficiency of inputs to outputs	Process of inputs Input roles (e.g.: assessment, diagnosis)
Training and skills	Improved and updated professional and managerial core competencies	Relationship of competencies and skills with judgments about context	Relevance of skills and knowledge and their application to presenting social needs
Accountability focus	Political-Managerial	Multiple stakeholders and accountability tensions	Professional and legal accountabilities

dependent on the judgment about what methods to use, when and where, and an ability to use managerial models and practices flexibly, rather than following rigid, standardized approaches.

The tension of political accountability versus market (consumer) accountability and the attempt to separate macro political strategies and micro managerial operations

The model of public administration delivery argued to have existed in the immediate post Second World War period in developed countries had its core in an ideal of political pluralist elections. A hierarchy of democratic elections at national, regional and local level resulted in politicians being appointed to oversee the public services delivered at the respective levels. Citizens could call politicians to account over specific service issues by contacting their representative at the relevant level. This accountability was much more likely to be achieved at local level. National and regional politics are dominated by political party coalitions of interests that form an overall political strategy for nation and region. Such political strategies represent ideological and value driven approaches to macro policy issues and are articulated as macro policy programs, like increasing affordability and access to welfare services, and stimulating economic development. With these macro political programs, accountability is via the voter's choice at major elections. They use this empowerment to judge the strategic management of the political party in power at the end of a government's period of office. In the macro political environment, specific service issues and experiences are remote from political accountability.

The limitations of representative political democracy in pluralist democracies created a growing interest in the 1970s and 1980s in forms of participation that could complement such macro party based representation. In many OECD countries, there was a growing acknowledgement of the part that other groups could play in assisting the process of representative accountability, for example pressure group lobbying on single issues, via organizations like Trades Unions, NGO campaigns and local action groups. These groups could influence regional and national governments and political parties more effectively on specific issues. Such groups have also become more important in local politics, and in some countries are partially or formally linked to local planning and management processes. It is argued these forms of representation offer a creative expansion of traditional representative politics. A counter argument is that such innovations in representation and participation confuse the public about political accountability and make them less likely to vote in elections.

If pressure from user and community groups cannot increase the specific accountability of services to local people, an alternative approach is to make the local manager of a service more publicly visible, so that service users know how to make direct complaints about individual services. The manager can then call professional service providers to account on the service users' behalf. This approach is termed, managerial accountability.

The evolving of public managerialism to create managerial accountability has led to new opportunities for the avoidance of accountability by politicians. The devolving of budgets to the managers of services results in some notable conflict between political government ministers and managers of provider agencies. In the UK, The Director of the Prison Service Agency was forced to resign after some prominent escapes of dangerous prisoners on the Isle of Wight, while the Minister could side step responsibility. Yet politicians could still intervene on some occasions. Interference was still possible when an issue was important enough to require good media presentation of political involvement and seek popular support. A senior manager in the UK NHS Management Executive resigned due to what he saw as political interference in his decision making.

If managerialism removes public services from the gaze of politicians and people express their views directly to local services, this has implications for political democracy. This may increase the disillusionment with representative democracy and the lack of willingness of people to vote in political elections. Civil involvement (for example taking an active part as a local school or hospital governor) might replace political involvement (joining a local political party). Ultimately, this creates some gaps in the accountability framework of the modern state and potentially creates power vacuums that might be filled by some unaccountable individual or extremist group. Low turnouts at local, regional and national elections increase the opportunities for unpopular extremists to be elected. Market managerialism has depoliticized local life and brought with it a new politics of service consumption.

Beyond New Public Management

Given the limitations of NPM and the insight in the mid-1990s that it had as many weaknesses as strengths, an alternative discourse of government administration began to develop referred to as Governance, Policy Networks, or simply, as one book title put it, *Beyond the New Public Managerialism* (Minogue, Polidano, and Hulme 1998). Another approach is to see the digital transformation of new technology as providing new opportunities for integrating, coordinating and democratizing public administration and management (Dunleavy *et al.* 2005). These approaches are notable for their wide view of the public sector and the need to reintegrate representative politics and civil society with the operational management of policy. Governance theories examine the fragmentation of public sector behavior. Government decisions are seen as primarily governmental rather than managerial, but decisions become entangled with private companies, NGOs, community groups, and other tiers of political government and inter-governmental bodies (Rhodes 2000). Policy networks (Klijn and Koppenjan 2000) try to explain the horizontal coordination and facilitation of these diverse agencies.

Thompson (1991: 171) described networks in the following way: "The key feature of networks is the way cooperation and trust are formed and sustained … in contrast to either hierarchy or market, networks coordinate through less formal, more egalitarian cooperative means." Somewhat in contrast to the above view, Rhodes (1997) has noted the distribution of power in policy networks. Membership may be exclusive. Similarly, networks can be horizontally or vertically dependent on bodies or other networks who have delegated to them power and authority to act. This will contextualize and limit their own cooperative stances. Stacey (1995) notes the importance of the soft structures of horizontal networks in organizations and between organizations, as opposed to the hard hierarchical structures of organizational and pyramid bureaucracies. Horizontal inter-department working requires that persuasion is by negotiation and bargaining, rather than via authority and issuing directives. Power is established through influence rather than formal authority. As a result, for managers to function in networks, certain personal skills of the manager or professional have to come to the fore. The nurturing of relationships in networks is important if the network is to be effective and responsive to new circumstances and challenges. This is different to the clearly structured form of hierarchical bureaucratic organization where roles are prescribed and not easily re-negotiated.

The language of practice changed in the last decade, with talk of governance appearing in policy documentation and leadership receiving as much attention as management. Whole Systems is another conceptual approach to appear in government policy documents in recent years, which reflects the evolution of managerialism into something beyond new public managerialism. "Whole Systems" approaches capture the need for a wide view—a view of policy that embraces much more than the operational system of inputs and outputs (Attwood *et al.* 2003). There are some similarities between the whole systems approach and practices that result from the application of complexity theory.

These accounts of public sector change offered by the governance and network based literature are more descriptive and wide ranging than the NPM literature. It is in contrast to the prescriptive and deterministic tone of a management ideal, where writers describe a focused project of change that is prescriptive. Governance and networks describe the dismantling of the modern state and see its fragmentation into the marketplace and civil society as an evolutionary process. There is little in the way of a normative comment on why this has happened or where it is leading. Rhodes prefers the broad scope of this account, distrusting the limitations of the managerial model precisely because NPM cannot account for democratic and institutional political change at a national and international level:

> After 1979, function-based policy networks based on central departments (or sections of them) changed in two ways. First, the membership of networks became broader, incorporating both the private and voluntary sectors. Second, the government swapped direct for indirect controls.
>
> (Rhodes 2000: 5)

This descriptive and less critical account of network change can be linked to Third Way ideology. On the one hand, the politics of the twenty-first century are concluded to be less ideological and more about pragmatics, while on the other the new pragmatism is cast into a rethinking of traditional ideologies that arguably does have a value base of its own (Giddens 1998, 2000). The entanglement of market and public/state organizations is now so intense that to talk of a dichotomy or dualism between private and public no longer makes organizational or managerial sense. In some cases, there are still distinct differences between private and public (as has been argued here with certain forms of management practice), but in other contexts, such as in the macro national economy, the terms private and public are entangled. For example, this interdependence is shown in the financial model for public-private partnership projects, and the resourcing of private banks that needed rescuing by the state after the international financial crisis of 2007–08.

Many private companies are dependent on their relationship with government and public contracts for profitability. This makes the public sector dependent on the performance of private companies. Even where the circumstances of service delivery appear entirely privatized, for example in the telecom and power utilities, here public regulation and licencing remain critical aspects for public policy and managers to consider. The state still has a lead role.

There is an evolution in the private sector towards service management practice (rather than production management), but it is argued (e.g., by Osborne *et al.* 2013) that the public sector has its own distinctive service approach which needs an appropriate theoretical and conceptual base.

Another major and important theoretical development in the last decade has been the development of the public values literature (Alford and Hughes 2008; Benington and Moore 2011). This approach places public management and administration back into a public context with an important attempt to redefine the public sphere as not consisting of only large public organizations, but also necessarily including civil and communities groups. The need for the public to experience collective identity and purpose allows for politics and political philosophy to find a linkage with public management as the operational machinery of government and public services.

Public values seem like a good foundation on which to revisit a coherent model of managing public services. The sculpturing of public management practice following the financial crisis of 2007–08 has felt for many like a return to the dominant privatization and marketization agenda of the 1980s. In some countries, like the UK, the austerity agenda has been articulated as the need for the government to withdraw from aspects of service delivery. This has politicized the public management debate. Immediately before the crisis, the impact of governance, leadership, whole systems and public value discourses had left many concluding that for managers to identify best practice required a necessity to recognize the contingency of any organizational context (given the difficulty of generalizing organizational and managerial lessons learnt in one organization to another). The post crisis politics have returned the discussion about the primacy of market structures and values to the front of debate. However, the failure of some large private organizations that now need state support has created a new opportunity to revisit ownership within the market debate. The ability of civil society and NGOs to influence and progress this debate is therefore critical. These organizations offer a meaningful method to the project of promoting public values in public management that has proved largely elusive to the privatization experiments. Civil society and NGOs can make important arguments about their forms of public ownership that are neither state nor private.

The preference and task for this book is to bring public values into the explanations offered by complexity theory and the idea of seeing society and its organizations as complex adaptive systems. This approach lies somewhere between systems contingency and systems fragmentation. It offers a view of systems that are inherently complex and at times unstable and unpredictable, but it still requires the advancement of management practice and organizational understanding. Values offer a key means to bring stability in this troublesome environment.

Why consider complexity theory?

Accounts of public organizations based on complexity theory stress the indeterminacy of organizational systems and the difficulty with isolating cause and effect. Organizational systems are complex adaptive systems (CAS) because the creative and dynamic feedback between the numerous elements and individuals is the defining aspect of the organization in any one time and space and these define how it further evolves and emerges.

Boundaries between organizations and their neighboring organizations and social systems are seen as permeable and soft. The soft boundaries between organizations lead to "entanglement". This is a mutual dependence on each other and inability to maintain rigid separations and boundaries. This is what observers increasingly witness when understanding the relationship between the private, public and non-governmental parts of society and the managerial and professional roles in these organizations.

Entanglements are formed by interactions, as different individual elements are drawn together and required to redefine themselves by communication. All this happens through a process of feedback. Interaction and feedback are most important to determining the pace and direction of change, rather than a few individual factors causing and determining a result. Teachers listen and interact with colleagues, government reports, academics, the media, children and parents of children. How they corporately react to this is the process of feedback that will determine the future of the profession.

Progress in understanding an organization is made by understanding the time periods of relative stability and similarity that do exist within its subsystems. Dynamic processes and associated outputs can be observed that are similar, based around forces that are in effect partial laws and social practices, but these "stabilizers" never lead to identical processes, only those that are similar. Complexity theory refers to these organizing stabilizers as "attractors", because they attract patterns of behavior. It is possible to observe many similarities in the way teachers behave towards the children in their care. These practices are informed by social and educational values, behavioral expectations, and aspects of wider social culture. These factors are the discourses that attract some similarity in teaching practice and draw teachers' experience together. In addition, there are important differences in the way that individual teachers behave and interact with a particular class. Similarity is different to uniformity.

Occasionally large-scale shifts in society cause fundamental change throughout organizations and break up traditional values and patterns of behavior. The stabilizing attractor forces that create similarity are displaced into transformed new patterns of order. A new dominant attractor has emerged. Thus, Byrne (1998) has written of the impact of marketization on public services in the 1980s and the phase shift that this caused in social systems. The key beliefs of public service, "one job for life" and bureaucratic standardization, were the attractor value and belief forces around which public servants had interacted for so long. In the 1980s, the attractor forces shifted to give public servants a new orbit of values and ideas based on less job stability, market values, and the need for regular change and innovation.

Kontopoulos (1993) has described a similar organizational dynamic where the numerous logics and beliefs that construct the culture of an organization are in a constant state of change and evolution. No logically constructed subsystem of ideas is ever the truth; there are always contradictions and tensions. A simplified view of logics is necessary to allow limited periods of predictability and stability. In this sense "totalizing" logics, like the marketization of public services and the managerial performance efficiency ethos, emerge as dominant logics over certain time periods (Haynes 1999, 2007).

Contradictory logics, such as the high value of professional knowledge, may also be held in an organization and policy system, but their evolution and power base is constrained by the more dominant logic. Again, at certain times in history, major shifts in the dominant logics occur, and these have a profound effect on everything else. This is similar to Bourdieu's (1977: 10) idea of the economy of logic, "no more logic is mobilised than is required by the needs of practice … making them subject to over determination." This helps us to understand why business managerial models can be appealing to politicians and managers in the public sector, even though they are inadequate logical accounts of social complexity. They are "an economy of logic." People seek simple accounts in a highly complex environment as a method for dealing with complexity and uncertainty. For a limited time, simple models may appear to be doing rather well, but in the longer term, their inability to deal with complexity is increasingly highlighted by contradictions and tensions.

The practice issue is to take what is useful and relevant from management and organizational theory and to reflect on this in a situational context. Managerial applications need to be reflective and able to embrace organizational complexity and the likely contingencies that make comparisons between similar circumstances difficult, but not impossible. They also need to be constructed on appropriate values.

Differences between complexity theory and general systems theory

Systems theory has influenced management and organizational theory practice for many decades. It is a macro approach that uses synthesis as much as analysis and has the theme of acknowledging contingencies and the contextual nature of managing.

Merali and Allen summarize general systems approaches:

> systems thinking ... asserts that systems cannot be understood by analysis—the properties of the parts can only be understood within the larger context of the whole ... Developments in the earlier part of the twentieth century were predicated on the design paradigm for management and problem solving. The emphasis was predominantly on the design of organizations as systems that could be regulated and controlled by management intervention.
>
> (Merali and Allen 2011: 32)

So what is the difference between systems theory and complexity theory?

Figure 1.1 illustrates a simplified management system. The core system is a process made possible by inputs that lead to activities that result in some outputs. A manager seeks to operate this system process in an efficient manner, with a key focus on the deployment of input resources, the defining of activities and the measurement of resulting outputs. General systems theory still tends towards a view that there is some optimal type of predictable rational state of equilibrium within a system. System equilibrium may be stable, or settled for long periods of time, or dynamic and likely to fluctuate to a limited extent. Classical economics have long been founded on this type of view, that complex economic systems can still be illustrated to follow some longer-term trends towards equilibrium in terms of the laws of supply, demand, price variability and inflation. These types of systems, if they do exist, are rather holistic, in the sense that the properties of the whole mitigate the movement of lower aspects and the behavior of individuals.

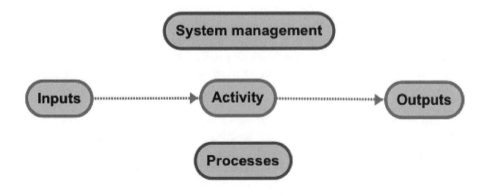

Figure 1.1 A simplified management system

The systems approach has been linked in recent decades to the business process reengineering and lean system management approaches (Harmon 2007). These have become popular as holistic and system based approaches in the public and NGO sectors. A recent seminal review of the popularity of lean system approaches by Radnor and Osborne (2013) criticized these classical systems approaches because of their being based on static production rather than dynamic service provision. More specifically, their criticism of the failures of the classical version of lean, in its applicability to public services, was attributed to: an inability to understand public service logics and domains; a failure to understand service user experience and outcome as the key performance aspect (rather than internal input–output efficiencies); a need to understand the relational effect of public service processes on their users; the importance of co-production between service users and professionals within public service processes; and whether lean can be applied to cultural change rather than change in physical production.

Complex systems approaches place much importance on the individual actor and the constant creative feedback between the system and the individual. Therefore, in any economy we cannot be sure that a group of individuals will respond in exactly the same way to certain economic feedback on each subsequent occasion:

> We should be sensitive to complex and self-organizing interactions and appreciate the play of patterns that perpetually transforms the system itself as well as the environment in which it operates.
>
> (Cilliers 1998: 107)

Complex systems are prone to periods of unpredictable instability and occasional extreme events that may happen more often than expected (Taleb 2007).

Dynamic feedback between individuals and the system introduces a strong non-linear effect and gives difficulties in predicting trends, particularly in the longer term.

The Norwegian philosopher Am (1996: 14) has defined a complex system as having four key attributes:

1   it consists of many independent components,
2   these components interact locally,
3   the overall behavior is independent of the internal structure of the components,
4   the overall behavior of the system is well defined.

Of resulting importance for the management perspective is the need for an overview or synthesis of the system, rather than focusing too much on any one detail in isolation. Public service managers need a good sense of overview if they are to do well and they must avoid the peril of getting fixated with a few points of detail at the expense of the wider picture.

Cilliers (1998) raised six key differences between traditional systems and complex systems and these are paraphrased below:

> Traditional systems are assumed to submit to some dominant and discernible rules that can be used to calculate the potential equilibrium or similar stable state of the system. Complex systems, in comparison, tend to defy a calculated equilibrium, but rather settle into a condition that satisfies external constraints for a given time period.
>
> Traditional systems have some kind of control system, for example a type of thermostat, while complex systems have no static regulatory element, but rather a self organizing and evolving regulatory system.

Elements in systems can be understood as separate elements and symbols. Alternatively, elements in a complex system have a tendency to derive their meaning almost entirely from the complex system and therefore the meanings attached to the elements and symbols will change and evolve as the system evolves.

Systems theory proposes that systems have some rational processes that lead to predictable results under given conditions in the system. Complex systems come to solutions via dynamic processes that are evolving and not likely to result in a single, final conclusion.

Traditional systems change their structures in accordance with rule-based learning and lessons about what does and does not work. This means that change occurs through explicit procedures. In complex systems, change occurs through self-organization where learning is a constant factor. It is therefore difficult to isolate change and attach it to key learning events.

Systems models have active and passive data, symbols and rules. These are used to program a future state. Complex system models are characterized by a dynamic, continuous exchange of data. The complex system has a memory and is always trying to reinterpret this memory in the light of current events.

Conclusion

Given that public services are examples of CAS what does this mean for the future of managerialism in public services? The argument of this book is that because public services are complex systems they do not always respond well to traditional business managerial approaches. Simplistic practices of organizational redesign, structural change, performance management and quality standards based on static definitions, look unlikely to be able to master the unpredictability and turbulent world of social complexity. An approach is needed where: "the focus of management has shifted from things to processes; from entities to interactions" (Lissack and Roos 1999: 3). The complexity approach then is relational, cultural and interactive. It requires managers to be creative and good communicators.

In the world of complex human networks, it is the myriad of connections and interactions shaping and forming within the network that gives life to the public policy world (Medd 2001). Public service managers have often been told to "network" more widely. This implies a broad vision of policy issues and good communication skills, rather than a narrow approach within one's own agency. As Wood says:

> The art of management in the 21st century thus lies in the ability to spot the potential for adding value in the construction and deconstruction of networks. This enables the creation of new knowledge and applying it so as to increase the value of existing offerings to customers, or the creation of brand new offerings that provide superior value to existing ways of doing things.
>
> (Wood 2000: 258)

Finding a coherent approach in such a complex world is not straightforward. In the remainder of this book, an argument is made to define further the managerial and leadership approach that is needed.

Before applying complexity theory to a better understanding of public systems, that has implications for specific areas of management practice (strategic, performance, information and knowledge, and people) the second chapter looks first in more detail at the scope of complexity theory and its general relevance to public service management.

2   What is complexity?

Introduction

This chapter explores the substantial and growing impact of complexity theory on the applied social sciences and its application in recent decades. The key methodological concepts and their application are reviewed. Finally, the chapter reviews the current relationship between complexity theory and its application to public policy and public management. It is argued that public management is the art of intervening in complex social systems, but this inevitably becomes linked with political and social values. Such values provide the underpinning ethos and order to justify management action.

Science and complexity: the roots of the theory

Complexity theory has been applied to the social science theory and management applications for several decades, but the roots of the theory were established in the natural sciences rather than the social sciences. In scientific theory, complexity has a longer history of explaining phenomena that are difficult to predict. One of the best examples of a physical and natural system that is difficult to predict is the meteorological weather system. Despite an exponential growth in the collection of information about the weather, via satellites, buoys and land based automated collection points, and with more data readings taken across the globe than ever before, the analytical forecasting system that results from this extraordinary amount of information has only made slow progress to its end precision. High-speed digital information systems pass the collection of meteorological data across the globe in seconds. Computers store this data and automatically synthesize it into historical patterns and can look for overall patterns that seem to be repeating. All this data collection and computer power adds up to significant progress. Arguably it does improve forecasting, to some extent, but the precision of the final detail can never be improved to give certainty of the detail for localized community and neighborhood weather. This is because the weather system always has a high degree of instability, and small changes in one part of the system can rapidly affect the stability elsewhere and thereby change forecasting and predictions. It is the inherent instability in the system caused by the interactions between its physical elements that defies deterministic prediction.

Not all natural and physical systems are like this. For example, the tidal system is predictable both in the long and short term. Tidal timetables can be issued many months ahead. Differences in the range over the year can also be predicted to a great point of accuracy. The reason for this is that the system is entirely dependent on a mechanistic and deterministic causal relationship: the orbit of the moon around the earth. This system is not inter-dependent with the changing and unstable interaction of the key properties that drive it. Other physical systems that behave in complex and unpredictable ways like the weather system are: the human brain, the outbreak of diseases, population growth and the decline of species.

In 2013, there were a number of high impact weather events across the world. In October, national weather forecasting agencies and models disagreed over the likely degree of impact of a cyclone about to hit the south east of India. India's own national service predicted a very severe cyclone. Another international system in the southern hemisphere made a forecast of a worse "super cyclone". This forecast came from the Joint Typhoon Warning Center, a high tech state of the art system that was made possible by resource cooperation between the USA and UK meteorology organizations. After the cyclone made landfall, the Indian media sensed and claimed a national scientific victory (www.ndtv.com/article/india/cyclone-phailin-india-meteorological-department-wins-battle-over-forecasts-431657).   The storm surge had not been as high as a super cyclone and the wind speeds not as strong as over 300 kilometers per hour as associated with a super cyclone.

Could a scientific victory of superior prediction really be claimed? The overall weather event—a cyclone that was predicted to threaten lives and damage economic and social infrastructure did happen, and thankfully the Indian authorities did achieve what was described as their biggest ever evacuation of citizens before the storm made landfall (www.bbc.co.uk/news/world-asia-india-24546015). Given the topography of the south east Indian coast and the social and economic vulnerability of its population, the mass evacuation was needed regardless of whether the storm was very severe or "super". The encouraging synthesis was that all the international meteorology services with an interest in forecasting got the overall pattern and forecast correct. In this sense, further detail can be argued as not important.

In addition, it might be argued by scientific theorists with an understanding of complexity theory that the victory claimed in the Indian media on behalf of its forecasts was due to chance and not because of their superior forecasting. The final details of the direction and geographical range and exact path of a storm in the final hours before it makes landfall are the precise events where the path of a complex system cannot be predicted. Clever science can forecast the overall emergence and likely dynamic of the system, but not exactly what will happen next. The power of such forecasting models decreases rapidly as the geographical area of interest is localized and the longer that the time horizon of interest expands into the future. Predicting an hour ahead might be possible, but not several hours, and a forecast has to expect some possible variations and scenarios rather than one possible future. As expectations about the ability to forecast within precise geographies and across future time grow, complex systems remain difficult to forecast.

This large scale uncertainty and difficulty in the understanding of the behavior of systems in the physical sciences also reflects some of the great challenges in understanding the human condition and its interaction with society (Castellani and Hafferty 2009). Social systems often have these complex characteristics. While the natural sciences have used complexity approaches to try and understand dynamic systems like the weather that defy simple linear and deterministic prediction, the social sciences similarly have come to see that the methods and metaphors of complexity science are of formidable use in understanding social systems.

Complexity, social science and management

Metaphors and methods

While complexity theory explains natural scientific systems that look and behave like complex social systems (that is they demonstrate unstable dynamics that can only forecast certain patterns and cannot predict with precision) some important differences remain between a scientific approach to complexity and a social science approach.

Scientific studies of complex instability and unstable interactions can be based on real physical measurement of the characteristics of these interactions. As Byrne and Callaghan (2014: 43) note: "Scientism always seeks to render its abstractions, its metaphors as real." For example, a weather system is measured by key instrumental readings of fundamental variables such as barometric pressure, humidity, and wind speed. Readings are dependent on the reliability of the measuring instrument and the ability to record this at a precise time and to communicate it correctly to a computer. A computer system then forms a synthesis of such observations and plots change over time and space. Social science measurements are not only dependent on issues of reliable measurement but more fundamentally depend on the social and cultural construction of the variable being measured. For example, a complex model of an economic system will depend on measures of variables like price inflation, employment, and output growth. There are important issues in social science about the validity of a variable and its definition, even before one faces issues of consistency of measurement. Price inflation is a composite of many thousands of items that can be bought or sold. These items are hugely diverse, ranging from the cheapest item of food costing only a few cents, to an asset, like a house, worth many thousands of dollars. These prices will vary across geographies, both locally and nationally. Employment is usually restricted to definitions of paid work and excludes important social labor such as caring for children and relatives. Casual and temporary work may not be captured by official statistics. For example, in societies with high unemployment rates, it is generally accepted that there is a large hidden economy where people undertake some tasks for others for small cash payments, but these are not captured in official employment statistics. A variable like economic growth is even more slippery in its relationship to precise and reliable measurement. What counts as growth? In recent years, since the financial crisis, there has been a growing debate about the validity of the international economic measure of growth (GDP—gross domestic product) and whether there might be a better way of measuring international economic wellbeing (Stiglitz, Sen and Fitoussi 2010).

Fundamental measurement differences between the physical and social sciences lead some to conclude that the application of complexity science to social science can never be conceptualized and operationalized in exactly the same way. For example, some of the theoretical concepts in complexity science that are examined in this book, like attractors, cannot be empirically demonstrated to the same high degree of evidence and rigor. This is because of the underlying social construction and cultural debate as to whether some of the social phenomena argued to be experiencing complex theoretical manifestations really exist or not. Byrne and Callaghan (2014: Chapter 2) discuss the difference between "restricted" and "general" complexity. Quoting Morin (2006) they discuss how restricted complexity remains closer to the empiricism of science, requiring a stronger emphasis on observation and measurement. In contrast, general complexity requires more abstract theorizing and inductive conceptualization. General complexity invites social scientists to attempt to understand the interactions of both human agency and social structures. They conclude (2014: 56): "Any general complexity social science has to get beyond micro determined emergence. It has to allow for structures with causal powers and it has to address human agency as capable of transcending narrow rules for behaviour."

Merali and Allen (2011: 50) note that: "Some of the objections to using concepts from the natural sciences to explain human social systems have focused on the inadequacy of these concepts to deal with issues of free will, intentionality and purposiveness." The application of complexity science to social science and management practice will therefore require some differences in approach and in this edition of this book a key focus is to make progress in understanding the interaction of human values with social and organizational systems.

Stability and instability

The relative stability and instability of a complex system is one key aspect that social science researchers use when researching the economy, society and its different forms of organization. Systems analysis seeks to differentiate between the places of occurrence of instability and those that are relatively stable. For example, where local instability is identified, it may be important to try to manage its containment, to prevent an escalation at a higher more macro level. This has been a key issue in economic management and intervention in recent years, especially since the outbreak of the global financial crisis in 2007–08. Could early containment of the US subprime mortgage market have prevented an international financial crisis (Financial Crisis Inquiry Commission 2011)? However, with regard to normative influences on the application of management practice, it should not be universally assumed that instability is always a bad influence. Some management practitioners will argue that, in some contexts, instability is welcome and it presents an opportunity for necessary change. Often complexity theorists and practitioners will argue that instability is an inevitable feature of evolving complex systems that results at certain times and places because of systemic dynamic and evolving emergent interactions. Public organizations evolve through relative periods of stability and instability related to external events and influences, such as economic crisis, or political change. Management is in part an exercise of responding to these destabilizing events (Meadows 2009). However, instability can also arise from within, from changing management and professional practices, or the dynamic interaction of people and their values and behaviors. One logic in a complexity based approach to management is therefore that one should respect this inability to always control and stabilize the organizational context, and that a lack of control may well be symptomatic of complex instability rather than managerial failure (Kernick 2004).

Chaos is a concept used by complexity theory to identify a particular type of instability. Battram (1996: 141) describes chaos as: "the point in a complex system when ordered behaviour gives way to a turbulent behaviour". In the physical and natural sciences, chaos has specific mathematical properties. In nonlinear models, chaos occurs when a very small change in perimeters causes an exponentially different outcome later. Edward Lorenz noticed this when developing early computer based weather system models in the 1960s. It is said that he discovered a dramatic effect after a very small change was made by an input error during a data entry. The mathematical effect can be demonstrated in a simple spreadsheet exercise (Kiel 1994). When the rate of change t-1 reaches a critical value, the resulting graph no longer presents a predictably linear or periodic cycle but begins to oscillate at apparently random intervals. Some mathematicians have also argued that these unpredictable oscillations are different to random events and do have aspects of a repeated emerging order and patterning to them. Similar patterns arise, but not in predictable precise ways. Some social science studies, predominantly in North America (Kiel and Elliott 1997) have tried to prove the existence of chaotic patterns in social science data, like voting trends. There is some debate over whether attempts to measure chaos in social data like this are appropriate given the social construction of the indicators used. Nevertheless, the use of chaos as a conceptual "metaphor" to describe certain types of instability and change has become popular. This also has its problems, and has led to the accusation that complexity concepts are under-defined, and not empirically demonstrated in practice (Pollitt 2009). These accusations are important for complexity theorists to address if the theory is to gain in both intellectual credibility and pragmatic use.

Discerning critical points of time and places in the evolution of instability and stability is referred to by complexity theorists as "the edge of chaos": a key moment of substantive significance in a social or organizational system when the overall characteristics of the system "tip" from one state into another. A similar explanation is the idea of a "tipping point", as a key point of change in the time path of a social system (Gladwell 2001). Byrne and Callaghan (2014: 38) remark that "the vocabulary of chaos has had too much influence on our approach to complex systems … most complex systems are actually remarkably robust".

Order and disorder

For managers, the experience of stability and instability is often expressed in terms of order and disorder. Management is, in a large part, assumed to be a practice that should bring order to an organization and its productive process. Management is a word that in modernist culture is often juxtaposed with order. Complexity and chaos theory demonstrate that in complex systems, the nature of emergent and interdependent interactions is dynamic, and therefore inevitably disorderly to some extent. It becomes possible that by imposing too much order a manager will harm such an interactive and dynamic system. John Urry (2003: 14) says: "chaos and order are always interconnected in any such system." The manager has to administer and make sense of this interconnection.

Democracy is an unstable and sometimes chaotic system, but it is not anarchy. The untidiness of representative democratic politics and plural party based elections still results in a form of order and organization that many people consider works well for society. It checks and counterweights a monopoly of power. Democracy has time periods of instability, like the end of a government and an election, but also points of complexity where there is both uncertainty and some stability also. Certainly, it can be said that democracy appears to have some negative characteristics. Planning is not always carried through. Politics is rather short-term in its focus. The combined compromises and negotiations of the political process often leave out some important single issues and progress some rather less important ones. However, all this takes place in the context of a synthesis over time, where at the end of a period government generally cannot escape the big economic and social issues of the day, and if they try to ignore too many key issues for too long they risk losing power.

Another word used by complexity theorists to describe this process is emergence. Cohen and Stewart (1994: 169) describe the emergence of the human mind out of the observable neurons in the brain. A higher order of process results from the biology. Coveney and Highfield (1995: 7) comment that: "interactions lead to coherent collective phenomena, so called emergent properties that can be described only at higher levels than those of the individual units".

Several writers have discussed the tendency for modern states and their forms of government, governance and organization to emerge and evolve towards greater complexity. For example, Geyer and Rihani (2010: 78) say that: "average complexity tends to increase and entities with higher complexity stand a good chance of making the most gain in new situations". In a special edition of the journal *The Leadership Quarterly*, Marion and Uhl-Bien provide a summary definition of emergence:

> Like natural selection, complexity theory provides an explanation of how new things emerge. Whereas selection attributes newness to random mutations, however, complexity attributes it to the transformative nature of interactive mechanisms. Very simply put, the

interaction of different "things" (people, ideas, chemicals, species, etc.), combined with various mechanisms that emerge when adaptive entities interact (catalysis, elaboration, alteration, interdependency, etc.), produce novel outcomes. Like natural selection, this process is driven by adaptive tension, but whereas selection tension comes from outside the system (e.g., competition from other species), tension in complex systems can be derived from internal mechanisms (e.g., pressure to adapt to demands generated by conflicting constraints, or difficulty reconciling differences among agents).

(Marion and Uhl-Bien 2007: 293)

The dynamic interaction of instability and stability leads to greater complexity and from disorder emerge new forms of order. Kickert (2010) studied the reorganization of sections of public administration in the Netherlands into governance networks with independent agencies and concluded that "emergent" change resulted.

Levels

Social systems, including public organizations, often have hierarchical structures of self similarity. They can be thought of as nested systems and may have the characteristics of fractal geometry where similar core patterns are repeated at different points in a hierarchy. Fractal geometry is the study of similar shapes that are irregular in their similarity. These are the units of similarity in organizations that take on many diverse forms. Examples are committees, projects, task forces, data processes, decision trees, and teams. They can be thought of as micro organizational patterns that may occur in similar, but slightly different ways, at different places in a large public organization.

Public systems of organization are also horizontally complex in addition to their hierarchical levels. Luhmann's (1995) work is particularly interesting in identifying how different aspects of complex social systems are paradoxically open and closed. Luhmann classifies systems in a part functional way, but his approach is holistic and dynamic rather than determined by reductionist individualism or structural domination. So for example, he talks of the subsystems of the "economy" and "law". In Luhmann's view, specialist and separate communication and language define these subsystems. While this gives them (and empowers) their specialist function it also serves to separate them from the rest of society. Luhmann's insight is how, in complex contemporary society, relatively closed these systems still are. His concept of "structural coupling" provides some insight into the limited ways that two subsystems as inherently complex and different as the economy and law can occasionally communicate with each other. His insight into these profound communication difficulties in modern complex societies helps provide understanding about the large-scale dysfunctions and crises modern complex societies still experience. The recent and on-going financial crisis is a good example. The legal system has found it profoundly difficult to hold the economic system to account. In a large part this was because the economic system managed to create a value base of powerful implicit norms around the creation and use of money that rejected explicit legal controls based on more traditional value notions of fairness, transparency, honesty and equity. Luhmann's insight explains why horizontal working across the specialist differentiated functions of large organizations or policy areas can be so difficult.

For Luhmann, the best sense we have of social structures is by understanding the communications, or lack of communications, between systems and subsystems. Essentially, it is the closure of interaction, the failure of communication, explicitly or implicitly, intended or unintended, that is the defining feature of social and organizational life. Therefore, the marketplace (economics) and the justice system (law) can only be structurally coupled by certain formal methods and points of communication. Subsystems like the justice system work to reduce social complexity to make their own sphere of social operation manageable. One of the consequences is a closure with other subsystems.

Managers operate in subsystems that are directed by rules, regulations and procedures, but the interpretation of these is a vital component and different staff will interpret and prioritize them differently depending on their own role, or professional allegiance, in the organization. Managers experience the paradox of openness and closure that Luhmann defines, whereby horizontal and innovative work requires particular skills of communication if progress is to be made.

What Luhmann's structural holism ignores is the micro agency of individual humans, that certain individual attributes and social memberships can transect system formalities in different social manifestations, for example, less formal social relations between a higher social class group. An example would be the elite behavior and shared social and economic aspirations of politicians and bankers in the financial crisis (see Haynes 2012: Chapter 4). Nevertheless, Kontopoulos (1993) also gives us the conjecture of hope: "Metaptations". Therefore, ideas and how they are communicated, can change and evolve, even on a grand and macro scale. Interactions between individual agents are dynamic and never completely determined, but they always take place under the restrictions imposed by complex levels of structure and culture.

Scale

The nature of dynamic change in complex systems is that change is not proportionate or consistent over time, and some change therefore takes off at an exponential rate and has a considerable growth of scale (Pierpaolo and McKelvey 2011). In mathematics such phenomena can be examined with Power Laws. As cities get to a certain population size the probability increases that they will grow at a faster rate, and a constant linear rate of growth is unlikely. Businesses that make their first million dollars are likely to find it easier and quicker to make their next million. Conversely many businesses fail to get off the ground at all and to make an income for their owner. Taleb (2007) and Mandelbrot and Hudson (2008) argued that this sort of effect means that so called outliers happen more often than one expects and trends such as price variations and product sales cannot be expected to follow Gaussian normal distributions. Events can also be "scale free", for example, "large, intermediate and small scale earthquakes and ava-lanches are forever at risk of taking place: there is no typical or average size to an event" (Room 2011: 22). Buchanan (2004: 4) concludes: "Large disruptive events are not only more frequent than intuition might dictate, they are also disproportionate in their effect." Fat tails result at the extremes of the distribution curve. Buchanan argues that these fat tailed dis-tributions when discovered in the data of social organizations reflect the interdependence of their people and parts. The rapid reinforcement of specific behaviors that appear successful is copied, and this creates the Power Law effect. Scale effects mean that innovations do not develop equally or with equal chance, but that, because some get recognition and are copied at a critical time, they take off exponentially and then success reinforces success. In contrast, many ideas and products do not get established, and fail (Ormerod 2005).

Interaction and feedback

Complexity moves method away from linear thinking about cause and effect to nonlinear models that seek to understand the association and interaction between factors. Linearity implies that some variables determine the path of another. For example, diagnosis and treatment determine patient outcome. It also implies that any causal effect is constant. Non-linearity challenges this. Any causal effect may not be constant. As a diagnosis is increasingly matched with treatment for a growing population, other intervening factors often either expand or reduce the effectiveness of the treatment so that it either does even better, or loses some impact. Non-linearity implies the relationship that a patient has with their medical team also determines the outcome. This is because good interaction ensures a careful sharing of precise information between the patient and doctor. In the context of an evolving condition, the communication needs to be dynamic to ensure a correct diagnosis is reached, and over time, the most beneficial outcome is possible. Complex systems are full of dynamic interactions from which the future state of the system emerges. Managers can take part in these interactions and thereby seek to influence the future of the system, but there are limits in their ability to determine outcomes and to control the direction that the emergence of new forms of order takes. It has been shown above that some of these restrictions to achievement are imposed by structures and cultures:

> Man made complex systems tend to develop cascades and runaway chains of reaction that decrease, even eliminate, predictability, and cause outsized events. So the modern world may be increasing in technological knowledge, but, paradoxically, it is making things a lot more unpredictable.
>
> (Taleb 2012: 7)

The importance of recognizing changing interactions rather than assuming causations can be applied to an understanding of many historical debates about political problem definition and the role of policy development and public service interventions. For example, various studies have been put forward to argue that parents should minimize their employment time when their children are young, and stay at home more with their child, or conversely that preschool education is vital to a child's long-term attainment. Here different arguments are put forward that parents' working behavior and use of preschool facilities directly affects the educational outcome for the child. However, much of this research is based on some underlying assumptions about what is likely to cause long-term educational attainment and a complex approach to the association and interaction between variables is rejected by the research. It may be that it is quite possible for a child to do well, regardless of whether both parents are employed full time, but that the critical factors are the quality of the interaction of the parents with the child and the services provided, to ensure a positive and caring network of relationships. Here the emphasis is not on a deterministic causal route but on the quality of feedback received in relationships. There may be different ways that a child can receive this quality of feedback, not one single path of patterns and events.

Complexity theory and its study of system dynamics put much emphasis on feedback interactions (Meadows 2009). Feedback is reinforcing (positive) or balancing (negative). Social scientists increasingly avoid the "positive" and "negative" labels, because they can be confused with normative value judgments, when the descriptions are intended as simple scientific language for observing system dynamics. For example, the increased use of sugary drinks by children could be argued to be positively reinforcing behavior. A pattern of increasing consumption is reinforced by peer behavior, cheap prices, clever advertising and product placement. But increased consumption of sugary drinks would not usually be seen as a positive in the normative sense. Conversely, government intervention to levy tax on sugary drinks designed as a counterbalance, and "negative" feedback to check the increased consumption, would be seen by health service professionals as a normatively positive intervention to benefit public health. Reinforcing and balancing feedbacks are important concepts for managers seeking to intervene in complex systems. They are responses to dynamic and unpredictable patterns and associations of human interactions. Poor judgments about when to respond to complex system dynamics can cause instability and social problems. As Sterman (2012: 37) notes: "Time delays in complex systems are common and particularly troublesome".

This interactive approach to causality implies different approaches to developing public policy interventions and their management. Lining up some key inputs like staff and the training of key skills will not be enough. A complex system is an ongoing myriad of interactions, some that reinforce certain behavior patterns, and some that do not. The degree of openness and closure in these communications is at the core of social science debate, given that some actors will have more power and status than others will. Human interactions are interpersonal communications and the quality of these is likely to be at the core of many public service outcomes.

The links between people in the system and flow of communications between them are highly creative and dynamic, but also restricted by codes and controls that reinforce the powerful and their authority. This context of communications and interactions ebbs and flows through the system, and dynamically defines it, moving the system through periods of relative stability and instability and change. One method for analyzing and managing this complexity of communication is to use network approaches. Put simply, this is observing what type of human networks are operating in a policy system or an organizational process, and then seeking to intervene in these networks to achieve desired managerial ends.

Networks

As described in Chapter 1, one of the theoretical areas that has been developed by academics concurrent with NPM relates to the existence of public policy networks. The conceptual interweaving of theories about networks with management practices is not without its epistemological challenges (Klijn 1997; McGuire and Agranoff 2011). Paul Ormerod (2012) has argued that networks in society and the economy perpetuate powerful processes of reinforcement, and at their most simple, these can reinforce certain trends of behavior change at exponential rates of growth. This in part explains the scaling up of consumer trends, where bubbles in assets like house purchasing can quickly take hold when credit finance for such purchasers is available. If the network reinforcement of scale takes off, the influence increasingly falls with the few who become more and more successful. Therefore, a distribution of similar products, or the popularity of people in a social network, can end up far from the Gaussian normal distribution, instead showing an outlier tail of the highly successful. Getting to a thousand followers on Twitter is difficult, but getting the next thousand does not usually involve the same amount of message prodding and creative tweeting: success and popularity is highly likely to rise at an exponential rate.

Once a specific media product takes hold and is copied, massive gains in the market place are rapidly established, even though a given song, book or film might not necessarily have rational advantages to the consumer over other similar products. In such volatile markets, positioning a new product alongside something that is already successful and communicating on a mass scale with those likely to be persuaded of the similarity, may improve the limited chances one has of being successful and becoming well established.

Other social networks can be highly dispersed and based on localized clusters. The ability to understand and intervene in these networks becomes dependent on identifying possible "connectors" who have the most history, power and influence with these dispersed or clustered interactions. Thinking about people and their networks in organizations, or across collaborative organizations, suggests a rather different approach to the management of public services. The focus becomes identifying some key individuals because of their social placement and the possible impact for certain tasks, and seeking their assistance in delivering effective communication. Classical approaches towards policy design and implementation that focus on the design of new vertical structures and processes, while still of some importance, are often less predictable than might be hoped and subject to a range of unintended consequences. Identifying, working, and communicating with existing key policy actors can be an important strategy for success.

The idea of managing boundaries and instability and allowing for self-organization with the creative tensions that exist requires that managers need to understand the concept of networks. Networking emphasizes the permeable structures between people, teams and organizations and the need to build up trusting relationships that allow efficient inter-organizational partnerships. Collaboration becomes as important as competition. Organizations have to find the correct dynamic mix of collaboration and competition that is appropriate for their context. Many writers, like Lipnack and Stamps, believe that network organizations have come of age:

> Life has become too complicated for hierarchy and bureaucracy. With change as the underlying driver, organizations need more speed and flexibility, greater scope and sharper intelligence, more creativity and shared responsibility. Teams offer part of the answer – our collective rediscovery of ancient human knowledge about the power of small groups. Networks – of teams and other groups joined together, which we call 'teamnets' – offer another, newer part of the answer.
>
> (Lipnack and Stamps 1994: xvii)

Public service networks do not have to be tied to lots of rigid rules and bureaucracy that make them slow to change and progress, but some degree of coordination is required. As Battram (1996: 3) concludes: "Networks need hierarchies and hierarchies need networks." Managers must intervene in these networks, as brokers and diplomats, trying to facilitate positive developments in policy activities and outputs. Managers established at certain levels are often the network connectors who give an organization this chance for cooperation and coordination.

The downside is that this new network policy environment can feel unaccountable to the public when compared to the traditional idea of a directly accountable political system that manages a monopoly public sector. Power inequalities are a key concern when examining social networks and there is often an inability of networks to break social and professional inequalities perpetuated elsewhere in social structures. For example, racial minorities and women may continue to be excluded from new governance networks (Newman 2001: 172). But complexity theory does imply that understanding networks aids the dynamic potential to create opportunities for social change that can include the redistribution of power and accountability.

The new policy environment of governance, markets and networks can feel fragmented and lacking in clear lines of communication, but the key to its evolution is in maximizing its transparent self-organization, so that the cross linking of different types of accountability—managerial, professional, political, consumerism—actually leave the public with more options to hold services accountable, rather than fewer. Rhodes (2000) has suggested that in such circumstances the network mix of stakeholders and structures will be different in each policy context. Hill and Hupe's (2002) analysis of policy implementation suggests a similar framework. Some degree of coordination will be needed to stabilize the evolving and changing organizational patterns. Too much flexibility will freeze the network (Battram 1996: 47). There is no single network structure blueprint for a mix of politics, markets, management and civil society.

Ormerod (2012) sees networks and their links as the key form of social organization for policy makers and public managers to understand and influence. He proposes three core types of networks: scale free, random and small world.

Scale free networks are in the main highly dispersed. Most people in these networks only have a limited number of connections and contacts with each other, but there are a small number who have many connections and contacts. Those who do have many connections are potentially highly influential because of their ability to understand the characteristics of the network, its values, behaviors and forms of communications. Attachment to the network will not be on "a random basis but preferential in relation to those who are already popular" (Room 2011: 176). In part this influence will depend on a further typology of the network, such as its degree of organizational formality or informality, and its dominant logics and values. Formality, like in a large public organization, adds network leverage to certain formal roles in those organizations. For example, in many large public organizations middle managers become the connector hubs because so much communication traffic has to pass through them on its way "up" and "down" the organizational hierarchy (see Table 2.1). In a softer and informal type of organization, for example an internet based network of professional doctors sharing information about the treatment of a particular disease or health condition, it will be less obvious that a role is correlated with communication hubs or with people with managerial roles at the centre. A few doctors will become the hub simply because the number of connections they establish is greater. This might be linked to their knowledge and knowledge sharing, and the credibility of their opinion, or it may be linked to their social persistence in using the network and seeking out the network for developing their own

Table 2.1 Network types and organizational features: formal public organizations and informal social organization

Network Type	Organizational type	
	Formal	*Informal*
Scale Free Complex web of many interactions. A large proportion go through a small number of connector hubs	*Large organization* Middle managers are the connector hubs	*National or International Professional network* Professional enthusiasts are the connector hubs
Small World Localized intensity of interactions, with occasional links out	*Division or team* Operational managers have intense communication with their local team. They are also the long distance connector who carries messages in and out	*Close knit social group* Locally intense communications. Occasional links to dispersed long distance connectors, these are identified by personality type or personal circumstances
Random Apparently random interactions, with no pattern	Opportunity to form "creative" randomness within formal organizations: i.e.: interprofessonal or interdisciplinary networking events	Emergence of social connections via social behavior patterns and weak networks, such as: commuting to work, holidays, internet chat rooms etc.

connections and influence. In the informal professional network, it is less easy for outsiders to identify the connector hubs, and it will not be obvious to insiders who the hub connectors are. For example, if an internet based professional network is primarily resulting in small group clusters of email contacts and one to one emails that sometimes lead to face to face meetings, neither an insider nor outsider will easily be able to identify the people who are the core network hubs. In all forms of scale free networks it is possible that a relatively small number of people can exercise maximum influence on the outcomes of policy and practice. Older nodes are more likely to be better connected, and once established, tend to be enduring, although it is difficult for an external assessor of the network to look beyond the quantity of communications and to understand much about the quality of the communications (Room 2011). This is why middle managers occupy such important roles in large public organizations. Judgments and decisions about the quality of communications in a scale free network are likely to require qualitative reflections and insights taken from a subsample of people belonging to that network. Each member of the sample should have a different status and membership history.

Small scale networks share the characteristic of scale free networks in that in the main connections and communications are dispersed. But in small scale networks there is less of an organized structure. Small scale networks connect people in small groups because of some predominant social reason, for example, because they are required to communicate at work, or because they share the same professional boundaries. These are small groups of people who often communicate with each other, because that is the routine of their lives. There may be long periods of predictability and consistency of the quantity in these communications, even though the quality and depth of the communications might be very different depending on the periodic social circumstances. Small scale networks may have strong spatial characteristics, although this may be declining in the digital age. Nevertheless, there is likely to be an overlap between face to face and digital communication rather than an exclusive type of communication. So people in an office team both talk at meetings and via email. Groups of children at school meet in the class room but also continue to communicate on mobile phones and social media in the evenings and at weekends. Arguably digital communication has intensified the local quantity of communications in small scale networks. Ormerod (2012) notes that the nature of these networks is that they are fairly difficult to intervene in, from a distance, in terms of whether they can be accessed by senior managers, partner organizations, or any form of outsider. In a formal setting there will be an operational front line manager or team leaders whose job it is to present formal communication outwards (Table 2.1). In families and friendship groups, external penetrations of the small network of communication may be near impossible, for good reasons of privacy and confidentiality.

The added layer of complexity with understanding small scale networks is identifying and understanding more about the communication routes going outwards. If there is organizational formality, the route in and out will be clearly specified, and that person can be communicated with and asked to communicate into their small network. For example, this might be a team leader within a large public organization. In less formal kinds of organizations, this is much more difficult. But clearly the nature of small scale networks is that people are likely to be members of several such networks: employment, family, friendship groups, hobbies and interests. So occasional connections across and between these small scale networks will occur, even if they are infrequent and difficult to understand. Ormerod (2012) calls these aspects "long distance" connections. An associated issue is whether long distance connectors can be identified as people with shared characteristics: in other words those in small scale networks who are more likely, due to their personality, or personal circumstances, to send messages out to elsewhere. If managers and policy makers are to identify legitimate and ethical reasons for intervening into small scale networks outside of their own organizations, in ways other than through a formally identified "connector", they will start by conceptualizing where the long distance connections and connectors are in the networks they are interested in.

Random networks describe the casual and chance connections that people have, rather than those that take place in deliberate and planned forms of organization. Random networks are characterized by time limited or superficial communication rather than long-term relationships. Examples would be people who all share a train journey, drivers who become stuck in the same traffic jam, or people who happen to use an open discussion forum on the internet because they all share the same problem with a consumer product at a similar moment of time. One interesting thing about random networks is that they seem to be on the increase in a global and digitalized world where there are many more opportunities for people to potentially interact in unplanned ways. Public health specialists have a particular interest in random physical networks, in order to understand the spread of global diseases, such as new strains of influenza.

It is argued that relatively passive forms of communication, for example observing web based advertising, can lead to random network effects, as even though these are not strictly speaking synchronous interactions, they can cause similar behavior patterns, if it leads to a consumer interaction such as purchasing an item at a later date. Therefore "random" phone calls have become a commonplace form of advertising where a company targets a very large population with its product, knowing that a very small subsample of that large population can be persuaded to make a purchase, albeit a random group from that target population. (If they knew more about who was going to buy, they would have targeted the group more tightly at the beginning of the operation.)

If policy makers and managers want to influence random networks they have to accept that mass forms of superficial communication into that network are probably the only method of influence, and that the precise result is rather unpredictable, but some small return on a large scale intervention is possible. Public policy interventions may require such approaches if the benefits of making connections with just a few relevant individuals are substantial. Examples would be subpopulations who are likely to need expensive support in the future if they cannot be identified early in an event path: children who have missed critical inoculations, teenagers with the early signs of severe conditions like depression, or young adult holiday makers at risk of excessive hedonistic behavior. In these examples, even if only a few can be reached and respond, the longer-term public service costs saved are substantial.

In summary, the importance of network theory to operationalizing complexity theory is that network theory provides a method for understanding patterns and similarity within a complex social system. It provides a theoretical basis for communication, given that communication and interaction are likely to have some relationship with behavior and behavior change. In the unstable and evolving world of complex systems, having a theoretical framework for understanding patterns and similarity is one of the best methods managers have for deciding where and how to intervene. Rather than reorganizing roles in an organization on the basis of perceived optimal structures, organizations may do better to ensure the correct functioning of managers and leaders as communication connectors within networks (Kickert 2010).

Attractors

Another method for understanding complexity, and its relationship with organizations over time, is to think of the idea of "boundaries of instability". This means that the future situation looks unpredictable, but that it is unlikely to move outside of certain boundaries. It is for this reason that the economist, Paul Ormerod (1998), has implied that economists should forecast the range of likely data, rather than making exact predictions. In other words— economists should forecast that inflation will be between 2% and 3%, rather than predicting it will be 2.34%. Boundaries of instability are maintained by what complexity theorists call attractors. These are the forces that direct the fluctuation of data and behavior back and forth into some recognizable pattern. Byrne and Callaghan (2014: 27) remark that: "An attractor is something to which a dynamical system evolves over time. When the system is close to an attractor it tends to remain in that location."

A mathematical attractor can be identified as a trajectory, a set of coordinates, in a dynamic system. It is not a precise central point, but a movement around an area, within fixed boundaries. A "strange attractor" is one where the trajectory of coordinates is more difficult to predict, but where there is still a sense of boundaries and partial order. With the presence of a strange attractor, there are breaks in the symmetry, so a similar pattern flips onto a different trajectory (Williams 2000). Battram (1996: 150) says: "the concept of the attractor reminds us that there are organising principles at work in all systems; values, goals, theories, leadership in groups: all can be considered as attractors bringing people together." So where a system is dynamic (not static, and predictable) there is very often a hidden sense of order, keeping action and behavior within a certain range of perimeters. Attractors are characterized by fluctuations around a common pattern, with some of the fluctuations being more extreme than others. These patterns of similarity are often described as attractors because there seems to be some kind of central point of order (almost like a magnetic attraction) around which the patterns of data change. Attractors can also be described as fluctuations within boundaries of instability. Accurate prediction is impossible, but most of the time there is a reasonable chance of forecasting within boundaries. The mathematical calculation and plotting of attractors in social science seems to have some, but limited, uses in public policy and management. One example is the pattern that changes in price inflation take over time and the extent to which patterns emerge that can be identified with particular periods of economic management or economic history (Haynes 2012). This may be useful to learning in economic policy management for the purpose of setting central bank interest rates, or the purchase of financial assets by central banks (often referred to as Quantitative Easing).

A qualitative approach to applying the concept of attractors to organizations is to try and understand the influence of rules and values on organizations and public policy and the extent to which certain rules or dominant values can generate periods of order and future behavior patterns. In this sense, there is an "attraction" to social order in social systems and organizations that is caused by "attractors" and these attractors may well take the form of values expressed as "norms of behavior" or "logics of operation".

Values are about thinking (cognitions) and they influence behavior, and are linked to the choices and decisions that people make. If not demonstrated in direct manifestations of behavior they can be expressed and revealed in the attitudes that people have. Values are inherently social and collective in that they link individual thinking, attitudes, and behavior to collective group attitudes and behavior, with the consequence that some values when translated to individual behavior deny the ability of others to make choices and decisions. Values are relational and can assist in explaining power distribution and conflicts. Their working definition is often dynamic and evolves through constant comparative judgments. Values are taught and reproduced in social groups, like families and communities; and in institutions like religious organizations and educational establishments, and also in places of employment. Values, however, are in a constant state of change. Social values are dynamic not static. They derive from a constant dialogue of communication and interaction, of feedback, between the individual and society. There are strong conceptual features of social values that can be linked to an understanding of complex social systems: they exist due to interaction, feedback and a dynamic state.

Can researchers understand social values as system patterns and make any general forecasts about their likely future direction? The World Values Survey (http://www.worldvaluessurvey.org) is a longitudinal international social science project to map the changing nature of social values with a particular emphasis on cross-national comparison. The Survey team argues that many social values are correlated and can be simplified by reductionist scientific methods to two cross-cultural dimensions. One dimension is traditional versus secular-rational values. The second dimension is self-expression values (World Values Survey 2012). Since 1990, the Survey has mapped the changing national patterns of international social values every five years.

Values can also be thought of as relative and absolute. Relative values are hierarchical. At the top of this hierarchy the majority of the population will share the value that it is wrong to kill a human being and it is only in extreme circumstances that they will temporarily suspend such a dominant value. Such powerful values might also be thought of as absolute because of their tendency to exert strong control over personal behavior, and their scope is universal in that they are shared by many cultures. In contrast, some values are much weaker in their relative impact and are at the bottom of the hierarchy and can be overruled by other values, so that they have little effect beyond cognitions and attitudes, and are not easily translated into behavior. An example might be a value that a person holds believing migrants are less likely to be good citizens and employees, but as soon as they have an experience of close contact with a migrant who they see behaving as an excellent citizen or employee the internalized value is no longer reinforced and less likely to be articulated as an attitude. Instead, it is superseded by a more important relative value: that other people should be judged according to one's experience of the evidence of their behavior and actions, rather than simplistic media stereotypes. Thus a person's real experience of how they value an individual person and relationships, in the context of a recent close encounter (and the norms and logics they apply to such key personal interactions) takes on a much higher relative influence in their own cognitions and behavior. Real experience interacts with any generalized value base that comes from historical and external sources. Real experience is a powerful reinforcement, or balance check, over internalized values and causes one's own hierarchical value system to change and evolve.

In sociology the concept of "Norms" has been used to understand rules and conventions of behavior derived from social values. Norms provide implicit conventions and explicit rules for social behavior. Norms are value-based expectations of future social behavior that are associated with behavioral outcomes. These are enforced by cultural pressures to conform, or by more formal rules of law and institutional enforcement and sanction. An implicit norm in most western societies is to pay men and women equal income for the same task. Not all comply. In some countries, explicit legal action, like enforcement in the courts, is possible. The underpinning social value here is that men and women are of equal human and productive value.

A major sociological study of complex social systems by Kontopoulos (1993) preferred to use the concept of logics rather than norms. A criticism of Kontopoulos' formidable work is that logics as a category are underdefined, but essentially, he applies logics as a synthesis, as patterns of reason, where values, alongside objective observation and learning, are constructed and bonded into more substantial social ideas. These ideas have a profound impact on social behavior and interaction.

Logics then are interactive and relational and linked to constructing and deconstructing norms of behavior, and these interactions and communications are social debates and arguments where changes in norms and partial closure between people and subsystems can have a powerful future consequence on other parts of the system.

Kontopoulos' (1993) major work proposed 40 logics of social stratification with groups of logics operating at different levels of scale (micro logics, meso logics, macro logics). He argues micro logics are applied at the level of the individual, although when being applied simultaneously by many, or in close time proximity, they can have higher scale effects. An example of a micro logic would be reasons for people to flow in and out of social systems: for example, an individual reaches a rule bound age and enters a school and then flows out on acquiring a certain grade level or when reaching a specific age. The logic here is that a child should attend school and receive an education because history has demonstrated numerous individual and social benefits of such behavior.

A meso logic interconnects individual and local structures. Differentiation (Kontopoulos 1993: 355) of groups is thus triggered over time by indeterminate evolution of self-organizing behavior patterns, so groupings that sociologists recognize as "gangs", "tribes" or "classes" can be evidenced. Allometry (p. 355) dictates that these groups are dynamic over time and not static and that at some point in time will have an optimal reason for existence that is likely to be impossible to maintain at a continuing and constant state.

Macrologics "operate simultaneously with (and on) the previous levels and produce global systems of structure at the higher level" (p. 335). An example is Capitalism as a historical collection and amalgamation of logics at lower levels that comes to control and regulate social life at the scale of national and international societies. Kontopoulos' work illustrates how in a sea of complex logics, totalizing logics come to dominate and are remarkably difficult to shift. In Chapter 1, we examined how NPM had become a form of macro logic.

The interaction of values, norms and logics

It has been argued that attractors in complex social systems are comprised of norms and logics, and can combine with rules to impose order and stability (Haynes 2012: 10–12). These forms of order can still be dynamic, but with instability restricted by the operation of a strong rule (like a law or policy statute) to achieve stable boundaries of activity, and with certain trajectory patterns likely to be achieved going forward. These rules are not deterministic in cause and effect, but result in similar patterns. It is suggested here that attractors can be thought of in human systems as norms and logics. In addition, formal forms of order in organizations like public services are highly likely to be constructed around norms and logics. If managers understand the interaction of values, cognitions, norms, logics and rules in their organizations they will be better able to manage and steer the future direction of that organization. Table 2.2 indicates the interaction of individual values with societal logics, through the interactive and hierarchical process that defines norms and specifies rules.

When the links between employees' values are in conflict with the norms and rules of senior managers and policy organizations, considerable problems can develop with the implementation of policy and delivery of services. Such difficulties can be considered as forms of bottom up, or "self" organized resistance. Attractors like norms and logics provide social stability and order, but they are a dynamic "soup" of ideas and their powerful patterns of influence are subject to constant feedback, evolution and change.

Self-organization

Complexity theory changes the perception that managers and professionals have about the nature of order in organizations. There is never any perfect or attainable sense of complete control and order, because if there were, there would be no meaningful and creative interaction

Table 2.2 Values, norms and logics: as attractors to order in public organization

Attractor	Implicit	Explicit	Micro	Meso	Macro
Values	Cognitive beliefs expressed in language	Influence social behavior	Community action	Political parties Single issue campaign groups Religious organizations Professional organizations	Universal and shared cross cultural beliefs
Norms	Family and neighborhood expectations	Public value Public ethos	Civic action	Dominant professional values	Universal professional values
Logics (Reasoning)	Collective responsibilities	Set up of public services to achieve collective public goals	Local government institutions	National government and governance	International governance
Rules	Professional ethics and values, expressed in contract	Organizational rules in the context of government and governance	Local government rules	National and continental laws	Universal laws and rights

and feedback in the organization. Total control of events is not possible. Organizational structure and hierarchy is seen by senior managers as the visible form of order and control, making the assumption that such a form of control can be managed, led and implemented. But structural solutions are rarely straightforward forms of successful management interventions. Often there are dysfunctions and unintended consequences when structures are changed. People in organizations frequently get anxious and worried by such changes, failing to share the vision and perspective of those who impose them. Reinforcing feedback can amplify negative responses to such change, and if people persist in believing that such imposed change via structural reorganizations will not work, organizational failure becomes a self-fulfilling prophecy as resistance builds and motivation declines.

A seminal study in the Netherlands (Boons *et al.* 2009: 235–236) about the existence and influence of self-organization in public organization concluded:

1   Self-Organisation is a driving force of governance processes that sheds light on why government steering ambitions often fail.
2   Self-Organisation causes processes to follow unexpected trajectories. Self-organisation stems from the free choices of people in charge often oriented at maintaining their position and stability, but occasionally oriented at chance and adjustment to new demands or circumstances.
3   Self-Organisation can and often will be driven by the ambition or need to survive (often this is called self-interest; we use the complexity theoretical term autopoietic or

conservative self-organisation), but also by the ambition to contribute to and have an impact on a larger system (often this is called public interest; we use the term adaptive or dissipative self-organisation).

4 Self-Organisation is closely related to the boundary judgements regarding the system as defined by the actors in a certain case. Boundary judgements that are based on partial knowledge and that are poorly investigated tend to generate discontinuities and conflicts or non-interaction between systems, while more holistic judgements could help to generate synchronicity.

Order in organizations is created by the human interaction and the feedback processes within the organization: through committee meetings, working groups, accepted practices, bureaucracy, and work routines. Formal and informal sanctions apply to those who do not comply. Power and authority as exercised by managers and senior professionals are the explicit disciplines in this process, but there will also be powerful implicit disciplines that act as controls on behavior that are reinforced by the peer pressures of colleagues.

Self-organization is a form of social construction whereby people in public organizations make sense of the order imposed upon them, sometimes choosing their own version or type of order in response. Therefore order can evolve and emerge from dynamic and innovative human interaction. Self-organization is bottom up. At first it is small scale, but sometimes it evolves into a dominant culture at a higher level of operation. Self-organization is a form of interaction that public policy makers and managers ignore at their peril. It is surely better to work with it, to seek to understand its powers and possibilities and to find ethical ways of working with the phenomenon. In a research study to understand the power and influence of self-organization in government policy networks Ricaurte-Quijano (2013: 76) provides the following helpful definition: "Self organisation is a property of complex systems that enables them to re-produce or re-arrange their internal structure in order to cope with internal or external perturbations and instability." She also distinguishes between "conservative" and "dissipative" self-organization. Conservative self-organization is orientated towards preserving existing social structures and cultures. Dissipative self-organization is destabilizing, leading to new dynamics and changes in the system.

Parallels can be drawn here with bottom up political movements in western democracies. A conservative self-organization is the Tea Party in the USA. Although a grass roots political movement that evolved primarily to reduce the budget deficit with this based on a fear of rising taxation, it has become linked with the established Republican Party on many issues, although sometimes in conflict with it. It seeks to preserve liberal economic values based on individualism, and therefore campaigns to prevent much progressive social change such as collective health care reforms based on redistribution. This is in marked contrast to a dissipative self-organization like Occupy Wall Street, a radical political protest movement that exists outside of main stream political parties in the USA and aims to achieve social and economic change by non-violent direct action rather than leverage via voting in elections. It argues that the established political system cannot achieve changes in the distribution of income that are needed to achieve a decline in relative poverty and that only direct action from the public can achieve such change. These are high impact examples of political self-organization with scaling up effects. They illustrate how some bottom up movements can quickly become identifiable at a higher level in society and reproduced elsewhere. This is a further example of reinforcing feedback.

It is the interaction of the members of the organization with each other and with the organizational group processes that gives the organization its collective life and meaning. This human interaction within organizations is dynamic and a living process; it can only be partly controlled by formal and informal sanctions. There will always be some dynamics of self-organization and self-determination within an organization, and the individuals concerned and their relationships with each other will create this. In many organizational contexts it is best for managers to harness this creative force and to try and use it for the good of the organization, rather than trying to suppress it through an increase in formal procedures and bureaucracy. Too much deliberate control can be counterproductive. In part this will depend on the exact context of the public organization, but even within an authority based institution like the Police, Fire Service and Armed Forces there will be strong creative elements of self-organization that need to be understood and worked with. Battram (1998: 120) comments: "Order will result from self organisation. The way is open to a new and adaptive form of teamwork in which individuals manage themselves within clear boundaries."

A variety of human relations management research has shown the need for people working in organizations to find a positive meaning to their role and working experience (see Chapter 6). In contrast, performance driven and control based management styles are in danger of creating fragmentation and conflict for those who seek positive social value in their public sector work (see Chapter 4). Self-organization is often demonstrated in resistance to higher top down institutional and organizational processes. Workers are very creative in giving a local meaning and value to their employment activities. This is illustrated by the concept of self-organization.

Types of change

Much of management activity involves change. The management of change has been the focus of much activity and interest in recent decades generating thousands of publications and considerable management consultancy output. Many management and business degrees have a unit or module of study that focuses on the management of change. One common approach is to maximize communication, thus encouraging expression of all anxieties and misgivings about change, but seeking to argue the positive element of what a particular change in a management program can achieve for the organization (while acknowledging some risks and losses).

When seeking to develop a rational argument to persuade others of the need for change, history is not always an accurate assessment of the future. This is described by some commentators as looking in the driving mirror to see the road ahead (Sanderson 2000). The English Audit Commission's (1995: 5) inquiry into the work of the Fire Service criticized the fact that response standards were based on historical data rather than recent realities. The Audit Commission argued that this meant the Fire Service had not updated itself to face new external challenges and opportunities.

Figure 2.1 indicates the different types of mathematical change that can occur in one variable. These are: incremental linear changes (1–7), periodic cycles (8–14), nonlinear changes (15–26) and transformations (27–35). The public sector needs to give thought to the types of change that can occur. This is one of the central ideas of complexity theory.

Although transformation is described in Figure 2.1 with a simple steep straight line followed by fluctuations at a higher point, transformations are not always best understood with such quantitative methods, especially when one is considering the multiple effects that large-scale social changes have. The key aspect of transformations is that the relationship and interaction between key variables change substantially. The global financial crisis of 2007–08, when there was loss of confidence in the money credit market, is one example of such a transformation (Haynes 2012).

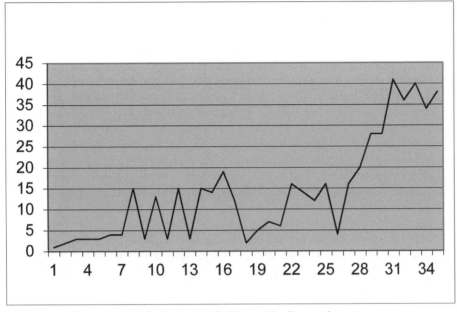

1-6=linear, incremental change; 7-13=periodic cycle;
14-26=nonlinear; 27-49=transformation

Figure 2.1 Types of change

Path dependency

Path dependency offers a differing account of the nature of public policy change to complexity, but there are some shared aspects. It puts emphasis on the importance of the early stages of the evolution of the nation state and public organizations and that thereafter, contemporary societies tend to settle in a macro policy world that is largely stable and conservative and resistant to transformation. In a competitive business situation, this path dependency may create first mover advantage, reinforcing that others follow but do not have the first and potentially most dominant position in the market: "If a firm is wondering where to site its operations, there may well be benefits in locating close to other firms in the same industry" (Room 2011: 17). Path dependency sees the importance of the early historical stages of establishing new levels of government and public institutions, as this is when change and instability are most likely before people and processes settle into patterns. Cairney (2012: 348) links complex systems to path dependence: "Complex systems are particularly sensitive to initial conditions that produce a long-term momentum or 'path dependence'".

The Punctuated Equilibrium theory of the public sector is similar, in that, it states there will be long periods of macro level stability, but occasional large scale transformations are still possible. If we juxtapose this with a complexity view of the public sector, complexity puts more relative emphasis on instability and the frequency of occurrences of instability, especially below the macro level and in meso and micro places.

Bifurcation paradigm shifts and transformations

Bifurcation is a term used in chaos and complexity theory to describe the critical points in time when systems and organizations are most likely to change dramatically. This is related to the concept of dramatic change, or transformation, or phase transition. The concept of bifurcation is one attempt to gain a greater understanding about how social and organizational transformations occur. As Urry (2003: 28) explains, organizational systems "reach points of bifurcation when their behaviour and future pathways become unpredictable and new higher order, more differentiated, structures may emerge."

Bifurcation is the point of time when organizations and systems are both on the edge of chaos and subject to dramatic change. At its most spectacular, it is at these times that public organizations may grow exponentially or die altogether. It is at this point of time that organizations and economies can stray outside of the patterns of what is apparently "normal" or expected behavior and change. As a consequence of this, the key attractor influences that have provided previous patterns of stability may also change. The organization enters a new phase in its evolution, referred to as phase transition, or transformation—completely new periodic trends may then follow. The biologist Richard May, cited in Sardar and Abrams (1999), called these phase transitions, bifurcations, because when he studied the mathematics of animal population evolution, he found that at certain points of growth, similar populations of species might suddenly divide into two different patterns. Cairney (2012: 348) describes this as, "long periods of stability are interrupted by short bursts of change".

Byrne (2001) has discussed the examples of a school at the micro level being transformed from a failing set of statistical results to a set that is more politically acceptable, or the transition of an entire welfare system at the macro level moving from one based on Keynesian public expenditure to one based on a reduced public sector and privatization.

At a societal level, Byrne and Rogers (1996) have talked about social and economic bifurcations that divide groups of people into different neighborhoods and social experiences. For example, social and economic changes in policy and free market behavior result in a separation of rich and poor neighborhoods. This places the challenge for managing change with political government which must prevent the chaotic aspects of social change from driving people apart into social groups that are unable to integrate and co-exist, and become defined by their stark differences and conflicts with each other. In this sense, recession, war, riots, terrorism, and other forms of turbulent unrest can be thought of as undesirable manifestations of chaos, or more explicitly, the reinforcing feedback derived from rapid social and economic change. Therefore, it cannot be assumed that unstable and disorderly change will automatically evolve to socially acceptable expressions of social complexity. Continued chaos, ineffectiveness and a divided society are the less attractive result of the instability paradigm that some of the writings on this subject refuse to consider.

Meadows (2009) has made a link between public and social transformations and major changes in dominant values and logics. Thus, she concludes, that such paradigm shifts if reflections of ideological and political changes in dominant social values are much more substantial than managerial changes at the meso and micro levels of society and within specific public organizations.

Box 2.1 Summary of complexity concepts

Attractors

Complex systems are in a large part indeterminate and unpredictable, but they do have important elements of order as defined by patterns of replicated behavior for given periods. This feature prevents a continuous saturation of instability and chaos. While system feedback, such as checking and balancing, can contribute to order and help establish relative boundaries around instability and disorder, attractors provide a further source of order.

Attractors are not communication feedbacks in themselves, but influences—like a cultural conscience—that lead to partially ordered patterns of behavior. Examples are values, beliefs and logics. In their basic form, these are internal cognitions, but the extent to which they attract order and persist over time and become dominant powers of persuasion, depends on how much influence they have on determining human behavior.

Attractors are hierarchical, in that in any one time and place one attractor will be contributing to social order more than others will, but these hierarchies are unstable over time and likely to evolve and fluctuate in their relative influence on behavior.

Government rules and procedures can also be conceptualized as creating an attraction to order. For example, central bank interest rate setting will often influence patterns of economic behavior, but such interventions can also be considered as communication feedback mechanisms.

Chaos

Chaos is present when a relatively high degree of instability defines the behavior of the system, or the local subsystem. Chaos can also be evident in a macro system and examples would be the outbreak of war, or the failure of a national banking system.

Dynamic

The complex web of interactions and feedbacks in a complex system makes these systems dynamic rather than static. Things never stay precisely the same and are always changing, if only in small and incremental ways.

Edge of chaos

This is the key point in time when a system, or sub system, is argued to be passing from stability to instability. This creates a critical challenge to politicians, policy makers and managers and there is a range of difficult decision options that result.

Emergence

People in complex systems are, to some extent, independent and local operatives who adopt some particular novel forms of localized and "bottom up" behavior. Therefore, their behavior can never be totally determined by "top down" rules and structures. This leads to the emergence of new and sometimes unpredicted forms of interaction, communication and behavior.

Feedback

Many interactions in complex systems take the form of feedback. A characteristic of feedback is similar responses to previous communications. Feedback can be "reinforcing" and thereby stimulating similar behavior. Alternatively, it can be "balancing" that checks the reinforcement of similar behavior and seeks to change a pattern and to break repetition. Feedback can take place in different social contexts and is not always part of a formal organizational process. For example, customers in a market often copy each other and buy similar products, thus reinforcing a consumer trend. Politicians and public managers may seek to use more formal public policy processes like taxation or trading rules as forms of feedback to check and balance collective behaviors.

Interaction

Complex systems, like public organizations are in a large part defined by interaction and communication. This includes interactions between the people within the organization, and the interactive communications flowing in and out of the system through its relationship with other organizations, and through those people who enter and then leave the system.

Levels

One defining aspect of complex systems is that many of their patterns and similarities are defined by reference to a hierarchical level within the system. Management, for example, as a key system role, takes place at different levels: senior, middle and operational. Similarly, different politicians operate at national, regional and local levels. While these levels can be differentiated by their geographical location or functions of responsibility, they nevertheless share common approaches to values and models of practice. Levels can also demarcate system difference: for example with an outbreak of instability or chaos being limited to one level and one place. On other occasions, instability is contagious across levels.

Networks

The interactions in systems and their subsystems form patterns. These patterns of communication can sometimes be identified as networks. For example, where some places and people are more substantially connected than others through "connector nodes". Here interaction is structured and repeated more often as a result. Nodes can be people of a particular social type or with a particular social role, or nodes may be created in a specific network because of a relatively random and evolving process of communication. Network communication patterns and flows are also in a large part defined by feedback responses and interactions. These evolve into patterns across time and place.

Scale

Like level, scale also provides another dimension to the understanding of complex systems. Up scaling of a change effect through a system from bottom to top, from micro local to macro, or small to large, is not consistently proportionate. For example, the larger a city grows over time, the even more likely it is to grow ever more rapidly than its immediate similar neighbors do. Likewise, a business that makes a million dollars will be more likely to make $100 million than a business that has made half a million is to make $50 million.

> **Self-organization**
>
> Given that order can emerge in complex systems in novel and creative ways, innovation and resistance, and other forms of local behavior are a common feature. Dissipative self-organization refers to the creation of new ideas and practices as a local response to system dysfunctions, like ineffectiveness and inefficiency. Conservative self-organization refers to the local defence of traditional and long-standing practices, this manifests as localized resistance to larger scale or external change.

The complexity journey—What have we learnt?

Box 2.1 summarizes the key conceptual issues discussed in this chapter. For the remainder of this chapter the text examines the current application of complexity theory to practice and how this might evolve further.

A synthesis of issues is more likely to lead to a better forecast of the future. As a seminal article in *Harvard Business Review* by Snowden and Boone (2007: 71) advised: "Leaders need to avoid micromanaging and stay connected to what is happening in order to spot a change in context." For example, the public manager assessing property values not only needs to consider the property price trend line, but also levels of economic confidence, income and household debt forecasts, consumer price inflation, asset inflation, and the wider economic climate. To make a good judgment, one will need to consider a lot of information and then make a decision based on this overview. The old scientific methods of analysis tended to place the emphasis on understanding specific detail. The key to the wider picture was felt to be in the detail. Detail may still be important, but complexity challenges managers and policy makers to have a good sense of global issues and the wider picture, before making decisions. Clearly the danger of focusing too much on the detail is that some large and newly evolving contingency or external factor might get missed. Synthesis becomes as important, if not more important, than analysis.

Snowden and Boone's (2007) research is one of the best current examples of a practice framework that combines the theoretical observations of complexity theory about the operation of organizations and interorganizational behavior with a model of practice for leaders and managers. They concluded that different approaches to decisions and action were needed in differing organizational situations. Not all situations managers faced were complex, some were simple and predictable, or more complicated, or at worst, chaotic. Complicated situations were potentially understandable and manageable given a collective and reflective managerial approach. The most challenging situations were either complex or chaotic. Complex situations were unpredictable, while still operating within some degree of stability. Here managers could not easily apply traditional and classical approaches, but needed to enable creative communication and innovation, so as to make decisions on the basis of identifying likely patterns of behavior and their likely trajectories. Chaotic situations were very unpredictable but also unstable. Often they presented as a threatening crisis situation. In these highly unstable situations managers needed to first intervene decisively and to communicate clearly and directly, and then to set up responsive and creative collaborative approaches that could restore complex stability and begin to develop a pattern-based approach. Table 2.3 summarizes the core elements of the Snowden and Boone (2007) approach.

Table 2.3 Applying complexity theory to management interventions

Type of situation	Simple	Complicated	Complex	Chaotic
Application of Science	Predictable	Analyse to predict	Unpredictable	Unstable
Degree of determinism	Clear cause and effect	Hidden cause and effect	Changing Interactions	Unstable interactions
Management approach	Apply known facts	Discover and use facts	Identify and use patterns	Crisis Intervention, to achieve some stability

Source: Adapted from Snowden and Boone 2007: 73.

Complexity and praxis—bringing in values

David Byrne, one of the best known international scholars to promote the methodology of complexity theory in the social sciences, says that a structural approach to scientific knowledge must be combined with a call to action on the basis of that knowledge:

> Praxis is in considerable part action which must be taken on the basis of knowledge, because when you know, you have a moral imperative to do ... complex realism operates as a constitutive in immensely important ways in the contemporary world, and has the potential for informing critical practice in order to make the world a better place.
> (Byrne 2011a: 38)

Action and interaction

Matrix processes result where employees have to be released from rigid allegiance to one part of an organizational structure, so that they can follow a multitude of new purposes across and through other departments and outside bodies. Many organizations have found such a bifurcation of processes and purposes in recent years. The challenge is to find new and less rigidly defined structures and processes that assist what is required, rather than hindering it. Often such organizations feel that they really are on the edge of chaos. What this means is that boundaries are less clear and managers have to find a new dynamic comprising of formal and informal agreements about what is good and acceptable practice with a flexibility of approach.

Constructing practice

Complexity theory implies the inevitability of change, and the determinism of events over time that cannot be re-run. Complexity theory enables people to understand that change is inevitable. The long term may be so unclear that it is better for new projects to focus on short- and medium-term goals. A large number of public sector IT projects in the last decade, for example, proved to be far too ambitious—resulting in expensive failures. A rapidly changing policy and technological environment dictates that the vision of a complex integrated IT system cannot be easily achieved (see Chapter 5). Beautement and Broenner (2011: 25) have argued the imperative of taking the lessons of complexity theory and applying them in an organized way to management and professional practice: "It requires a change of mindset and behaviour in general in order to be able to embrace complexity and grasp opportunities."

Large scale change involves attention to numerous aspects over the longer term (Attwood *et al.* 2003). Take the example of the peak of price rises in the housing market. Trend lines, as a method of linear modelling, are certainly useful here. They show how "out of trend" a given periodic price rise is. Over time, the curved real world data will usually fall back to the trend line, but knowing how long it will take is where the judgment comes in. The point in the trend at which a property is sold or purchased can make all the difference to key factors such as income in relation to debt and future capital and revenue ratios. Many individuals know the difficulty with making this judgment. The issue is also paramount in a policy environment where the public sector is leasing and purchasing services from private sector companies. For example, some private rest homes established in England in the late 1980s, but having places purchased by the state on behalf of poorer people, ended up paying high amounts of revenue funding on mortgage repayment due to interest rate rises on their loans. This undermines the quality of the nursing and social care they were able to provide to local authority and NHS purchasers. The selling of state assets in former Eastern European countries required impossible estimation of market value where there was no real market competition and comparison. This resulted in exponential value and profits for some of those who purchased at the right time. There have been concerns in the UK about the Private Finance Initiative (PFI), where prices for capital projects have been agreed at the height of property and land price fluctuations. Short-term political requirements have to be weighed against market valuations, trends, and long-term debt ratios. Managers and politicians involved in such decisions need a good overall synthesis of the market and economic environment. Politicians and managers in such circumstances need to assess the likelihood of a range of alternative forecasts occurring, and try to plan action that can cope with moving targets. As Hirst (2003: 19) concluded, when reviewing the then UK Chancellor of the Exchequer, Gordon Brown's November 2002 approach to public finance, "the Treasury should produce estimates for public borrowing that set both the worst and best-case scenarios". In the same article, she quotes Martin Weale of the National Institute of Economic and Social Research (NIESR) as saying: "Not having a clear idea of how likely things are to go wrong is a lot more worrying than getting the figures out on one individual forecast". As Eve, Horsfall and Lee (1997: 271) say: "the problem is not one of chaos in the sense of no pattern at all; it is merely a lack of predictable, specific solutions within certain mathematical limits." Feedback over time combines to give us a future that is largely unknowable, but that is likely to resemble some aspects of previous patterns. Complexity theory, while presenting challenging epistemological questions and a danger of ontological ambivalence, paradoxically, "appears more likely to be used to produce practical advice to practitioners than to inform the wider theological debate on structure and agency" (Cairney 2012: 355). Barnes, Matka and Sullivan (2003) are concerned as to the consequences of complexity for methods of evaluating public policy programs. Beautement and Broenner (2011: 48) describe preparing practitioners for a complex world as developing "Complexity Worthiness".

Complex organizations do not necessarily require complex processes. Collinson and Jay (2012) argue that while simple organizations evolve to become more complex this often leads to inefficiencies and managers need to often revisit the core processes of activity and work to ensure the organization does things as simply as it can. This is necessary to ensure efficiency of process and effectiveness of outcome.

Likewise Taleb says:

> A complex system, contrary to what people believe, does not require complicated systems and regulations and intricate policies. The simpler, the better. Complications lead

to multiplicative chains of unanticipated effects. Because of opacity, an intervention leads to unforeseen consequences, followed by apologies about the "unforeseen" aspect of the consequences, then to another intervention to correct the secondary effects, leading to an explosive series of branching "unforeseen" responses, each one worse than the preceding one.

(Taleb 2012: 11)

In a tweet on March 29, 2014 Taleb further summarizes this to a basic rule: "General Principle: the solution on balance needs to be simpler than the problems. (Otherwise the system collapses under its complexity.)"

Collinson and Jay (2012) take a holistic management approach to working with complex systems. Public services work in highly complex social systems and create complex organizations and processes to deal with this complexity, nevertheless there are dangers that such responses evolve towards mirroring the instability of the external world rather than offering well organized responses to social problems. Managing complexity therefore has a strong sense of appreciating complexity but not seeking to reproduce it or to add to it, but rather to manage it assertively. They document that an inefficient complexity of process can be generated from a number of aspects in any organization: people, organizational structures, strategy, processes, products or services and everyday routines.

Conclusion

The management of complexity in public organizations requires clarity and focus. It is the identification of patterns and the management of these patterns. It is the management of change via excellent interactions and communication, and the development of an appropriate shared value based strategy. At the heart of the management of complexity in public services is the need to enhance the understanding of what complexity is and facilitating appropriate public values. Complexity theory therefore is not just about functional understanding, but also about the ethics of practice:

> Organisations are an inextricable part of the social fabric. The future of humanity depends on their role. We should therefore not only think of organisations in a functional way, but also perhaps primarily in an ethical way. The development of an understanding of organisations and what they do, which takes the provisional ethics of Complexity seriously, stands as a challenge.

(Cilliers 2011: 152)

In response to the challenge to develop complexity informed practice, beneficial and necessary collective public outcomes will result. For the remainder of this book the task is for the chapters to align the complexity perspective with the core areas of management practice: strategic management, performance management, information management and human resources management.

3   Strategy and planning in an unstable world

Introduction

There have been many strategic planning initiatives in the public services in the last 40 years since the arrival of the NPM phenomenon. The business and market approach to the public sector that was endemic in the new managerialism brought with it a focus on strategic management and planning models used in the private sector. These provided a wide assessment of both the internal and external environment and attempted to focus an organization on its key objectives and performance. This chapter looks at the implications for public services of implementing strategic management and strategic planning models in the unstable world of government policy.

Theories of planning

Planning and rational decision making

A major theme in post-war literature about organizational behavior was an emerging debate about the nature of decision making and this was of relevance to the public sector (Simon 1957). A key issue for debate was the extent to which government decisions could be rational. There are major theoretical problems with raising the status of rational techniques in the social sciences, as summarized by Oakeshott (1994). Scientific rationality inevitably becomes linked with values and ideology. The task of applying rationality is fraught with difficulties, not least because there are differing accounts of rationality in public administration and management that have become linked to differing ideological or disciplinary based bias. The word rationality is used differently in politics, economics and management literature. The early post-war organizational literature appeared to be founded on an idealized scientific notion of rationality, where all possibilities would be researched and considered in an objective manner. This can be linked to Taylorist accounts of classical management (see Pugh, Hickson and Hinings 1983). Such an approach was of interest to public administrators but was impossible to reconcile with the short-termism and ideological objectives of politicians. Other literatures on public policy making began to identify short-term political and ideological rationalities for developing policies that were often in conflict with rational-scientific research (Lindbolm 1959; Hill 1997). The political desire to produce policies that are popular with the electorate and public opinion is often about the rationality of getting re-elected rather than a scientific review of research. An example of this is immigration policy where for politicians to win votes may require them to talk "tough" on immigration and promise limits, but businesses in a growing economy may need migrant labor to meet output demands.

Finally, a growing literature in the 1970s and1980s linked classical economic rationality to policy supply and the consumption of public services (Self 1993). This was the idea of a predictable and selective consumer who could make "rational" choices about which school, hospital or university to attend. This implied that public services should be organized around competitive market systems. The apolitical rationality of strategic planning and management practice developed in Business Schools and related literature is based on profit motives and surviving in a competitive supply side global world. Important questions remain about the application of such practices in the world of the public and non-government sector that needs to be underpinned by public values.

Lindbolm (1959) talked of "political rationality", or what became better known as incrementalism. This account stressed the short-term nature of plural democratic decision making and the bias of political parties towards gradual adjustment, rather than radical change. Incrementalism is certainly the experience that many managers and professionals have of public sector budgeting and financial planning, where last year's budget codes and corresponding figures are marginally adjusted to reflect the slowly evolving priorities of the next budget year. This suggests that politicians are cautious in a pluralist democracy and reluctant to suddenly change the fundamental direction of policy. Complexity theory questions the stable notion of this incremental adjustment and risk avoidance. While complexity acknowledges periods of stability that may evidence incremental adjustment these are contrasted with times and places that demonstrate instability. It is these occurrences of instability that can generate periodic transformations, where fundamental shifts in values and logics take place. Incrementalism is a pragmatic approach to periods of stability, but strategists and planners also need to be prepared for what happens in periods of sudden and unexpected change and instability. That is when public strategies and plans must adapt rapidly. A number of different views of rationality are each having their own impact on public service management, rather than a single unified approach.

Some attempt has been made by academics to combine types of political and managerial rationality. One historical approach, for example, was to suggest that scientific research rationality was only achievable for the occasional macro policy decision, and the day-to-day operational reality of the public service is best described by incremental adjustment (Etzioni 1967). This explanation might inform why so many long-term planning initiatives fail, and fall into disrepute. They are frequently overtaken by political and economic change, and so pragmatic political adjustments occur, and the focus for any long-term vision is lost. During the aftermath of the financial crisis government agencies and services often had to adapt quickly to dramatic changes and an austere funding environment.

In an attempt to drive a new academic approach to political rationality that challenged market orthodoxy, Alan Walker (1984) published an account of a radical socialist approach to local planning that sought to maximize local democratic involvement and control of resources. He argued that political and managerial rationalities could be combined, but around a highly localized and active local democratic system. This type of planning was never implemented on a grand scale as the ideological direction was turning against his model and those in practice increasingly looked away from the idea of a planning model written especially for the public sector, moving instead to models being used in private business and economics.

Recent developments of local planning practice have put less emphasis on direct political participation and more on administrative and managerial led dialogue within the local state. Nevertheless, these attempts have also experimented with new forms of participation and democracy alongside managerial based strategies. There have been some much talked about examples of community involvement in South America (Oropeza and Perron 2013). Other examples were the local Community Care Planning exercise in the 1990s and the Local Strategic Partnerships (2000s), both in England.

Government systems in South America have attempted to combine local politics and administration in interesting ways, with a strong emphasis on local participation where people meet and talk about local issues in considerable detail with the aim of informing local administration (Ricaurte-Quijano 2013). This is so called deliberative planning where new approaches to deliberative democracy meet with ideas from organizational strategy (Lee and Zachary 2013).

In the late 1970s, economic rationality had become increasingly influential in the public sector and this paved the way for the market value base of the new managerialism. This was founded on a classical economist's notion of the "rational man", this being individual self-interested consumers of public services who would behave in such a way as to maximize their own benefits. The implication was for policy managers to build a diverse supply-side with a strong competitive element. The rational intention being that consumers, with a choice about their service provider, would drive competition and increase the efficiency of services being offered. As a result, in the 1980s, in countries where central governments were ideologically sympathetic to this economic and market driven model, some regional and local government planning exercises changed to a short term economic model, where the focus was on understanding market principles and supply side strategies (see Table 3.1). Strategic planning models from the private sector were imported to achieve this aim. Market and business planning language was pervading the public service environment. Strategies and plans were developing that sought to give choices to those using services like schools and hospitals. These were strategies to dismantle monopoly administrative structures and facilitate a managed market place with a diversity of suppliers.

Corporate planning

The corporate planning initiatives of the 1970s influenced large government departments, including regional and local government at their core and central points. The key aspect of corporatism is the central coordination of large and complex organizations, with the focus

Table 3.1 Competing rationalities in the public strategy and planning process

	Economic	Political	Managerial
Driving ethos of rationality	Market values	Need for popular support	Managerial efficiency
Strategic paradigm	Supply side competition Consumer choice	Government want to be re-elected Select popular strategic choices	Improve delivery of efficient outputs
Key weakness with the rationality	Market failure Need-demand mismatch	Changing public opinion Inconsistent compromise	Efficiency and effectiveness mismatch (outputs not evidenced to longer-term social outcomes)
Operational counterbalance	Local participation	Civil service and agencies with longer-term perspective	Local participation
Time horizon	Medium	Short	Medium

being internal and horizontal, across the organization in focus. In the past, corporate planning has been criticized for giving too little consideration to the relationships of the host organization with outside bodies. Corporate planning depends on a key policy, planning and resources unit at the center of the organization. This unit seeks to pull together the different specialist functions of the organization and to give a control and command direction, and often it seeks to achieve economies of scale. In UK local government this was the development of the "centre of the local" (Leach, Stewart and Walsh 1994). Since the 1980s corporate and strategic planning initiatives in large government organizations are often combined. These may be ambitious attempts to align the internal structure and culture of the organization with evolving changes in the external environment. Sometimes changes are made to devolve incremental department budgeting systems with the redirection of some central funding towards priority tasks. Department managers are encouraged to bid for strategic funds that can be used to develop projects that can be argued to deliver on the center's corporate objectives. In the highly centralized UK National Health Service, attempts were made via Corporate Planning to break up one of the largest public organizations in the world into new more devolved geographical and market type structures. These strategies and plans have generated new approaches towards the allocation of resources that were designed to be more equitable and efficient at meeting health needs. The hope was that this might drive a more radical approach to health inequalities and public health approaches based on prevention rather than cure. Nevertheless, public health data in the UK show that inequalities in health outcome related to social class and ethnicity remain stubbornly high (Marmot 2010).

Corporatism has become synonymous with a rational scientific managerialism characterized by centralism and re-structuring. Corporate planning can be driven by a managerial obsession with redesigning organizational structures and seeking a perfected organization process. In some cases, politicians drive these idealized managerial plans, in other circumstances politicians complain they are too removed from systematic managerial approaches. Corporate driven strategies and plans can result in a drift towards larger government organizations, as they attempt to clarify and empower decision making at the center and top of the organization. In other circumstances, corporate plans can result in new forms of devolution, such as the tendency in the UK NHS, after the 1980s, to introduce a marketized form of administration via the separation of staff and activities into purchaser and provider sub-organizations. If corporate planning is to be successful it needs to clarify organizational processes, roles and responsibilities, as much as it changes structures. Similarly, understanding what happens to staff cultures and values in such large scale internal changes is paramount. If these details are not managed, large scale corporate restructuring can add additional instability, rather than allowing the organization to deal better with external changes.

Historical examples offer little hope that such corporate planning initiatives are a straightforward management tool for improving public services, but this may have had more to do with difficult public sector funding environments. While the 1970s were marked by the attempt to use corporatism for ambitious reorganizations accompanied by medium- and long-term plans, the 1980s saw a move to short-termism. This was accompanied by a minimal government who put their faith in market economics and the use of strategies to replicate market structures in government and its activities.

Strategic planning and strategic management

Strategic planning was growing in popularity in the private sector in the late 1970s. It is characterized by a more competitive external focus, rather than an internal organizational focus. Strategies were about looking outside the organization, at the wider market environment, in an attempt to make resulting internal changes that would make the organization more competitive, market focused and understanding of the need to change its production of services. Porter's (1980) classic text documented many methods of environmental analysis that companies could execute in order to achieve competitive advantage. These practices spread rapidly through the public sector in the early 1980s and began to have a growing influence in NGOs. The public sector could no longer assume that similar expenditure and staffing patterns would evolve from year to year, given increased privatization and marketization of service delivery. The public sector was to strategize for increased community, civil and market involvement in services. Managers had to begin to look outside their own service to understand competitive advantage and see where innovation was taking place and what efficiencies might result. SWOT analysis, that is the strategic planning exercise of assessing Strengths, Weaknesses, Opportunities and Threats became commonplace. The academic and professional literature available to students of politics and political administration and to those undertaking professional training in civil service and government administration started to define the use of strategic planning in the public sphere:

> What distinguishes strategic planning from more traditional planning is its emphasis on: action, consideration of a broad and diverse set of stakeholders; attention to external opportunities and threats and internal strengths and weaknesses; and attention to actual or potential competitors.
>
> (Bryson and Roering 1988: 15)

Owen Hughes' (2012: 213–214) seminal text book, *Public Management and Administration*, now in its fourth edition, notes that: "Strategic planning in the public sector is a phenomenon of the early 1980s—significantly later than its development in the private sector. It became commonplace for governments to require their agencies to prepare strategic plans." Such an outward looking strategic review was often accompanied by a process of internal review, where management by objectives, and similar performance management methods were used to identify key output areas where performance could be improved. In many cases strategic planning in the public sector became co-terminus with the pressure to be subjected to market ideology and disciplines and hence one key model of strategic planning referred to is "business planning" (Joyce 1999). Many public service organizations whose key function is service delivery are now compelled to write an annual business plan. Sometimes this is very "business explicit", being linked to ideas like market testing and competitive tending for a fixed price. Here government agencies and authorities are required to plan the devolution and fragmentation of service provision in a contracted market environment and there is no opportunity to protect provider services within a single large corporate system. In these circumstances, consumer accountability in the market place has directly replaced political accountability through the ballot box (Day and Klein 1987).

This is not the only variant of strategy being used in government and public bodies. Joyce (1999) has recorded the diversity of approaches, using case studies from UK based local and central government. Some models are more long term and creative and less short-term and market based, these being founded on vision and foresight for the future. Joyce (1999: Chapter 1) has documented four types of strategic management in public services:

- The classical planning approach;
- The business like strategic model;

- The visionary strategic model; and
- The foresight based strategic management model.

The classical planning approach is described by Joyce as a rational approach to management that is goal led and linked to performance measurement and targets. In many cases, such an approach is embedded in statutory requirements and the requirement to publish a formal strategic plan. This type of approach has been influential in many areas of the public sector, including health and education.

The business like strategic model is described as placing more emphasis on strategy than planning. The strategy is one of using a market place within the public sector, where senior managers are often distant from front line "provider" managers. This distance creates the purchaser-provider relationship that resembles a competitive market place. Senior managers have a strategy of using this market dynamic in their dealings with front line services. The senior managers who commission and purchase the providers of services approve the detailed operational plans of front line services and respond accordingly with contracting and budget decisions that are linked to a broad strategic mission and values. The language in such a public service environment is the language of the market, with service users being seen as customers.

The visionary strategic planning model focuses on the senior management team achieving a long-term view of where the organization wants to be in the future. This uses creative thinking and techniques. This vision is then communicated with the workforce through team work that develops an organizational culture and value system that will make the change possible. The advantage with this approach is that it can help define the hierarchy of values linked with service delivery and development making explicit any value based conflicts and contradictions.

Finally, Joyce outlines the foresight based strategic management model. This model also takes a long-term view, but attempts to be more pragmatic and to make clear links between the present state of the organization and where it should be in the future. A strategic vision is created. A variety of scenarios and methods are examined to see how they can contribute to achieving the vision, with a sense of realism that one method alone is likely to fail. The organization will look to make strategic alliances with other organizations that help secure the environment and the likelihood of the vision being achieved. The emphasis is on developing the overall capacity and flexibility of the organization to achieve strategic change, given uncertainties in the external environment.

The complexity approach

The final foresight based approach to strategic management outlined by Joyce has some sympathy with the view of the world put forward by complexity theory. Complexity theory raises some serious questions about the ability of strategic managing and planning to work because of high levels of uncertainty in the global and national public policy environment. Building a strong and resilient organizational culture that is founded on shared values becomes central to the strategy of a public service organization.

Applying complexity theory to strategic management raised challenges that are both theoretical and pragmatic. On a theoretical basis, complexity suggests that the future is largely unknowable and subject to periods of unpredictable change. This implies that detailed planning should be short-term and subject to regular review. At the more extreme end of theoretical debate, some writers have argued that complexity and chaos provide evidence that many forms of planning cannot take place in a market economy (Parker and Stacey 1994). A number of other writers, however, suggest that government strategic planning is still an imperative, but that it needs to pursue a radically different model (Allen, Clark and Perez-Trejo 1992; Haynes 1999). Longer-term strategic management and planning cannot really be planning in the traditional sense, but needs to be a more open and creative method where there is an imagination of possible futures and a consideration of their consequences. It is inevitable that any long-term plans will have to be amended and adapted in parallel with evolving events in the external environment. This has led to the idea of scenario building, that is, thinking through how different possible futures might work out, this coupled with the idea of visioning broad principles about what kind of future government and public organizations see as desirable. More detailed operational planning is subject to short-term timescales and subjected to regular reviews and changes. Buchanan (2004: 10) advises: "Expect change to arrive not gradually in a way that will allow the organization to adjust in real time, but in sudden discontinuities".

On a pragmatic basis such fundamental questions about the instability of the future and the pressing need for organizations to face sudden periods of change, have led to a modification of strategic planning practice into what is often referred to as strategic management. This evolution is not explicitly the result of chaos and complexity theory, but it shows the need for strategic planning practice to adapt so that all managers begin to share an organization's need for strategic direction. Strategic management as a core aspect of general management practice is implicitly linked to the major concerns of those like Mintzberg (1994) who stressed the incongruence between unpredictable systems and the very idea of a rigid planning system. Hamel and Prahalad (1994) challenged some of the more institutionalized approaches to strategic planning and suggested that a new practice of "crafting strategic architecture" was needed where creative thinking and forecasting were encouraged throughout the organization. All managers should become involved in thinking about the future and how the external world is changing and how the organization and its activities might adapt. Managers may do best when: "pursuing strategies across several terrains and using their advantage on one to create positional leverage on others" (Room 2011: 76).

Strategic management moves the focus of strategy making, and the associated detailed analysis of data and information, away from a specialist planning unit. Responsibility for strategy and planning is devolved into the whole organization. It facilitates a holistic and integrated organizational approach. As Hughes (2012: 219) says: "strategic management aims to integrate the planning function within the overall management task." This allows an organization to think creatively about the future and for strategy to be on the agenda of all managers and teams. In short, the approach is one way of ensuring that all managers address necessary change. As a result, many public service organizations now expect managers at all levels to undertake an annual strategic review and to relate this to general changes in the overall strategy of the senior management team and politicians or board members.

All managers have to have a good command of the wider issues affecting their service, in terms of general demographic, social and economic indicators. This will enable them to develop strategies that make the most of identified opportunities and to minimize the threats to the organization. In some areas of public sector work this takes on a market component as managers identify competitors and competitor's behavior, and benchmark this against their own organization. Overall strategic management puts a lot of emphasis on "looking outside" when compared to historical public planning models where the focus was much more inside the organization. Strategic management is about reconciling external and internal change, with the emphasis on the external environment as a driver, but with an interest in the interaction and feedback between the external and internal aspects of the organizational system.

Within strategic management practice there should be less focus on a single planning document that is widely disseminated as a glossy publication, but instead the building of a long-term process where annual documents are little more than drafts that can be regularly revisited and adjusted. The publishing of such documents on an organization's web site lends itself well to this type of adjustment approach, as such documents can easily be removed and updated. File formats like the international standard, portable document format (pdf), allow draft documents to be published in paper and electronic form that are professionally presented, but easily updated and changed. This is preferable to the highly expensive publication of one hard copy in color that is widely disseminated, but never really finalized or achieved. The result of such hard publications is often that the organization and outsiders focus on a permanent document that is quickly out of date and missing new developments (Mintzberg 1994). The experience of organizations involved in trying to edit annual plans ready for publication is that it is extremely difficult to draw a clear line at the point of publication and there is often a temptation to hold back for new policy announcements and data updates. The problem is the longer the organization waits for new information to become available, the more out of date and irrelevant the general document becomes. Planning is by nature dynamic and not a static activity. Table 3.2 summarizes the influence of planning theory on public service practice.

Dealing with complexity in the strategy making process

This book illustrates the difficulty with building public services around tight and hard organizational structures that are inflexible and problematic to change. While a minimal core hard structure, with a small senior management team at the top, is needed to define larger

Table 3.2 Summary of the theoretical influences on strategic planning

Theoretical approach	Key characteristics
Rationalism	Scientific and research based Comprehensive Long-term
Incrementalism	Politically driven Gradual adjustment Pragmatic adaptation Short-term
Corporate	Large organizations Internal focus on reorganization Scientific and research based Centralized planning unit Long-term
Strategic	External environment Politically aware External and market assessment Short- to medium-term Performance and data based
Complexity	External environment Forecasting risks, examining scenarios and possible transformations Adaptable, inclusive process Short-term

organizations, public services—like the private business sector—are increasingly making use of soft network structures where roles and processes can adjust more easily to changing circumstances. Typical elements of such adaptive structures are project groups, task forces, and working parties. Adaptive strategies often require such adaptive and soft forms of organization.

Modern strategic management processes have to make good use of soft structures. Traditionally public planning has been built around bureaucratic cyclic processes with set committees and meetings feeding into an annual process where the end point is an annual planning document. Newer, more innovative approaches will be open to influence from much of the organization, in addition to the necessary co-opted elements from outside. The key is that core managers can co-opt important players into the strategic planning process as they are needed.

Collinson and Jay's (2012: Chapter 5) important research on simplifying management in the face of evolving complexity found that strategic management activity was one of the main areas where organizations could become inefficient. They found that the most problematic examples of management practice were when managers were involved in too many strategic planning projects simultaneously, the processes were overly complex and the resulting strategies failed to be clear and concise. All this inefficiency could result in considerable communication problems. Further evidence of problems was when senior managers were too preoccupied with detail in meetings to debate and review priorities, and decisions failed to be made. An inability to agree and set priorities resulted in professionals and employees having different understanding and perception of what the organizational priorities were. Some organizations tried to analyze too much information and data, leading to what Collinson and Jay term "analysis-paralysis", and resulting in no concise data based priorities being communicated. A lack of strategic clarity at the core of an organization could lead to confused values, different perceptions of what was important and conflicting and stressful cultures and behaviors. As a result, managers lower down the organization might avoid being innovative and taking risk, feeling instead that the safest and most appropriate behavior was to maintain the status quo. The resulting outside perception of such strategic inertia was service users being unsure what the organization stood for and what could be reasonably expected in the service provision. Staff providing the service might mirror the strategic ambivalence in the organization, appearing indecisive and ambivalent about what they were offering.

Avoiding the setting up of a new, permanent and hard institutional system of committees and meetings to design and deliver strategic planning seems particularly important given Collinson and Jay's (2012) research. Otherwise, process overload and the inertia that can result from an overly complex response become inevitable. The core decisions and process can be linked to management teams, meetings and communications that are already taking place rather than forming a new and different planning substructure. Any new meetings should be "soft" as argued above and formed temporarily to meet the needs of the immediate planning task. In effect such a meeting would report back and into the existing management and decision making process.

It is important to note that the dominant focus of Collinson and Jay's (2012) work is private business organizations and, as argued in this book, there are some important differences in managing public service organizations, not least the driver of public values and the need to involve elected politicians and other public representatives.

The key is that core and senior managers can co-opt important players into the strategic planning process as they are needed. It may be useful to hold some very wide ranging stakeholder consultation events, rather than relying on one or two stakeholder representatives in a cyclic process of formal meetings (where it is difficult for representatives to be proactive and they are left struggling to work out who they are supposed to be representing). This leads to the challenge of designing a process of participation that is relevant for strategic management and planning.

Participation

Less formal structures and processes might at worst be used as an opportunity by senior managers to close opportunities for participation and to keep the strategic process closed so that the senior management team can force its own agenda. This is unlikely to be a satisfactory application of such a method, as a good strategic management and planning process will need to fully understand change, and convince all players of the best way of dealing with it. Such an approach requires an undertaking that at least attempts to make all feel valued and included. A good strategic management process needs to find a dynamic between inclusion, to hear and consider different points of view, and decisive leadership, where appropriate responsibility is taken for direction and decision making. Maximum inclusion of stakeholders must not result in drift and lack of direction. It is a vital leadership task to argue for a way forward in the face of difficult circumstances when there are both diverse voices and a need for change in order to survive.

This will involve the identification of conflicts and tensions that are not always resolvable. Better to have these acknowledged and out in the open as part of the change process, rather than hidden or not properly acknowledged by senior managers. Again the key is to deconstruct and restructure conflicts into creative tensions, wherever this is possible. It is unlikely to be possible to reduce all conflicts into acceptable agendas for change and the majority of organizations have to move forward with strategies that include the carrying of a number of tensions and conflicts into the future, with close monitoring and continuing debate about how they will be progressed. However, open acknowledgement and recognition of such tensions can in itself be one way forward (Healey 1997). Such a process is demanding on managers and leaders. It takes time, and those involved in carrying such tensions forward, need peer support, perhaps mentors in other organizations, or managers elsewhere under similar pressures. Emotional intelligence skills (Goleman 1996) become highly useful when some stakeholders are reluctant to allow a strategy to move forward. Relationships can become severely strained.

Traditional approaches to participation have focused on the extent to which participants are representative of a wider population and the degree of engagement that they have in decision making. Approaches to participation in the new policy environment, with its dispersed decision making and softer structures raise concerns about how participants can represent any wider grouping, especially if they are beginning to replace the traditional political lines of accountability in national and local politics (Jeffrey 1997). Much participation in public administration has been criticized as consultative on a limited choice of agenda items, rather than proactive in setting agendas and the scope for decisions.

Complexity implies that participation needs to be pursued on two additional fronts, firstly the need for "on-going" involvement and interaction with participants over time, and secondly the need to incorporate a diversity of participants as combatants in representative issues. Both ideas are akin to the idea of an open and adaptive system approach (Healey 1997). In some public circumstances, it can take years to establish and build the capacity of representation, given the nature of exclusion and alienation experienced by some social groups.

Complexity models of strategy making imply the evolution of an ongoing dynamic process, rather than a predefined limited cycle of events. Therefore participation is not solely about consulting individuals at key points in the cycle, but rather about forming an institutionalized level of engagement that allows stakeholders to define their own approach to long-term issues. This is not easy. As mentioned in the previous paragraphs, it is likely to result in conflicting interpretations of events and additional tensions, but ultimately a healthier and transparent process should result. This will allow arguments to be articulated and carefully considered, rather than a single view of the future recreated each year. Stakeholders will need open access to a range of data and information and the skills (or access to the skills) to analyze and synthesize about the policy environment. Healey (1997: 305) has talked about the emergence of different arguments in the policy process, rather than a single rationalized view of events. She talks of the "plan being a store of arguments". Such a difficult process of reflection seems more likely to come to terms with complex events and the best methods for dealing with them.

One example of this was the development of a local government drug action strategy where up to a hundred different stakeholders were involved in two open, explorative days. Some difficult issues about performance had been set by central government and these had to be adapted into the local strategy. The local management team did not want to impose a simple top down performance plan that did not have the endorsement of a majority of stakeholders. Waiting lists for services were at the top of the central government performance agenda, but some stakeholders felt very vulnerable, they being at the front line of demands for service and needing adequate time to assess a complex and sometimes dangerous problem.

The open style of the stakeholder days generally worked well and reduced the top down impact of the performance agenda and allowed a more inclusive approach to strategy development. The most sensitive of local service providers were allowed to develop their own version of a service plan, rather than an overall strategy, and they published this on the health commissioner's website. This allowed an open expression of different ideas and encouraged the overall sense of inclusiveness, rather than undermining the general strategy with its performance focus.

When the service commissioners came to publish the first annual document of the three year strategy that had been nurtured carefully, they hit another problem. Just before a glossy local document was launched several new key central government documents were issued that altered national priorities slightly. The importance of a regular review of the three year local strategy and its adaptability were quickly reinforced.

In terms of participation, Healey (1997: 292) comments that the challenge is to: "remake political life in the image, not of instrumentally rational bureaucracies, not competitively rational markets, but mirroring the organizational forms and dialogic processes of everyday life."

Participation methods

One approach towards making public participation more central in the planning process has developed by importing methods from developing countries. Here, in poorer countries where social and public policy is at an earlier stage of development in terms of the evolution and growth of complexity in systems, attempts are being made to involve whole communities in the development of appropriate new social policies. Participation methods used in developing countries have emerged as a key method for institutionalizing a pragmatic and "real" approach to participation. Such approaches are noted for their long-term inclusion, rather than being one off consultations. Participatory Rural Appraisal (PRA) has been used in poor countries to attempt to empower local people to raise their own agendas, in a way that is not prescribed or directed by government or powerful corporations. It is now being usefully applied in the neighborhood and local planning as required by governments in many developed countries.

In essence, groups of local people analyze their own conditions and how they should be improved. Outside government officials, or professionals, are there to facilitate the process, rather than direct it. It is a method of action research where ideas emerge and change throughout the process. A significant period of time is needed and "one off" consultations cannot easily be applied with the method. A variety of tools and methods have been used, including many visual tools such as maps and diagrams. These are preferred to technical text based representations and methods such as interviews and questionnaires. Groups can use tools like time lines to understand the contextual history of recent local events or use a sketch map to identify patterns of incidents that need public service attention. A neighborhood planning group in a poor area of a city found a time line to be a useful method for documenting the decline of the area. The time line led them to record some past events including: reduced public transport, closure of a bar, the demolition of older housing stock and associated rehousing of families with strong local ties. This then gave them some ideas about how the area could be regenerated.

Inputting data and data analysis into strategies

Strategies and planning processes invariably need to draw on a wide range of data and current strategic initiatives have access to large amounts of data. A key part of the process becomes the selection of appropriate data, their analysis, and how such analysis is entered into the strategy and planning process.

An understanding of change over time becomes a key point of analysis for managers seeking strategies in a complex and changing environment. Similarly, geographical data offer another hard data route for understanding relatively simple manifestations of complex phenomena. Time and space are two key variables that offer relative stability in the unstable world of high complexity.

Trend analysis has long been a popular method in traditional approaches to economics and business planning in the private sector, but it should be used more in the public services. This is probably because of the complexity and short-termism of the public sector, with a wrongly held view that political short-term goals are the main driver of trends, and that any other trends are largely insignificant. In reality there are a number of social and economic trends that affect the public sector substantially and are not necessarily linked to political changes. Examples are periods of economic growth and decline, population demographic changes and energy supply and demand and resulting price changes.

Population change, especially the birth rate and migration, is notoriously difficult to predict accurately, especially in terms of detailed changes in local areas and age subcategories. And yet key age groups have an exponential effect on public expenditure, namely children and older people. Economic factors may create strong reinforcing feedback incentives that encourage the migration of certain age groups within a national and regional geography. Hence, single people and partners without children tend to live in the most expensive inner city areas, while those with children and older people live in areas where property values are lower. Expensive inner city areas can be polarized between social housing neighborhoods, where there are relatively excluded neighborhoods that include children and older people who have high needs for public services, as contrasted with wealthy neighborhoods which are often self-sufficient. Some regions and cities contain rising retirement geographies, where coastal towns in particular without much manufacturing industry prove attractive good value retirement areas to older people moving out of the crowded and expensive inner city. Local services often experience rapidly rising demands as a result of these sorts of migration patterns.

Public service managers need to identify the different types of data change that can emerge over time. Incremental (or linear) change is the gradual year on year rises in costs and demand, possibly linked to consumer price inflation, which can be predicted to some extent in the short term, although longer-term prediction of such increments can be difficult given the arrival of unexpected instability.

Much incremental change settles into cycles, particularly over a standard period such as a calendar or financial year. For example, the recruitment of low paid, part time support workers will be easier at certain times of the year, when competition in the labor market is not strong. Fuel costs will rise and fall during the year, meaning that in some months the running of emergency vehicles is more expensive than others. Accident rates will peak at certain time points. There will be more accidents in the winter than the summer and more in the morning and evening rush hours than at other times. To some extent, these cycles are predictable, not so much in the short term, but because of their likelihood of returning to an average over the longer term. Allowances and estimates can be made based on these sorts of cyclic patterns and the likelihood of a regression to the mean average.

The real challenge for planners is what complexity theorists call transformations, the feedback patterns and influences on data that result in major shifts from previous patterns of incremental adjustment and trend cycles. In 2008 the economic instability created by the global financial crisis resulted in some dramatic and difficult changes for many public services around the world. So called austerity policies meant unexpected cuts in real expenditure were applied to many services.

The key point about transformations is not so much observing critical changes in the pattern of individual data, but judging what changing feedback mechanisms have started in a range of other social and economic variables. In the 2007–08 financial crisis a number of financial organizations like banks, started to behave in different ways and to interact differently, and this was then expressed in the variables that monitored their collective behavior.

Transformations are essentially a synthesis of changes, built on changes in the inter-relationship of a whole host of inter-dependent variables. Established theories of cause and effect between variables may be terminated or even reversed. Economists learnt in the economic crisis that conventional monetary approaches of lowering or raising central bank interest rates might no longer be a lever for dealing with the supply of money and price inflation. Instead some countries had to turn to a new policy called Quantitative Easing (QE) to prevent price deflation. Transformations cannot be properly understood by analyzing a few variables, instead managers need to grasp a number of different interactions and patterns at the same time and to summarize their combined effects. Traditional assumptions have to be challenged. Public service organizations need to spot social and economic transformations taking place and do their best to describe and understand them accordingly. Strategies provide an opportunity to better understand such changes and to make decisions about appropriate changes in government and community interventions and practices. Examples of such major social changes in recent years have been: the growth of women's activity in the labor market, an increased need and demand for education and training, digital transformation in media and communications, increased longevity, and a rising incidence of morbidity in older age resulting from increased longevity.

The turn to narrative

In the last decade, the international strategic management literature has grown ever larger with a vast array of general texts, many of which are historical and instrumental accounts of what strategic management is, based on previous case histories and offering records of "how to do it". An interesting area of difference is the cluster of literature and research that examines strategy as a form of organizational behavior and communication, examining it as a relational area of practice and through research seeking to understand it via narrative and textual analysis (Fenton and Langley 2011).

One of the best known international writers to link strategic management practice with complexity theory is Ralph Stacey (2000) and his accounts very much focus on the importance of narrative, conversation and communication as core processes and methods for developing a strategic approach. As a complexity theorist he emphasizes that strategy formulation takes place in organizations that are characterized by complex and unstable operating environments. Stacey therefore creates a radically different approach whereby managers have to accept they have little direct control over the future but must work to achieve a good collective response to change that allows the organization to adapt and evolve, to achieve an adequate level of stability and purpose in the sea of changes it constantly faces.

Stacey summarizes this approach as:

> strategies emerge … in the ongoing conversational life of an organisation and in the ongoing conversations between people in different organisations. Strategic management is the process of actively participating in the conversations around important emerging issues. Strategic direction is not set in advance but understood in hindsight as it is emerging or after it has emerged.
>
> (Stacey 2000: 413)

Fenton and Langley (2011) proposed that strategies and strategic plans (strategic text) result from three different forms of organizational conversation: practitioner narratives, practice narratives and praxis narratives. These three forms were defined previously by Whittington (2006). The strategic practitioners are those whose roles require them to become involved in strategy: senior managers, middle managers and practitioners. Strategic praxis is the specific activities that managers and practitioners undertake in formulating and producing strategy through research and meetings. These activities are "intra-organizational", that is they take place within the host organization. These are manager's specific activities. In contrast, strategic practices are more cultural and include shared routines and the articulation of organizational norms of behavior. Therefore these practices are likely to be more holistic and widely influenced by external professional and public values, or "extra-organizational":

> Although many strategy practices are unique to organisations – specific planning routines, for example – many other strategy practices – such as away days or portfolio management – are common across organisations. From a practice perspective, it is such common practices that become the units of analysis, and is their performance, rather than that of particular organisations that needs to be explained.
>
> (Whittington 2006: 629)

Fenton and Langley's (2011) interest in strategic documentation as strategic texts gives additional scope for a structured analysis of how strategy is more formally articulated as text based communication and what the dominant practices are that are consistently drawn on by practitioners. But any reliance on a static textual planning record is rather at odds with Stacey's dynamic relational approach. For him, the evolving complexity and instability of the policy environment requires managers to focus on building strong relationships and a quality of communication. This allows organizations to reach a mature state of reflection about the external threats and drives for change that it faces. Stacey's inter-personal model of strategic management implies that strategic management is a constant adapting and innovating of people in the organization, rather than pausing for a static articulation of a single and shared vision of the future. Similarly, Iszatt-White (2010) expresses a clear leadership role for managers in such uncertainty where they must engage in strategic practices that clarify, rehearse, uphold and elaborate for the organization and its workforce.

Planning for risk and uncertainty

There has been much discussion in the public sector about planning for future risks and the management of risks. Much of the work produced is described as facilitating the management of risk, but in effect, it is strategic thinking about what can be done to prepare for negative events, or to turn possible future challenges into opportunities.

The focus on risk is in response to particular global difficulties for government and public services. The outbreak of swine flu in Mexico in 2012, the Deep Water Horizon oil spill in the Gulf of Mexico in 2010, and the terrorist attacks on the United States of America in 2001 all illustrate events that were not foreseen, but that had large scale consequences for public services. Similarly, less dramatic, but expensive mistakes, such as the failure of major new public service computer systems, can have large scale negative consequences. Some of this change in management approach that places more emphasis on the ability to respond to what is unpredictable also reflects the disillusionment with rational long-term planning and a growing sense of reality that sudden events can undermine plans and cause a public agency to drastically change its priorities. The idea is that public managers should think through some of the possible extreme events, developments and system failures that can occur and rehearse the possible courses of action that would be necessary in response. This is scenario and contingency planning.

The former UK Auditor General (2000: 2) defined risk as: "having in place a corporate and systematic process for evaluating and addressing the impact of risks in a cost effective way and having staff with the appropriate skills to identify and assess the potential for risks to arise". Public service managers are today encouraged to assess risks at different levels of the organization. This involves a number of stages.

Risks are categorized as existing on a number of dimensions, based on a notional hierarchy of their likelihood of occurring, and/or according to the type of consequences for the public. Risks can also be defined by their level or scale: for example the UK Office of Government Commerce (2002a) identified four levels of risk: strategic/corporate, program, project, and operations. Table 3.3 illustrates the basic components of strategic risk management and this can be used to facilitate contingency planning. The key dimensions are the likelihood of occurrence and the degree of disruption that would follow. Different aspects of risk will then be rehearsed and practiced at different levels of government. More detail can be added to working examples. The "likelihood of occurrence" can be further defined on the basis of a ten point probability score and linked with historical evidence, although the danger with this is that history is not always a good guide to future probability of an occurrence. Similarly, the degree of disruption can be measured more sophisticatedly, with reference to detailed scenarios and contingency plans, including rehearsing responses to major events. Rehearsals with the deployment of operation services are expensive but do allow for much more precise operational plans to be formed on the basis of what is learnt from an exercise. Rehearsals also give a much clearer indication of what financial contingencies need to be put aside as buffers for such future shocks. The decision to invoke full scale operational rehearsals is related to an

Table 3.3 The basic components for risk strategies and contingency planning

	Likelihood of occurring	Degree of disruption resulting	Main level management focus of any first management response

Event	Low/medium/high	Low/medium/high	• Strategic/Corporate
			  • Programme
			  • Project
			  • Operations
			  • (National or place specific?)

Civil war	Low	High	All levels, national
Terrorism	Medium	Medium	All levels, place specific
Floods	High	Medium	Operations, place specific
Major industrial relations dispute and labor strike	Low	Medium	Strategic/Corporate, national
Workplace fire	Low	High	Strategic/Corporate, Operational, place specific
Economic slowdown	Medium	Medium	Strategic/Coporate, place specific

assessment about the level of social and economic disruption likely to be experienced if the event occurs and therefore the importance of being confident that the containment can be managed and assured.

Large government services manage strategic and corporate risks. For example, when the commissioners of major projects assess the ability of future providers to deliver on large scale public contracts. With the increased linking of private and public interests in the UK through policies like Public Private Partnerships (PPP) and Private Finance Initiatives (PFI), changing economic circumstances can affect the quality of public services provided by private companies and NGOs and their ability to make adequate investments. In North America, some reversal in local privatization was observed in the 1990s (Warner 2008).

Corporate risks are of concern to politicians. Large scale failures in the public sector will undermine the credibility of elected governments and therefore be a source of unease to politicians. Senior civil servants and government officers are required to assess such risks on high profile political programs, giving impartial and objective accounts of the likelihood of success and failure. The stakes are particularly high in issues of civil disobedience, terrorism and war. Military experts will be asked to assess the likely consequences of different courses of action.

Program risks may still have some consequence for politicians but be of direct concern to strategic managers. This involves the likelihood that a particular public policy program will fail to deliver intended outputs. The level of political interest and investment may vary, depending on the issue. New surgical procedures, rail and road building programs, new psychological and genetic profiling in criminal justice are the type of large scale public program initiatives that offer significant benefits in long-term economic and public outcomes, but may be at risk of failure due to innovative technology, inadequate understanding and dialogue with professional workers and unrealistic expectations from stakeholders and the public. Risk management seeks to isolate the stages where things can go wrong, to anticipate such difficulties, meeting them head on and preventing them occurring before they have undermined efficiency and effectiveness.

Specific projects may be at risk from: human resource issues like an inability to recruit adequate staff, specific technology failures, new legal precedent judgments, stakeholder conflicts (for example with professional bodies, trades unions and user representatives) and unclear management and leadership. Thinking ahead and considering likely problems can allow at least some of these risks to be identified and avoided.

At the front line, individual day to day operational policy delivery can be subject to its own risks. These can include the disruption of human resources by an inability to retain staff; industrial relations disputes; the technical failure of support systems; external financial changes such as reductions in local budgets and grants; the inability of equipment providers to supply on time or with adequate quality; and environmental problems such as cold, flood, disease or fire.

A risk management exercise, or risk plan, seeks to identify the key elements of risk and what possible action can be taken to prevent risk, or deal with it, should it arise. It identifies the levels of responsibility with reference to the different geographies, scales of risk and consequences.

Risk management can become dysfunctional if it becomes hyper rational and assumes that there is a detailed answer for every conceivable risk. Risk planning is likely to be more functional if it is used as a creative process for anticipating future issues, rather than as a perfect and detailed checklist that pretends to do the impossible of planning for all future possibilities and eventualities. Some new methods and applications do go to this extreme.

The former UK Office of Government Commerce (2002a) proposed a number of stages in a risk management and planning process:

1   Risk identification
2   Risk ownership
3   Risk analysis probability
4   Appropriate action and response
5   Embedding risk management policy

Risk identification processes can attempt to be too rational and occupy large numbers of meetings where members seek to identify all possible risks to every person and place in an organization. It becomes impossible to see "the wood for the trees". Managers and professionals need to identify possible risks at their level of involvement in the organization and communicate these to senior managers who can take an overview.

Reflection on key risks identifies the interaction and feedback between them. This is often the case in a complex system. It was noted in Chapter 2 that reinforcing feedback in one positive aspect of public life could help prevent, or even cure, problems in other aspects of society. Conversely, there is a risk that reinforcing feedback of some anti-social behavior can have negative consequences which might start a spiral of decline in other areas of public life. The UK Office of Government Commerce (2001a: 8) calls these aspects "independencies". Organizational based strategic risk assessments may be critical to the survival of the organization and its employees.

Although risk management can be perceived as a rather negative approach to strategic management and planning, it offers a sobering and reflective approach to the complex policy environment and a degree of honesty about the possibility of change and uncertainty, and that certain outcomes are not always attainable and guaranteed over the medium and longer term. Better to take a broader assessment of the future and its possibilities, rather than to think it is possible to know exactly what will happen. In this sense risk management might help staff to be more forward thinking and better prepared for unexpected events. It might enable a culture that embraces complexity rather than assuming the organization can continue to act and behave exactly as it has always done. Risk management is helpful for clarifying what are the most important priority areas of work, especially when professional staff have many diverse tasks. By identifying reinforcing feedback patterns that have negative consequences early on, risk management can be used to prevent devastating feedback loops from occurring later. Nevertheless, risk assessment and management can go too far if it is applied in a mechanistic, scientific and rational manner that suggests an unrealistic level of reliability, probability assessment, and a comprehensiveness that cannot be realistically delivered in a complex and uncertain world. As Byrne says:

> The significance of the chaos/complexity approach lies precisely in the recognition that whilst there is no inevitable outcome, no linear law, no single answer, we can none-theless analyse in order to see what the possible set of outcomes might be, what the possible answers are.
>
> (Byrne 1998: 118)

A concern with hyper statistical rationality in risk management where it is erroneously claimed that precise historical probability calculations can be used to estimate future risks has been vigorously rejected in recent complexity writings. One of the best known examples of this literature is Taleb's (2012) *Antifragile*. He argues that risk is unmeasurable because it is about an unknowable future event, but that fragility and antifragility can be estimated because they focus on the property of an object or system rather than a specific event. It is possible to examine buildings and identify how fragile they are to future weather extremes, but not possible to predict when and if the extreme weather will appear. It is possible to examine banking records and to decide on the basis of comparisons of capital to lending ratios which banks are most likely to survive a future credit crisis, but it is not possible to predict when the next macro credit shortage will happen. Fragile systems do not like volatility because they are easily damaged. Robust systems aim to be resilient to volatility and survive. Antifragile systems can even benefit from volatility and evolve to become stronger.

Systems can prepare themselves by either becoming more robust, or as Taleb (2012) prefers, "Antifragile". Taleb gives the example of stories in historical literature and their survival in culture. Literature that is stored on the newest technology is fragile, as the story depends on the technology for survival. If the technology breaks or fails the account is gone, at least until it is reloaded or repurchased. A paper book is more robust. It is a more permanent physical record and can be re-found, even if the medium is vulnerable to deterioration and destruction over the longer term. In contrast, oral stories and legends as retold by extended families and communities over the generations are antifragile because they are imbedded in human culture and very difficult to destroy or lose. As Taleb (2012: 12–13) notes: "it is much easier to understand if something is harmed by volatility – hence fragile – than to try and forecast harmful events."

The Precautionary Principle (Bar-Yam, Read and Taleb 2014) is therefore focused on avoiding the occurrence of devastating events or so called "ruin". The central idea is the avoidance of fatal consequences. Such judgments cannot be easily based on evidence as the nature of evidence is that it might not be readily available until after the event has occurred. Interdependence and similarity in a system increases the likelihood of ruin: examples are the financial interdependence caused by being employed by the same large organization. This would not be as amplified if more of the employees were self-employed and had economic interdependencies elsewhere. Small scale and local action that evolves, rather than being centralized and over directed, are argued to be part of the antidote to ruin, as any errors or judgments made are comparatively small and not amplified by multiple interdependencies.

For example, selective breeding is argued by the authors to be very different and much lower risk when compared to genetic modification. Similarly the growing development of diverse local energy production, for example, via small scale renewable energy, reduces the risk of a large scale mass energy producer being unable to generate sufficient power to satisfy national demand.

Strategic management as systems interventions

At the core of strategic management is decision and action that is proactive rather than reactive. The manager is trying to anticipate an appropriate course of action given the alignment of their organization with the outside world. The methodology of this book is that such action is in a dynamic and evolving complex system and that this presents considerable challenges to management practice. Meadows' (2009) account of system interventions provides an important tool box to assist managers and organizations in deciding upon where and how to intervene. Meadows' seminal account of systems interventions has previously been adapted by the author and others, including the UK Economic and Social Research Council (ESRC) funded project Systems and Complex Systems Knowledge Exchange. Below it is adapted and presented as seven forms of strategic intervention in systems. This strategic approach is summarized in Table 3.4

Value based interventions

This ESRC project adapted Meadows' work into seven interventions for public service organizations. The first possible intervention is radical change that changes existing values or

Table 3.4 A model of strategic intervention

	Type of strategic approach	*Core focus*	*Output*	*Problematize*
Value based interventions	Vision and mission	Values	Changed behavior	Political and managerial conflicts
Finding direction and core purpose	Aims and objectives	Clarity of direction	Improved performance	Reductionist, over simplification
Intervening in self-organization	Corporate	Local innovations and projects	Pilots of new delivery sub-systems	Conservative self-organization
Intervening in internal bureaucracy	Corporate	Efficiency of rules and processes	Simplified and changed processes	Reduced flex-ibilities in per-iphery activities
Strategic informa-tion management	Corporate	Better use of information	Improved decision making	Management over standardization
Interventions for change and crisis	Crisis intervention Change management	Focused and priority interventions	Solve crisis, reduce high risks	Over corrections
Routine resource interventions	Corporate	General opera-tional management	Efficiency of inputs to outputs	Ignores effectiveness

builds new core and primary values. This is a cultural intervention where management aims to use a focus on changing and articulating values to transform an organization and its service. Examples would be where public services have experienced a high volume of complaints about discrimination, or a single high profile case with devastating negative consequences and impact—for example losing a major court case, loss of confidence from a minority community, or a decline in presentations of those requesting service delivery from that community. Large scale, high impact training programs are necessary to change values and behavior and to challenge inappropriate existing examples. Recruitment policies and changes must change to bring more minority staff. More direct dialogue and participation with the minority community is required as another aspect of achieving the required change. Similar value based strategies have been used in public services to implement environmental sustainability. Values of care have been reasserted in hospitals, where services have become too depersonalized and instrumental with dehumanizing and harmful results. Success depends on holistic approaches that assertively challenge inappropriate values and change behavior through actions that amplify the benefits of change. Joyce's (1999: 14) idea of visionary strategic planning notes that, "employees are engaged in a process of internalizing a set of values". Meadows' (2009) long-standing contribution was to argue for change in the political economy towards a sustainable environment and society and she argued that radical change of values was often the most effective strategic intervention for achieving large scale public change. Values can be changed by explicit debate alongside evidence that supports change.

Finding direction and core purpose

A common and important strategic intervention is a process that seeks to improve direction and purpose. Collinson and Jay (2012) note that many large complex organizations require strategies to simplify and clarify the priorities for action. In the private sector, this can be companies that have diversified and innovated too much, so they have lost sight of their core markets and where their customers are no longer as committed to a historical brand, and so customer loyalty is declining as a result. Direction and purpose is required to get the company back to its previous strengths and reconfirm its core business. There are similar issues for some public services, especially where they are providing front line services. One core purpose of strategic management is to clarify direction and purpose, often through stating clear goals.

Intervening in self-organization

Complexity theory places an important emphasis on self-organization. This is the order that evolves and emerges from the bottom up in an organizational system (see Chapter 2). Some elements of strategic planning need to focus specifically on understanding and utilizing self-organization. This is especially the case for corporate strategies that are taking an internal focus and seeking to understand how best to increase internal organizational efficiencies in relation to external needs and demands. Eisenhardt and Piezunka (2011) refer to the need for "rewiring" of corporate organizations, so that creative connections emerge from the bottom up and because of good and creative communication between different teams and organizational departments. Such rewiring is facilitated organically by leadership and managerial communication and cooperation rather than because of top down directives. The people who are appointed to these roles have the skills to build trust and develop productive working relationships that are in the corporate interest. Large complex organizations often inhibit places where local workers are working around dysfunctional parts of the system in a creative way (sometimes referred to as dissipative self-organization). Rewiring should foster such innovative activity rather than closing it down. Strategies can acknowledge and formally approve such evolution. Conversely strategies may discover negative self-organization (sometimes described as conservative self-organization) where a group of staff are defensively resisting change and protecting old and inefficient ways of working by refusing to engage with new practices. Positive adaptation through self-organization may need to be facilitated and grown more by interventions to create changes in rules and procedures. Such change can alter conservative behavior. Senior managers have to keep an overview of self-organization and its rewiring and ensure a central steer rather than autocratic directives. In particular, only a moderate number of emerging projects are likely to be successful at any one time (Eisenhardt and Piezunka 2011), and too much small scale innovation without such a steer will tip the organizational dynamic towards instability and overly complex internal relationships and processes.

Intervening in internal bureaucracy

Internal corporate strategies concerned with maximizing the efficiency of an organization can focus on the local rules and intervening to change rules to improve efficiency. Bureaucratic rules in the public sector can easily evolve to become very complex, with additional clauses added over the years to deal with differing cases and circumstances. Strategic intervention focused on refining rules offers a chance to simplify back to core principles, leaving some discretion for judgment about exceptional circumstances. Eisenhardt and Piezunka (2011) concluded on the application of complexity theory to corporate strategy that a strategy process should clarify the core and simplify corporate rules of operation around which operational units in the organization can evolve, innovate and adapt. These simple rules create the overall sense of purpose and direction while not becoming so complex as to create inefficient processes that prevent creativity and adaptation. Collinson and Jay (2012: 152–153) argue for simplifying rules to reduce organizational complexity. They argue that strategic intervention can aid clarity and efficiency by analyzing and clarifying borderlines (like reducing duplication and deciding where in the organization a task should happen or a decision should be taken), and defining the operation of priorities (for example, health care system formulas that rate and prioritize the use of treatment interventions based on scientific research). A related practice is the use of "stop rules". Boundaries are set for ending certain organizational activities. These boundaries can be set using mechanisms like the entry criteria for level of need, or the geographical sphere of operation. Changing rules can be a key part of strategic interventions to provide organizational clarity and focus.

Strategic information management

Information and its analysis is a key input to strategic management activity to assist decision making, but changes in the use of information can also be a strategic intervention. What information is routinely made available via databases and information systems will influence operational decision making. Strategic interventions can therefore focus on changing information systems. Their inputs and outputs are methods for changing organizational behavior. Too much information or poor quality information can be harmful. The key is getting the right information to staff when they need it to make decisions. A university had traditionally collected admissions data both centrally and at the local department level and this in the context of a national admissions agency who had their own complex data and process. An IT strategy focused on designing a web based portal that integrated the most essential information in dynamic real time, with daily updates. This improved decision making at all stages and levels and the university increased its offer making both in terms of time response and quantity. The quantity of those taking up offers was also improved as a result. This was core business for the survival and health of the university.

Interventions for change and crisis

Strategic action depends on a correct diagnosis of the external environment and its interaction with the organization. This should result in confident and appropriate strategic decisions about interventions. Good use of information and intelligence, like in the example above, will allow confident management decisions with local resources. Good intelligence and analysis will identify major risks and, as a result, allow for a higher impact intervention than the norm. This can identify reinforcing feedbacks that are out of trend, like higher disease outbreaks or escalating exam failures at school. Extra resources can be applied as a balancing intervention. The use of reserve stocks of resources can be important buffers against such instability at times of crisis.

Routine resource interventions

Strategic analysis routinely leads to decisions to better deploy resources or to use resources differently. Examples will be the input balance of where best to deploy different professional and quasi professional jobs, and setting up and directing staff towards training. It might include incremental adjustment to organizational structure to reflect changes in the environment. Seddon's (2008) application of systems to public performance focused on entry points to public services where needs and demands could get wrongly diagnosed and assessed leading to costly additions in later reprocessing. Good resource management and strategies about the forward use of resources require the identification of reserves and stocks that are used as buffers to retain stability at times of external instability and change. Eisenhardt and Piezunka (2011) describe the need for senior managers to "patch" the design of their organization so that it can adapt incrementally to map with the changing external environment. Such patching is easier to achieve if the organization has a flexible approach to structure and project team formation. It is more difficult if large organizations have long-standing structures that are institutionalized with embedded processes and these continue to be legitimized by conservative cultures and beliefs. While such permanent structures can be argued to have provided stability, they can nevertheless prove perilous if they prevent an organization from evolving to match changes in the wider environment.

A summary of the strategic interventions and their dynamic relationship with the core organizational system and its process of inputs, activities, and outputs are illustrated in Figure 3.1. The most ambitious intervention is to exert value change. It is less ambitious, and a more common management practice, to set clear goals and priorities, perhaps with measureable targets. There are a number of ways that internal processes can be improved, with regard to change seen in the external environment and ways of making the relationship of inputs to outputs more efficient as they interact with external forces. The interventions that follow can include the better management of resources, the revision of process rules and a different approach to the use and communication of information. Strategies may need to focus on making better use of dissipative self-organization, to promote innovation more than is already occurring, or rather managers may decide to confront conservative self-organization that is preventing necessary change. Operational process change can include strategies to better deploy resources with different input numbers, with changed rules of deployment and using a different informational and communicative approach to such routine management.

The flexible planning model

Public service planning and strategy needs to be flexible and adaptable. As the complexity economist Paul Ormerod (1998: 189) says: "business people realise that it is futile to search for the best plan, for the future is to a large extent unknowable." Strategic management and planning needs to be creative and not subject to rigid organizational processes that are institutionalized and lacking in creativity and flexibility. Planning processes that are overly formal and periodically institutionalized are in danger of being locked into wrong views of the world that cannot keep pace with external events. Conflicts and tensions need to be explored in planning processes rather than denied and suppressed. Planning and strategy needs to consider multiple futures, some of which may appear negative, but that the organization can then empower itself to avoid. Planning and successful strategy making can be one of the most demanding and time consuming tasks for the modern public service manager. It will expose complexity in the form of paradox and contradictions. Issues, decisions and choices can become linked to personal issues and some managers' over-investment in certain specific futures. Strategy making demands developed skills of leadership that strikes a balance between moving forward and listening and negotiating.

The main points of adaptive and flexible planning are summarized below:

- Allow as many people as possible to contribute their view on what the strategy of the organization should be, but senior leaders and managers should make it clear that while all views can be expressed and listened to, they have responsibility for deciding on the priorities for the organization's future direction and actions.
- Organizations need a good sense of strategic and operational levels and what major decisions need to be taken at the central core by senior managers and what details can be delegated for decisions at the operational level.
- Publish a wide range of data and encourage others to understand and use it. Keep updating core information and make people aware when it is updated. Encourage debate about data findings, but senior managers should make it clear which data arguments they think provide the most important evidence for change and action.
- Strategic documents should be presented as working documents to guide operational and business plans, they should not be seen as fixed end points.
- Expose and understand the key tensions and contradictions in the policy environment, including identifying possible opportunities and risks.
- Revisit key strategies and plans regularly and be ready to rewrite them, and realign priorities.

Conclusion

This chapter has evaluated the evolution of approaches towards planning and strategy making in the public sector since the middle of the last century. The early literature is notable for its tendency to draw on the classical approach, suggesting that planning can be a rational scientific exercise where many options are researched. Decisions are then based on scientific evidence. In the 1960s and 1970s there was an increasing awareness that the politics and value based agendas and conflicts of both private and public organizations prevented such a rational process being implemented and achieved. The reality was that the public sector in particular tended to be driven by short-term politics and reactions to sudden and unexpected events.

In the last two decades of the twentieth century many articles and texts were written about the strategic approach to management and organization. There is diversity in this literature, but there is a common theme. Managers need to get a realistic vision of the future so that they can attempt to make appropriate changes in their organization. Much of the strategic literature is notable for its attempt to find an idealized and rational process for designing strategy and implementing it. Complexity theory shows that managers should be more flexible than this, and seek to design a process that is relevant for a specific context. There is no single perfect strategic process model. Complexity theory implies that engagement in strategy and planning in the public sector is a highly dynamic process, where success in strategic planning paradoxically depends on an awareness and appreciation of disorder, risk and uncertainty. It is not possible to plan for the elimination of these challenges. The only real strategy is to engage with complexity, seeking to gain from it and to adapt and survive as the external social and economic landscape changes in unpredictable ways.

4   Complexity and the performance of public services

Introduction

This chapter examines public outputs and outcomes and performance management in the public services and asks how this can be understood in a world where the cause of social problems and the effect of policy interventions is complex, highly unpredictable and difficult to reduce to simple elements of cause and effect. As Byrne (2011b: 133) notes: "finding out 'what works' for complex governance systems of indeed any sort of complex organizational system, is not a straightforward business." After a discussion of the difficulties of implementing performance management in the public sector, the chapter explores realistic ways of achieving improvements in performance, given the complexity of the public services environment. A management process based on understanding the whole system's performance and attempting to intervene with reference to the complex whole is proposed. This model of practice is new for the second edition and made possible by an Economic and Social Research Council (ESRC) Project that funded a practice based knowledge exchange that produced a working toolkit on intervening in public policy and organizational systems (www.brighton.ac.uk/sass/complex-systems).

Public performance as business performance

The last 40 years have seen an increasing convergence of the private and public sectors. Performance management has become a central feature of NPM. As discussed in Chapter 1, this can, in part, be traced to the global economic crisis and associated public expenditure crisis of the 1970s in the USA and UK. The oil price hike of that time and the monetary crisis for the US dollar (Strange 1972) started a long period of preoccupation in many developed countries with controlling taxation and public expenditure and increasingly using private and voluntary bodies as providers of state services that offered a more flexible financial alternative to a state monopoly. This set the background to the rise of the New Right with its ideology of market liberalism and deregulation in America and the UK. A major part of this ideology was that bodies independent of the government, either trusts, associations or companies, could raise capital outside of the public sector borrowing requirement (PSBR) and thereby improve the appearance of public finances. Capital costs, in particular, were removed from the state and then funded by annual revenue costs to the public, in the form of leasing, contracting, or the annual purchase of private and voluntary services by the state. Fifty years on, the concern is that this model of the state withdrawing from certain aspects of public provision has actually increased opportunity and resource costs as private bodies monopolize provision and profiteer. Private profits and their distribution can be at the cost of public value.

If organizations that were independent of the government, operating in the capital and private markets, were to be successful in raising large scale funding on the international markets, then the market required them to have disciplines of operation that were similar to other private bodies, such as good financial management records and performance plans, business plans and targets. Performance management plans and planned output targets that were used in the private sector were increasingly implemented in the public and non-government sphere. As Hughes (1998: 63) comments on the drive to implement managerialism in public services: "managerial reforms have stressed performance by individuals and by agencies."

The idea of looking to the private sector for public sector ideas had started earlier, even before the crisis of the mid-1970s. Ideas from organization and management studies theorized in private companies were increasingly assumed to have some relevance to public bodies in the late 1960s. At that time planning systems and organizational structures in the public sector were beginning to be crudely based on private sector models. Management and organization writers and gurus increasingly began to turn their attention to the public sector, alongside their interest in business and commerce. It was argued that performance in public service might bear some resemblance to performance models in the private sector.

The use of an integrated Planning, Programming and Budgeting System (PPBS) in the USA in the 1960s has been argued by some academics to be an early form of performance management in the public sector (Van Dooren, Bouckaert and Halligan 2010). PPBS is an integration of planning and budgeting activities. It aims to link expenditure to priorities for policy expenditure. These priorities should be linked to research evidence about what interventions are most likely to have beneficial social results. The deployment of budgets and resources into priority activities is audited subsequently. This method of policy implementation was designed to move public services away from repeating routine activities and expanding activities based on demand, towards an assessment of social need and the likely outcome benefits of different options. PPBS as a macro form of policy intervention could be argued to be more a form of evidence based policy implementation rather than performance management. PPBS focuses primarily on the input process and the planning of the good use and economy of inputs towards achieving planned priorities (where priorities are based on historical evidence) and there are dangers that over time PPBS quickly loses its link with activities and outputs and any ongoing research into the outcomes of those outputs. For this reason, it has had maximum applicability and impact in government departments like National Defence where forward planning decisions have to be made about financing very large sums of public money on the production of items of equipment like planes and ships. While PPBS will want to ensure that technical outputs are achieved in production, the future use of the equipment, in terms of its performance at times of crisis and war, is many years after the planning of procurement, and may therefore occur in a different context to that which was anticipated in the planning stage.

The development of a culture of business ideas in the public sector became more firmly established in the UK in the early 1970s under the government of Edward Heath. He was concerned with making government more efficient and looked, in particular, for new ways to organize the processes that might increase efficiency. It is no coincidence that major reorganizations of local government and the National Health Service were established at this time. Peter Hennessy (2000: 337) writes of Heath: "At his first Tuesday evening audience with the Queen he placed at the top of the list, the formation of the government, civil service and the place of businessmen in the work of government."

Management by objectives

Corporate approaches to business performance began to be copied in government organizations, for example the centralized management systems of post-1974 UK local government. This included attempts to implement Peter Drucker's (1964) approach to management by objectives (MBO) as had been previously applied to the private sector. Drucker was one of the most influential management writers of the last century (Morris 1998: 88). He identified objective setting and plans for achieving objectives as one of the key tasks of managers. Similarly, he argued that managers should measure and analyze the success of all organizational activities undertaken by employees.

Mullins (1996: 447) defines MBO as: "the setting of objectives and targets; participation by individual managers in agreeing unit objectives and criteria of performance; and the continual review and appraisal of results."

Management by objectives sought to focus industry and commerce on clear output based objectives. Achievement was to be defined and measured more readily than activities. Hughes notes, when writing about the historical change in the operation of public policy from an administrative to a managerial paradigm, that:

> The main change in the managerial programme is for the organization to focus on outputs or outcomes, instead of inputs. Managerial reforms have stressed performance by individuals and by agencies. Agencies are expected to develop performance indicators as a way of measuring the progress the organisation has made towards achieving declared objectives.
>
> (Hughes 1998: 63)

Management by objectives as an elementary method to define performance and performance targets has been central to the management revolution in the public sector of the last 40 years. The setting of objectives requires the establishment of measurement indicators. The focus on performance indicators has been implemented to varying degrees in different countries. Pollitt and Bouckaert (2004) note that performance output targets were a strong feature of public management reforms in New Zealand.

Drucker argued that objectives are fundamental to a functional organization and need to be understood by all staff. Management by objectives attempts to link corporate objectives with team objectives and individual staff objectives. In this sense, MBO is often linked to staff development reviews and staff appraisals where individual work is placed in the context of what the organization needs to achieve. Explicit objectives are meant to ensure that all staff understand and embrace the difference between activities and achievements (Table 4.1). It is not sufficient for staff to be very active—they must focus their activity on the achievement of outputs and outcomes. Productive efficiency (Andrews and Entwistle 2014) is maximizing achievement for a standard input of resources. Staff and organizations must be efficient in their use of resources, including their time. Outputs are the numerical measurement of the primary achievements of activities; for example, the number of surgical operations completed successfully. Outcomes take a longer-term view of outputs and examine the more substantive impact that outputs have over time. For example, the quality of life benefits that result from surgical operations.

Many management consultants who practice MBO argue that a comprehensive system of objectives and individual objectives should be developed through consultation and participation with the work force. This can be difficult to achieve in practice and one problem is that when MBO is first implemented it can appear top-down and authoritarian. Developing public service objectives with professionals can be time consuming and require additional

Table 4.1 Simple management by objectives

Input	Activity	Achievement
Police Officers	Policing and investigations	Arrests, convictions, crime reduction
Surgeons	Operations	Health gain, quality of life improved, patient returns to employment
General Practice Doctors	Prescribing	Symptoms removed, pain removed, quality of life improved
Teachers	Lessons and classroom activities	Children achieve literacy and numeracy standards

meetings and periods of negotiation that may undermine other areas of workflow, increasing delays and lowering morale in the short term. This is also contradictory, in the sense that quite a lot of focus of the application of performance management in public services has been on the reduction of time to deliver services, based on the assumption that waiting time increases social problems. For example, the patient awaiting treatment becomes more ill, or the offender awaiting sentence on bail commits more crime.

In the example below (Table 4.2), the corporate objective of a criminal justice agency like the UK Ministry of Justice is crime reduction. Each individual police and probation officer and team should be able to argue how they contribute to this overall objective. The probation team needs to demonstrate the successful completion of probation orders without reoffending (Merrington and Hine 2001). The probation officer must assist the court in making judgments about risk, when selecting which offenders are likely to respond to probation treatment and not reoffend. Similarly, the police team needs to make arrests that can lead to prosecutions, but the individual police officer has to decide which crimes to pursue as priority targets on the basis of which are likely to lead to good arrest and prosecution results. Hudson (1999) has referred to this kind of framework of objectives as a hierarchy of objectives; it may also be helpful in assisting the appropriate level of detail for each level of the organization. Strategic managers will need an overview. Operational managers on the front line will need much more detailed objectives for their particular service.

Table 4.2 Corporate and divisional objectives: criminal justice system

	Corporate	Police		Probation	
		Team	Officer	Team	Officer
Objective	Crime reduction	Targeted prosecutions using evidence	Targeted arrests	Target offenders who will benefit from probation rehabilitation program	Increase attendance and completion of probation orders
Measure	Crime statistics	Ratio of successful prosecutions to the targeted category of offences	Increased arrest rate for reported target crimes	Percentage of those who reoffend while on community sentences	Satisfactory completion of probation orders

There is a concern in the public sector that this type of hierarchy of objectives and indicators, as dominated by corporate objectives, can become bureaucratic and lead to unintended consequences, especially when there is too much political focus on one output (Bevan and Hood 2006). For example, the focus on surgical waiting list reduction in the UK NHS led previously to longer periods of waiting to see a surgeon for the initial assessment. In contrast, once an initial assessment was made by the surgeon, surgical operations happened relatively quickly. This was because the achievement measurement (improving the speed of service delivery) was based on the time taken from surgical assessment to operation and excluded consideration of how long someone waited to get the surgeon's opinion. Such an unintended consequence of the management of time will not necessarily reduce the number of deaths of those with serious heart disease and cancers requiring urgent surgery to prolong their lives. The emphasis on school attainment created by the Organisation for Economic Co-operation and Development (OECD) comparative national league table of international achievement in core curriculum subjects, has led to more children with behavioral difficulties being excluded from school in developed countries, and this was then argued to be connected with rising levels of persistent youth crime, mental health difficulties and substance misuse.

Corporate, or centralized objectives are often too simplistic in a complex and local world. As a result, their implementation may not lead to the broad positive social outcomes required. They can fail to acknowledge and reward front line staff who show flexibility and resourcefulness in complex and difficult situations. Examples are a social worker who spends many hours with a family so as to try to prevent a depressed family member committing suicide. If a suicide does occur, a key objective has failed, but it would be erroneous to simply conclude that such support was unhelpful and undesirable. The intervention will likely have played a vital part in assisting the family to manage their own feelings of depression about the situation, and to raise the quality of life for other family members in the longer term. The flexibility of public service professionals to adapt rapidly in changing circumstances, when a particular intervention method does not appear to be working, is vital. Management by objectives methodologies can undermine such flexibility and the willingness of staff to work creatively. A UK Audit Commission (2002) report suggested that such MBO approaches can undermine morale and lead to professional staff leaving the public services.

This real anxiety about the power of performance indicators to distract politicians, senior leaders and ultimately professionals from the complexity of many social problems has resulted in a large scale degradation of simple performance indicators and some considerable debate about how performance indicators are best derived and applied. Some have talked of a need to move managerial practice from a focus on performance measurement to a focus on a performance culture where organizational and professional values demand a high quality experience for the service users. The UK NHS for example set up a major working group to consider this issue (Department of Health 2001b). Hughes (1998) acknowledged the considerable difficulties with measurement, but reminds us that performance indicators are ultimately indications of what should be considered, they are not—and should not be—ends in themselves. As will be seen later in the chapter, one result of this debate has been a growth in the range and type of indicator used. Table 4.3 shows some of the different types of indicators now used in the public service.

Performance management

Contemporary performance management is an extension of the concept of MBO. The most prominent feature of both models is their similarity and the attempt to separate means from ends, or process from achievement. Performance management and MBO try to isolate the results of

Table 4.3 Types of performance indicators

Type of indicator	Examples
Input	Salaries, building costs, training days
Activity	Cases processed, assessments undertaken, number of visits
Output	Interventions and treatments successfully completed
Outcomes	Personal satisfaction with intervention and treatment
	Personal satisfaction with user involvement in activity
	Evidence of additional benefit (added-value) resulting from intervention or treatment (for example, medical treatment results in return to employment)
Impact (Social impact beyond the benefit to the individual)	Community satisfaction
	Neighborhood satisfaction
	User group satisfaction
	Satisfaction for related social group (e.g.: a service for children increases quality of life for parents)

management from management activity and process. In private industry, MBO had encouraged firms to become more competitive by refocusing from the activity of work and the production of goods, towards the attainment of the increased output of quality products with better sales and increased competitive advantage. Some research argues that the implementation of performance management regimes can make important efficiency gains, especially in the early stages of public service reforms (Verheijen and Dobrolyubova 2007).

The language and structure of performance management builds on the earlier writings of MBO (Drucker 1964). Public service activities must be clearly defined and understood as separate from outputs and outcomes. An activity like a doctor's or nurse's assessment leads to an output like a prescribed medicine that in turn will result in an outcome of a happier and healthy patient. Activities produce outputs and outcomes. Similarly inputs are what make activities occur. Inputs are items like human resources, training, vehicles, and buildings—all of which can be usually traced back to income. Inputs provide for the process of work. Activities are the process of work. Outputs and outcomes are the results.

Figure 4.1 shows a classical performance system where the focus is on three management tasks: economy of inputs, the efficiency of inputs to outputs and the effectiveness of outputs to outcomes.

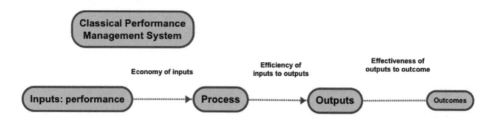

Figure 4.1 Adding input value

This division of means and ends is not without its difficulties. Academics refer to such a rigid separation as a dichotomy or as a dualism. Complexity science is rather suspicious of dualism. The rigid separation of two aspects of reality is not sympathetic to the complex notion that such features are linked and are likely to become entangled in some conditions. Dualism rejects the complex notion of dynamic feedback between different elements of a complex adapting system. Complexity theory sees feedback and interaction as central to the understanding of society and its social problems, policy interventions and public organizations.

The danger is that performance management sees issues in terms of simplistic cause and effect rather than complex entanglements and changing dynamics that occur due to interactions and feedback. It is a false separation of two aspects, an erroneous separation of means and ends, process and outcome. Farnham and Horton (1996) noted that a false and over-simplified separation of process and outcome was one feature of NPM theory.

For example, while the teaching activities of a school teacher are activities that can be argued to be separate from the actual learning outputs of literacy and numeracy standards achieved by a child (because one child can sit in a class and learn nothing), activity and output are always linked in complex ways. The teaching activities are highly likely to contribute to the learning of the child, in addition to the input of parental support and out of school activities. Different children will respond in a variety of ways to the different teaching activities offered. One approach may not suit all children, especially those with specific and special learning needs. Some general approaches may be shown to be more optimal for the majority, but they will not work for all children all of the time. While performance management might encourage the separation of teaching activity and learning outcomes, to be clear exactly what activity is achieving which outcome, complexity emphasizes the entanglement of activity and achievement and the difficulty with reducing the causes of outcome to some controlled teaching experiments. A simple example of this entanglement is positive reinforcing feedback, where the initial gain in a child's knowledge encourages the teacher so that the teacher is more successful over time. This is not because the teacher has changed their activity, but simply because they have experienced positive feedback and this has made them more confident and positive towards their class. As a result of the interaction, the children's esteem is raised and they continue to gain across a range of specific outcomes. A small amount of initial positive feedback has an exponential gain once a positive feedback loop is established. This is not to argue that a very specific teaching method might perform optimally with one key skill, but a number of important issues will also be involved, many of which are interpersonal and resulting from communication and interactive feedback.

Feedback and interactions

Complexity theory implies that achievement will be contingent on many factors and that it will be subject to some instability over time. Feedback is an important part of this process. We have seen that an example of positive reinforcing feedback would be children enjoying a particular activity and its repetition, thus increasing their learning performance over time. An example of negative feedback would be children growing bored with a particular activity, thus reducing their learning performance over time. Time scales can be critical. If an activity does not have an initial positive affect, it may, at some key moment in time, shift to become negative in effect. Conversely, some activities may take a long time to show a positive gain. Another added complexity is that activities that show short-term gain in some individuals, may take much longer to show success in others. While waiting for the long-term effect on one subgroup, the activity may start to be having a negative effect on those who got a short-term benefit. The variable of time and time effect is critical in the understanding of complex systems and the variability of individual effects.

There is a fundamental difficulty for the development of management practice here; management by objectives and performance management look to maximize the relationship between activity and achievement, by separating and reducing the two elements to a linear and causal understanding. MBO and performance management want to know exactly what causes good achievement. It is argued this enables resourcing to be standardized in a method that maximizes efficiency of inputs to activities, and activities to outputs (how many teachers spend exactly how much time, teaching a specific skill, with a specific method, to an optimal number of children). The complexity and entanglement of the public service and social context make this sort of rationalization of cause and effect extremely difficult. Every gain made is in reality highly contingent on hundreds of complicated factors. We cannot always be sure that one activity method will always replicate and achieve similar results. This is because there is much potential for change in numerous interrelated variables. In the example of educational activity and learning, variables like the prevalence of illness, what was on TV the previous night and the resulting time children went to bed, what was served at the school canteen for lunch, are examples of conditions that might have exponential feedback effects for limited time periods.

Similarly, a method of medical surgery might be seen to have very positive results with a high number of patients, but there is a significant minority who do better with other treatments. Individual difference and genetic variation dictates that such prediction is limited. This is especially true with drug treatments where contraindications are unpredictable and subject to individual differences. A key aspect here, once again, is interaction, the relationship that the human subject develops with the activity applied. What works for a majority, will not work for all. A significant minority remain who require a different method.

Evaluation work in higher education illustrates the different experience and learning styles that students bring to their learning and the resulting effect is that no single teaching method is superior, rather a mix is needed to keep all students engaged, but unfortunately each different method used is likely to be unpopular with one minority group at some point in time. This is sometimes referred to as "blended learning". Here diverse activities are used to ensure maximum gain for the whole group, even though at any one point in time it might appear that a minority is not gaining. The end result, over time, is the main consideration. The teacher needs to take an overview, or synthesis, over time. In this example, timescales are all important. An evaluation taken at the half way point in a course will be very different to an evaluation taken at the end, because not all the diverse learning styles will have been catered for in the mix and match of teaching activities. What is emerging is a picture of performance management that is at times non-linear and scale free, where performance gains are not neatly periodically located.

Processes and activities

Trends in management science need to be located in the context of history. The input of performance management into the public sector has its own history. There was in the post-World War Two public service a tradition of professionals working in a manner that focused on complexity of process and too little on outcome. General practice doctors, for example, traditionally focused on diagnosis rather than prognosis and treatment. A patient who could not gain a clear diagnosis after seeing several experts was in danger of not receiving any treatment plan or health gain. Hence psychiatry turned its back on those with a "personality disorder" and considered such patients to be untreatable precisely because they did not have a proper medical diagnosis, yet clearly such people had chronic psychological difficulties and multiple social problems. Thousands of patients were left without satisfactory treatment, many ended up homeless or in prison after repeated petty offending. This focus of public sector professionals on process was one of the reasons why professional discretion, that is the right of professionals in the public sector to apply their own personal judgment, fell into some disrepute from the 1970s onwards. The public and political representatives were no longer willing to accept these complex professional processes without asking some searching questions about their efficiency and the outcomes that resulted.

Teachers focused too much in the past on the process and activities of learning and teaching without enough reflection on the relationship between these processes with learning outcomes. The introduction of key attainment tests to evaluate the specific skills at certain ages was an internationalized attempt to raise output results (OECD 2012) used by many developed and developing countries. Methods like a standardized national curriculum attempted to focus professional input to agreed areas of content. Similarly, in several national health systems, large scale programs of cognitive behavioral psychological treatment have been implemented to help those with less severe mental health difficulties. Offender rehabilitation services in the UK tried something similar (Chapman and Hough 1998). These kinds of approaches seek to standardize the professional approaches to large numbers of service users. The attraction to managers is that the boundaries of operation are clear. Training and supervision is relatively easy to implement and a small number of input and activity variables can be used to evaluate the resulting outputs. New public managerialism has dictated the popularity of these approaches to service delivery.

Before the current contemporary policy of attempting to hold professional practice to account by performance management, professionals based their discretion and inherent right to exercise judgment over the process of their work, on the assumption that their work was highly complex and technically intangible. There was a resistance to reduce their skills to technical competence and instead an emphasis on a large quantitative range of skills that might need to be combined in any number of qualitative combinations at any one time and place. This placed more emphasis on the art of judgment about what to do in a unique situation rather than technical competence in a given situation (see Table 4.4).

One of the consequences of this was that professionals had a tendency to search for new ways of doing similar activities and a vast drive to increase the scope of their knowledge and understanding. This was the method they used to modify and improve their interaction with a complex environment. The last two decades have seen a change in this culture with an attempt by politicians and managers to impose a more standard technical competence on professional work, even where tasks are highly technical. There is also a stronger emphasis today when new methods are developed that they need to show their evidence base in terms of what outputs and outcomes they can really achieve.

Value maximization

Performance management goes a step further than MBO. It seeks to maximize value. To do this it seeks to maximize the quantitative value of the relationship between its key aspects: inputs, activities, outputs and outcomes. For this to happen the relationship between inputs and activities must be economic, in other words the minimum cost is paid to achieve a standard level of activities. The relationship between activities and outputs must be efficient,

Table 4.4 Differences in managerial and professional approaches to understanding performance

	Professional	*Managerial*
Skills	Judgment about application of a skills set or toolkit	Focus on specific skills and competencies
Use of skills in work based activities	Large number of skills needed	Focus on core, most relevant skills
Knowledge base	Identify many possibilities and relate knowledge to unique situations	Evidence practice is based on historical similarities from past cases
Performance indicators	Many, overlapping, perhaps contradictory	Few, focused
Time scale	Indeterminate	Determinate
Performance achieved by	Flexible trial and error, what works in practice and similar circumstances (Rules of Thumb)	Clarity of task and outcome, related to historical evidence (Reduction to core elements)

that is to say that activities must be the right ones, administered in the correct method, to achieve the outputs necessary (Andrews and Entwistle 2014). Finally, the relationship between outputs and outcomes should be effective. This requires the outputs to be producing the required outcomes. The last part of the value maximization triage is the most difficult to achieve. This is partly because outcomes in the public sector can be intangible and rather abstract, making them difficult to measure (Rouse 1999). Examples are public service outcomes like quality of life and community safety. The relationship between service outputs and these outcome wider goals is far from straightforward to prove when one is examining cause and effect.

Much performance management work in the public sector has failed to comprehensively consider the full value of the maximization process. When managers have talked of "value-added" for example, they are very often thinking of introducing an additional task to a professional or an administrator's workload without enough reflection on whether the extra output is really increasing outcomes. In addition, if no extra input is applied to get the added value, will value be lost in other areas of work because of the associated strain on the number of activities carried out? Consider the increase in students entering Higher Education in many countries in the last decade. In most countries, the financial input per student did not increase in line with the total number of students. It was not possible to retain generous teacher–student ratios. This achieved economy of input with education being delivered to more students without much added input. But the quality value of input for each student is argued by many in the sector to have declined, as less time was available for individual student tutorial support and to chase up students with personal difficulties. In some countries this led to increased university drop out rates and a problem with retaining students. This can be described as inefficient—too much wastage occurs before outputs and outcomes are achieved. Performance was improved in terms of economy of input, but not necessarily improved for efficiency.

Whole systems approaches to performance

These kinds of assumptions and errors in the application of performance management are based on the idea that a performance system (as identified in Figure 4.1) is a single and relatively isolated system. In reality, the complexity of the public services' operating environment dictates otherwise. The need for public service performance management to consider more than one dimension (or aspect) at a time is referred to by Holloway (1999: 12) as the "double loop feedback". A public service user may enter one part of a service system and then be referred into another. They may experience two interlinked subsystems at the same time, for example being treated both by a General Practice doctor and a surgeon. Another similar idea, related to measurement, is the balanced scorecard, where a range of performance indicators are chosen to reflect the overall performance of an organization, because single indicators are inappropriate (Hudson 1999: 180). Systems based approaches can consider multiple elements and subsystems (see Figure 4.2). Even these types of adaptations of practice may not suffice for dealing with some of the dysfunctions of public service performance management if additional influences on performance are unknown and therefore not identified in systems analysis, nor measured for their system impact.

Performance management has been applied too simplistically in public services. It has been used as a tool to save money and reduce the amount of input and activities in relation to activities and outputs, without enough real consideration of the resulting effect on efficiency and quality of outcomes. As a result of this, numerous management writers have looked to more complicated approaches to managing performance that can still be understood and used in the busy practice environment. Mwita (2000) has described a whole systems approach in the public service. Although still primarily based on economic measures of cost benefit, his argument is that personal factors, leadership, teams, procedures, facilities, finances and the external environment all need to be included in the implementation of a drive towards better performance. His model is, nevertheless, primarily based on a perception of a linear rational and inclusive process where there is little acknowledgement of conflict and rapidly changing political agendas, as is often the reality. The NCVO (National Council for Voluntary

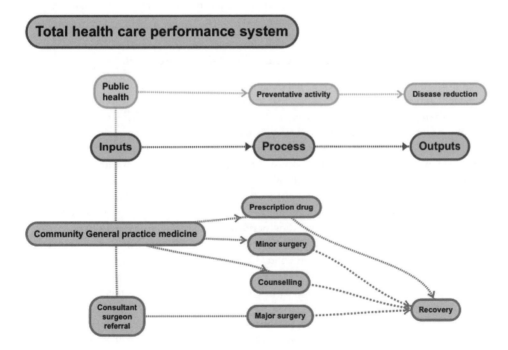

Figure 4.2 A total performance system

Organisations) Excellence Model as described by Hudson (1999: 194) can also be thought of as a whole systems approach to improving performance. Here the emphasis is on making links between a wide range of inputs (these include human resources and skills), with processes that determine a diversity of results that include people satisfaction, user satisfaction and general social impact.

An OECD review of Human Resource Management (HRM) in Belgium, part of a multinational approach to compare the implementation of new management techniques in government administration, concluded on the supreme difficulty of having a fully integrated HRM performance management system across the hierarchy of a large government department:

> The challenge of providing a coherent cascade of objectives and targets – where hierarchies of goals and priorities are established at each level from organisational, through departmental, divisional team and finally individual – to establish a good basis for the evaluation of performance, does not yet seem fully achieved in any of the governments under review.
>
> (OECD 2007: 91)

Beyond the criticism that whole systems approaches are still constructed based on unrealistic linear models, complexity theory raises some fundamental concerns about the theoretical basis of performance management. The separation of activities and outcomes goes too far, becoming as it does a dualism or dichotomy. Complexity approaches to performance management need to give more emphasis to the entanglement of the stages of performance management and this is rather different to a cause and effect understanding. Complexity accounts focus on the interaction and resulting feedback between different elements of the process and outputs. Complexity theory implies that it is the feedback process itself that offers us the best understanding of how performance is constructed.

Performance interaction and feedback in higher education

In higher education this feedback is a vital component of policy. Trying to economize on inputs has made it more difficult to give individual students support and this creates the feedback of students leaving the sector when they cannot find help. This inefficiency means that an economy of inputs has not been as effective in increasing the output of qualified graduates as it might have been. A complex approach to performance management needs to focus on the interaction and feedback between economy, efficiency and effectiveness rather than one-off static definitions of inputs or outputs. In other words, the approach needs to be dynamic and consider the changing relationship of constituent factors over time (Blackman 2001). One-off league tables of outputs are fairly meaningless, unless put into their dynamic context. Table 4.5 illustrates an example of some base line performance data for four universities.

Drop out statistics show that universities A and B in the SW and NE regions respectively are doing less well in retaining their students. University A is the only university where drop out rates have increased.

When this performance information is balanced against increased student capacity, University A has grown at a fast rate of over 4% for each of the three years. University B's reduction in wastage may be due to its more conservative growth in the last two years. Universities C and D have grown more conservatively while keeping their retention high (drop out low). Rapid expansion carries with it risks. Systems are more likely to be strained and student support diminished. The key is to maximize growth while reducing wastage,

Table 4.5 Comparison of university performance data

Univ	Location	3 yr average % entering employment on graduation	Year 1 annual % increase in students	annual % drop out rate	Year 2 annual % increase in students	annual % drop out rate	Year 3 annual % increase in students	annual % drop out rate
A	SW	90	4	7	5	8	4	9
B	NE	85	4	10	2	10	2	8
C	NW	90	2	6	2	6	1	5
D	SE	99	1	5	1	4	2	3

rather than seeing wastage increase with growth. How can one analyze this relationship in a complex way? The following dynamic could be suggested.

The central dynamic is the essential feedback relationship between academic teaching staff and students. Staff are the primary drivers in this relationship, but they need to be sensitive to student feedback and adjust their behavior accordingly. In addition, there are periodic outside contingencies that will affect the staff and student inputs. Academic staff will be under pressure to publish scholarly writing and to win research contracts. These can limit and disrupt their teaching activities and relationships with students.

Students will have a perception of the job market in accordance with the performance of the economy and the relative risk of leaving university prematurely to take paid employment with immediate prospects. Similarly this will be balanced with immediate debt and personal financial difficulties and any lack of government financial support to continue with their studies. Therefore, the wider economy and Higher Education policy environment will influence student behavior in a manner that may affect the specific performance indicator of student drop out rates.

In this example, performance can only be improved by understanding the interaction of critical components. Such feedback interactions are likely to be quite unstable and unpredictable, and subject to short-term patterns, rather than long-term cycles or linear trends. This means that performance management is a dynamic process and cannot be based on static definitions and processes. A regular review of the interaction of critical elements and how they are changing is needed (see Table 4.6). Some of the contextual factors relate to the performance of the economy and issues such as the wider job market and cost of borrowing to pay course fees and rents. These external factors may have a bigger short-term effect on public service performance than is sometimes appreciated.

Adding value to public service processes

Given that qualitative professional and user responses might be needed to address performance difficulties, as in the example of higher education teaching and tutoring, benchmarking might be one useful strategy to pursue. Hudson (1999: 186) describes performance benchmarking as "the search for best practices that leads to superior performance." Thus professionals and managers look to their competitors for best practice examples where performance has been improved. The collaborative ethos of the public sector makes this a real possibility. In recent years, governments and international organizations have set up bodies to try and encourage the collaborative development of best practice.

Table 4.6 Management of performance interactions

Process of change	Key dynamics for staff

Economy-efficiency	Changing workload for staff
	    Educating better with less resource per student, so that students still graduate successfully and with good results.
	    Supporting students with their studies and personal life, so that drop out is prevented.

Efficiency-effectiveness	New teaching methods and outputs lead to better quality of life for students and more favorable employment outcomes.

What is needed is a method that does not look to over-simplify the human condition and one that can embrace the potential for individual difference, including the dynamic relationships between people in the system, while searching for patterns of similarity. Complex public service management, as an art of practice, needs to embrace some responsibility for performance. While poor performance cannot always be blamed on external factors, this is one consideration. A manager will be one key part of a complex system that can influence performance. But this ability to influence performance needs to be based on an honest and realistic appraisal of exactly how an influence can be established. Managers should not underestimate or overestimate the influence of a particular method or activity. The manager is one key player in a complex system. Managers need to assess the interrelationship of aspects and attempt to appreciate the feedback mechanisms that influence performance. Understanding the operations of a system, its values, cultures, relationships and interdependencies is as important as understanding the flow and distribution of resources. Figure 4.3 begins to identify the impact of values on performance. Values of technical competency are often explicit and strong in public professional work with powerful quasi-legal consequences for those who do not deliver. They can be linked to explicit working standards. Training and qualifications reinforce these values and standards. Managers ensure these values are delivered to the public and apply the penalties when they are breached. Other professional peers are usually involved in the formal process for sanctioning breaches. Professional technical competency does not stand still, but is also dynamic, as new equipment is available and demands new applications and techniques. Training and skills updating are therefore important professional value bases themselves and a key method for improving operational performance.

Personalization refers to the ability of public service processes and activities to make service user experiences tailored to the user's individual needs (Barnes 2012) and relational in the sense that they are co-produced by the user and the professional (Radnor *et al.* 2014). This maximizes the opportunities for adding value and delivering appropriate outputs with excellent long-term outcomes.

Locally devised performance measures often prove to be as important as global measures. The contribution of front-line staff and service users to defining, measuring and implementing local performance measures becomes vital. The monitoring of team performance, in relation to similar teams, might be more appropriate than focusing on individual performance in some situations. In all situations analysis of qualitative and quantitative performance data needs to be holistic and reflective and draw conclusions from such an informed perspective.

It is argued here that true value maximization has largely been ignored in public services given the dominant austerity focus on quantitative performance indicators and economy of inputs. Focusing on such limited and narrow definitions of quality may reduce the

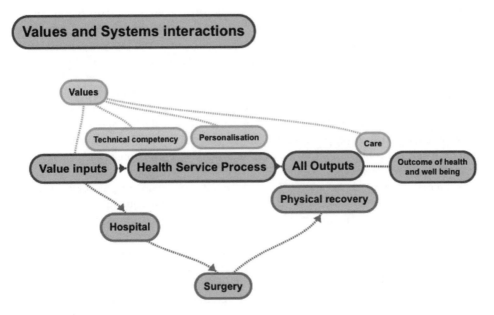

Figure 4.3 Values and systems interactions

opportunity for "value added". For example, the school teacher who is brilliant at coaching for academic examinations may not be so good at pastoral support and extracurricular activities like sport. These other skills give education important added value that may minimize children's personal and social problems in later life (many developed countries are noticing that their children are getting better at passing exams, but more overweight also). Complexity implies the need for a synthesis of performance management that looks beyond very focused and narrow definitions. Such management practice needs to understand how entangled aspects of a complex and dynamic system change over time. Managers will look for patterns and similarities and seek to see how stable or unstable those features are. Balancing short-term and long-term goals may require a different blend of initial activities and inputs.

Instead of starting with the premise of getting more for less inputs, which so often leads to a focus entirely on economy of inputs and not enough consideration of efficiency and effectiveness, many public services would do well to start with the premise of getting added-value from existing resources. This is about enhancing the efficiency and effectiveness of existing resources. Often this is a good point at which to involve service users and front line professionals in consideration of performance issues. It is a constructive point on which to initiate dialogue with those staff involved.

The care management process in social welfare departments is typical of the kind of reforms of professional work that have accompanied the public managerial reforms of the last 40 years. Care management has meant that professional staff increasingly assess need, and help a user make an informed choice about what future services are best for their situation. The emphasis has moved from a few alternative services being offered, many of which were owned and managed directly by government, to a greater range of services being offered, with the expectation that many will be managed separate to government, either by NGOs, or by private companies, or by both. In some countries, service users are given funding for personal budgets or vouchers to purchase a service directly themselves.

Much of the initial anxiety expressed by professional workers about market and persona-lized based reforms concerned the perception by them that they are not being allowed to use their full professional skills. Instead they are being asked to make a bureaucratic assessment for finding the cheapest option for long-term private or charitable care outside of the public sector. Professional staff perceived this as both undermining their professional skills (hence actually reducing the value of their input) while using them to economize on long-term service inputs (requiring them to find the cheapest long-term services). In some countries, governments contributed further to these anxieties about reducing and economizing on inputs by arguing that this new care management task did not need professional social work or nursing staff, but could be done by assistants trained in the core assessment and administration, finance and computing skills.

An alternative approach would have been to consult with the existing professional workers about the skills they possess and how they could be used to add value to a changing process that gave users and their families greater choice about the services and interventions available to them. This could have focused on the important process of crisis management when an older person falls sick with all the psychological and social traumas for the person and their immediate family. The highly trained worker becomes a key point of support in the midst of the crisis, rather than a calculating assessor. By clarifying the psychological aspects of the crisis involved and through sensitive negotiating with the user, medical services and family mem-bers, an inappropriate decision (perhaps for expensive residential care) could be avoided (Barnes 2012). Seen in this way, the social psychological and relational management of the distressing transition of becoming disabled, or experiencing a major illness, becomes a key opportunity for adding value to the process that can also maximize the output and outcome benefits. Taking care about making the best possible decision in such difficult circumstances can end up being the most efficient way of economizing on new inputs over the longer term. Later expensive additional costs in having to change care arrangements and re-assess again might be avoided by a high quality involvement in the early stages. Here the social worker or nurse is a dynamic manager of a complex adapting system and he or she is taking an important part within that system.

This is different to a reductionist view that only looks at the physical aspect of the social care materials and resources, where costs are rigidly defined and crisis counselling skills and resources assumed to be static and not cost specific. The dynamic approach to value adding emphasizes the constant instability in the system over time and the ability of the professional to potentially intervene and become positively involved in the feedback system, even though no final outcome can be easily predicted. Here the focus is constantly on adding value and positive input to the system and its self-organizing potential, rather than reduction and sim-plification (Figure 4.4). Performance may be defined by human actions as well as service achievements (Van Dooren, Bouckaert and Halligan 2010: 3).

Complex systems and performance

Complex systems present some substantial challenges to understanding how good perfor-mance can be managed not least because of the dynamic and changing nature of these sys-tems and the range of influences upon them. Byrne (2011b) discusses some important alternative approaches that use case based methods and take qualitative approaches seriously as an alternative to isolated quantitative indicators. Holloway (1999: 246) notes: "the need for approaches to performance management to be compatible with organizational cultures and political factors which may be rather less rational". Managers who are sympathetic to the

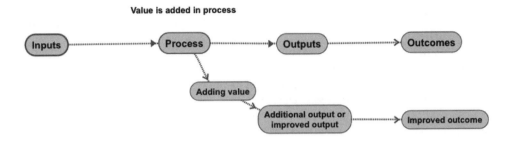

Figure 4.4 Adding value to systems

complexity of the public sector and its services will need to start their assessment and man-agement of performance by embracing and accepting the nature of the complexity in which they are engaged. An understanding of the political and economic context is crucial. Of course, it is sometimes necessary to simplify things in order to understand them in practice and to make decisions, but to enforce simplicity too early in a process of judgments about performance improvement is an error. An initial assessment requires an understanding of the nature of the complexity faced.

The first stage in understanding public service performance is, therefore, to assess the local management system, its key processes and interactions, and their associated levels of com-plexity. A central question at this point is the level of entanglement with other processes and tasks and the extent to which the task in question is contingent on other external factors. This may include and require reflection on the unintended consequences of intervening in performance as the manager and professionals are part of that dynamic performance system (Smith 1995).

An example is the attainment of school children in key stage tests. Crude measures will simply record the averages and data dispersion for children and then compare this to local and national averages and dispersion for the same age bands. This can have the effect of encouraging schools to be more selective and to attempt to exclude from intake those chil-dren whom it thinks will be less successful. Similarly more highly paid and qualified parents may have a better ability to "play this system", pursuing the best schools for their children either by campaigning on behalf of their child or by physically moving into the catchment area of a specific school to improve their chances of entry. The combined feedback effect begins to be the separation of schools into those that have poor average attainment and those that have good average attainment. The relative instability of allowing more choice at one point in the life of the system, interwoven with schools responding with selection criteria, can result in a bifurcation towards a system with two increasingly extreme points (Byrne and Rogers 1996). So in some circumstances, feedback will reproduce an increase in social separation. Instability in market economics, free labor markets and global trade without adequate regulation can have this effect on the economic distances between rich and poor and a lack of positive social outcomes for poorer groups in society (Haynes 2012).

Crude performance measures like average school key stage tests fail to take into account the socio-economic context. Schools in poorer areas may be the most important parts of the education system to address, as this is where skill gains are most needed, if unemployment and social deprivation are to be tackled. Socio-economic context will include a whole range of factors that are likely to influence a child's performance such as, parental attitudes to education, parental educational qualifications, household poverty, number of children with special needs, etc. In this kind of public policy situation, policy and managers might favor policy responses that are not universal, but targeted at particular marginalized social groups, or geographical neighborhoods, for maximum targeted gain.

In the context of performance in schools a focus on ability tests alone can have other unintended consequences. Most tests, like the OECD's (2012) international standard tests, focus on language, mathematics and science and so the subject disciplines that do not feature can suffer and not be developed. Children might become very good at taking tests in core subjects, and certain types of assessment, and teachers very good at coaching this aspect of performance, but will this actually give children the skills they need when they are having to rapidly adapt to new learning environments as young adults in the fast changing world of technology and work? Will children have creative skills, personal skills and the ability to judge when to use and apply the knowledge that they have?

This is a potential effectiveness gap, a gap between outputs and outcomes, a gap between educational qualifications gained and useful employment and life skills gained. The children who have performed very well at tests will not necessarily be the best workers or employees who are able to assimilate and create new knowledge and apply it in the context of teamwork and having the necessary interpersonal skills. Neither will they necessarily be the best citizens who become active and supportive community members.

Outcome measures often imply more of a synthesis of attributes. For example, quality of life as a social outcome can be linked to the elements of educational attainment, job satisfaction, personal relationship skills and health care. A health care treatment might cure a disease, but if that person has—in the process—lost their relationship with their partner and their enjoyable career, raising general quality of life will prove more difficult.

All this implies the need for a range of data, perhaps focusing on a number of key performance areas that on the face of it appear contradictory. In reality they will more likely be paradoxical than contradictory.

One step towards achieving this approach has been the introduction of different types of performance indicators—indicators that focus on different dimensions of performance in government (Department of Health 2001b). Boyne (2002: 19) argues that there is some improvement in the range of indicators applied to local government, because of the acknowledgement of different dimensions of performance. He notes the five dimensions now covered:

- outputs (qualitative and quantitative);
- efficiency (cost per unit of output);
- service outcomes (that deal with issues like impact and equity);
- responsiveness (consumer satisfaction with services); and
- and democratic outcomes (such as participation and accountability).

This is a framework of public service performance that embraces some complexity, but for it to prove satisfactory as a managerial tool it would have to lead to a consideration of the interaction and feedback tensions resulting from the various indicators that can be generated by such frameworks. The temptation and danger is that large numbers of indicators are added together simplistically to give an overall star rating or grading (Office of the Deputy Prime Minister 2001), for example the UK Comprehensive Performance Assessment (CPA) applied to local government or the "star" ratings applied to English hospitals and social care services (Cutler and Waine 2003).

If there is a large range of performance measures covering different areas, the danger is that services are over-audited and this creates too much data collection and analysis work for middle managers. In addition, front line workers can feel that their working environment is getting over-managed and bureaucratized. This can demotivate staff, a factor that is virtually guaranteed to undermine good performance (Audit Commission 2002). A large bureaucracy of performance and accountability can waste resources and be remote from the realities and pressures of service delivery. This implies the importance of peer performance evaluation, or keeping those on the front line close to the qualitative performance management and accountability process—so that they and their user population should be centrally involved in it (Lipsky 1980). Front line workers need to become involved in setting qualitative performance targets and their measurement. Professional ownership and bottom-up management that creates motivation and protects quality for service users is more important than an impressively large range of centrally controlled indicators.

This does not imply that professionals should acquire sole discretion over their own working environment. The key is finding the right dynamic for a given professional situation. In any situation, professionals will not manage performance alone; there will always have to be some involvement of politicians, managers and service users. This is a reality of a complex public service system. The OECD has encouraged more career movement of public managers and administrators, particularly between central departments and service provider agencies, so that good practices are better disseminated and shared as workers experience different environments: "International experience shows that in a performance based environment, careers back and forth from central departments to agencies should be encouraged to promote a high quality dialogue on outputs and outcomes of agencies" (OECD 2007: 125).

While there will be aspects that are defined by hard data and focus on clear structures and statistical data, there will also be just as many aspects that are soft. This is the "underbelly" of the performance system that allows different professional involvement to reflect on their unintended consequences, or other complex interactions. For example, in education, this is where a network of professional communication can allow general teachers to understand their contribution to child welfare, psychological well being, and diverse and special needs. It is erroneous to remove these aspects of performance quality from the general class teacher because their professional commitment is to all aspects of child welfare.

The central point in the complex system is the general professional, but to adapt successfully to a changing economic and social environment they rely on a network of specialists and resources; it is their complex entanglement with these aspects that gives the system its added value, its enhanced performance. A complex system is a response to a complex society and to attempt to over-simplify it is to reduce the ability of the system to respond to all social needs. It is the ability of the teacher to interact appropriately and with flexibility and creativity that is so important if the needs of all children are to be met. An aspect of this is appropriate referral to specialist support and related public services.

The process of understanding complexity can therefore add value to the end product. It should enable a process and product that is adaptable. It should enable the creation of many unique products, in terms of human experience, that are not standardized, but have many similarities: yet each is unique in how it is applied to an individual public citizen. Thousands may have the same medical operation, but each process is unique. Each patient has a different social and cultural context that is part of his or her state of health. Each has their genetic constitution. Each person's physical body and the way in which it adapts to ill health are slightly different, although of course this is in the context of similarities. It is how the patient is spoken to, fed, assessed, and discharged and what choice of medication they receive on discharge that will add value or undermine the standardized surgical operation. This means that there may be some variations in cost for the standardized activity, but variations of the experience are needed to ensure performance is maximized. This is because human beings are complex systems, not complicated machines. They are not the same as a jumbo jet. They are not as predictable in the mechanical sense. A jumbo jet cannot interact with its maker; a patient can interact with their surgeon.

Performance as communication and interaction

Process cannot be detached from output. It is precisely the manner in which the process is handled that allows the output to become a positive outcome. Process is an opportunity to add value to an outcome. Public service process is critical for adding value and enhancing performance. Many parents will tell you stories about the personal skills of a particular teacher who was able to help their child move on extra fast in a given year. Something about the process of interaction between that child and teacher maximizes the value of the educational output. These are the qualitative experiences that are of substantive significance, even if in quantitative terms they do not seem statistically significant.

When we look back to what we learnt at university or school, what is it that we remember? Is it the knowledge, the test answers—or the personal qualities of the person who enabled us to learn? How did we learn? Were we developing as a person or just acquiring focused knowledge? The answers to these questions tell us much about the nature of the performance management task in public services. It is not an impossible task, but it is an extremely difficult task, and one that the modern age requires us to do. If society underestimates the difficulty of the task, public performance management may do more harm than good.

Lawton has identified that value may well come from the ethical commitment that public service workers have to public institutions and public service and that a commitment to such a process creates a sense of accountability to positive social and democratic outcomes:

> There is a sense in which we live in "the evaluative state" where the prevailing ethos is "if it moves measure it!". We appear to be overwhelmingly goal-orientated and procedural issues and processes are downgraded. In so doing the quality of relationships within organisational life and the feelings of mutual trust and obligations and reciprocal rights and responsibilities are lost.
>
> (Lawton 1998: 128)

At worst, the reductionist and highly focused approach of performance measurement and MBO implemented in the public sector through the new managerial revolution has undermined some of the deep and historical added value culture that Lawton describes. But Hughes (1998: 186) says: "The absence of performance measures is not a serious option."

The key task then becomes the understanding of the emerging contradictions and tensions in the system data. Qualitative research may be the most satisfactory way of understanding what the contradictions between quantitative performance indicators really mean in a substantive sense, especially when front line service providers have to make immediate and pragmatic decisions. Qualitative case studies of public service users provide rich performance based data and should not be underestimated.

One approach to these qualitative aspects of performance is to designate them as soft outcomes (Dewson et al. 2000) and to distinguish them from hard outcomes set at a macro level and linked to statistical indicators. This was the approach of the UK Institute of

Employment Studies in its research into employment programs for the Department of Education and Skills (DES). Soft outcomes were defined as (Dewson *et al.* 2000: 2): intangible, subjective, relative, personal, and intermediate (in that they could be argued as steps towards hard outcomes). Van Dooren, Bouckaert and Halligan (2010: 101–103) also distinguish between soft and hard approaches to the use of performance information. They argue that managers must distinguish between loosely coupled low impact situations (soft) and tightly coupled high impact situations (hard). An example of a soft situation is a social worker using a relational approach to assess a low risk case for future referral to appropriate social support, whereas a hard situation is the referral of a heart disease diagnosis for urgent assessment and treatment.

Managing performance in a complex public system

Using the author's research with the Brighton Systems and Complex Systems Project (Haynes *et al.* 2011) a toolkit for intervening to understand and improve performance is proposed. It is based and refined on the early work of that project and its interdisciplinary and interprofessional members.

The performance of public systems is best understood through collective, creative and collaborative processes. There is no one single model or method for undertaking this, but the description below is based on the author's own experiences in practice.

The starting point, as with all systems based approaches to management, is a good and well informed understanding of the system being studied. This is best done by attempting to construct a diagram, or diagrams, of the system. A pitfall to avoid, that often inhibits the involvement of those involved, is that there is some holy grail or ultimate truth representation that can be drawn. The opposite is true. Complex systems can be illustrated as diagrams that are partial representations of complexity. Participants will produce different diagrams and representations of the same system. This is because any single diagram can only present one perspective and a few dimensions at a time.

Elements for the diagram to start with are:

- What, for the purposes of representation and considering performance is best considered as inside, outside and on the boundaries of the system?
- People: who are the key actors and where are they positioned in the system?
- Primary activities: what are the core activities and where do they take place?
- Secondary activities: what activities also take place to assist the delivery of primary activities?
- Where do outputs occur, and is it clear how these outputs relate to prior activities?
- Is there any logical order or connectivity of activities and if so can this be represented diagrammatically?
- What are the key points of connection, for the purposes of communication and linking complex processes of interaction, in the system?
- How do resources flow into inputs and activities?

This checklist should allow the working group to construct some interesting and meaningful descriptive representations of the systems they work in.

It is also worth noting at this point that these diagrams are often potentially fractal and recursive through levels: that is they can be subdivided into smaller micro elements, that will have some similar, but also some different, aspects. For example, an analysis of an education system will break off into schools, departments, year cohorts and classes. It depends at what level the management group is trying to understand performance that will dictate how many different levels they try to represent in a particular exercise.

Having formed some agreeable representations of the basic description of how the system operates, the exercise now moves to the second stage of defining performance. This can be done both quantitatively and qualitatively. For example, the group might take some performance issues already given to it by a senior manager, or an external audit body, or similar. The group then has to locate where these performance issues occur on the diagram and use the diagram as a method to start analyzing and debating what the issue is about. This leads to a further diagram, or "overlaying" on the first diagram. One popular method for "overlaying", is to use sticky "post it" notes. Adding quantitative information can include estimates of time, including how long a particular activity takes and indicators of volume and/or distribution of volume in a given time period.

Having debated and defined performance issues, with reference to the whole system, the next stage is to clarify management interventions to improve performance. This can be done either on the diagram, or off it. The key thing at this point is that the diagram and subsequent considerations have enabled the group to get to the stage of considering what needs to change. At the end of the process it is helpful to add the final decisions about agreed management actions to the diagrams, as a final record of what has been decided.

To summarize the application of complexity theory and complex problems to the performance management task, a number of key points can be identified:

- The choice of baseline indicators, some of which will appear contradictory. Some will be prescribed by outside organizations, but other indicators may be chosen by the host organization. This stage needs to clarify what the indicators are, who will collect the data and how regularly it will be presented and analyzed.
- There should be a process of consultation and involvement with both professionals and service users about what constitutes good performance and why, probably also reflecting on existing indicators and their usefulness.
- A performance review exercise, that uses a whole systems perspective and seeks to map with diagrams, and thereby identify interconnected performance issues, should be undertaken. Such an exercise should also aim to make decisions about which aspects of performance are most likely to be improved relative to the ability to change organizational behavior and move resources as required to achieve change.
- The above processes of reflection should lead to a complex performance management framework that uses the above process to identify key contradictions and tensions and the best strategies and objectives for intervention.
- Identify the key points of interaction and activity that related to the contradictions and tensions and the likely reinforcement patterns and how they can be changed or amplified (if already valuable). Explore ways of value maximizing valuable interactions and communications.
- Identify persistent negative feedback patterns and try to interfere with negative feedback loops by injecting alternative feedback mechanisms.
- Agree on a regular process for reviewing and updating the above.

Conclusion

In conclusion, there are some fundamental problems with the practice of classical approaches to management by objectives and performance management in the public sector. These relate to the attempt by such approaches to oversimplify the complex systems in which social and public policy operate. In particular, there is a tendency to reduce complex systems to simple assumptions of cause and effect that ignore many of the contingent and human or interpersonal factors that characterize the public policy environment.

This chapter has argued that performance is essentially about a type of reflective critical practice where managers and professionals engage in a process of understanding contradictory data patterns and trends and seek to identify critical points of interaction, where staff can take positive action to mediate an improvement in performance and perhaps end a negative feedback situation. Wherever possible these mediating actions should be identified, owned and refined by front line staff, perhaps with a manager acting as a facilitator. This has to be balanced against the process becoming bogged down in additional meetings and bureaucracy, so that it is unproductive and consumes too much valuable time.

5   Information management

Introduction

This chapter explores the extent to which managerial and professional narratives of public service generate conflicting perspectives about the implementation and use of Information Technology (IT). New managerialism has tended to present an argument that IT offers unique opportunities to the public sector for it to become more economic and efficient, especially in its processes of bureaucracy and administration. This chapter assesses whether this is really the case. Role conflicts and organizational tensions and paradoxes and their implications will be explored.

It has been a global characteristic of governments that they make bold claims about the possibilities that IT offers for increasing the efficiency of both democracy and public service delivery (OECD 2001a; 2001b). For example, *The Financial Times* recently argued that the US Air Force had wasted approximately US $1.1 billion trying to upgrade its IT system (Mance 2013). Research in the corporate private sector into attempts to implement major IT projects (Flyvbjerg and Budzier 2011) concluded that one in six projects had cost overruns of 200% or more.

Spectacular failures of computer projects have continued in the post-millennium age, despite the bold promises of governments to use IT to make government administration more efficient. But many attempts to implement IT systems in the public sector in numerous countries in recent decades have failed (OECD 2001a). This chapter explores the reasons behind this failure and begins to explore what the solutions to increase the effective use of IT might be.

It is argued here that IT systems increase the complexity of public service organizations rather than simplifying procedures and practices, but that IT can still present opportunities for more efficient and flexible soft structures that support professional working. IT systems can, therefore, present opportunities for the creative organization of complex information and processes in the public services. The danger is that they are used to add layers of bureaucracy and as methods of inappropriate organizational control. The chapter will conclude by exploring the possibility of collaborative implementation of IT systems where both managerial and professional goals can be realized.

Managerialism and IT in public services

Like the narrative account of new managerialism with its supply side and consumer ideals, the managerial implementation of IT in the public sector carried many assumptions that came from the market place. Bellamy (1999: 129) notes that this was "strongly encouraged by global business", and "constructed around the widespread assumption that the government have much to learn from corporate business, particularly those sectors which engage heavily in analogous transactions."

Public management practice after the technological revolution of the 1980s was in great danger of over-simplifying the task of using IT and assuming that it automatically offered some determinist path to greater efficiency and effectiveness. "By exploiting the power of ICT, they offer to square an apparently unsquareable circle; to drive costs out of public services while by the same means enhancing their effectiveness and quality" (Bellamy 1999: 128.).

By 2005 academics were arguing that some of the problems of NPM could be resolved by a new era of governance founded on digitalization where the use of technology could reinvigorate public participation and this coupled with organizational efficiency and effectiveness (Dunleavy et al. 2005). However, such bold visions have to be set against the reality that as technology is implemented, in many cases the implementation of such systems leads to costly mistakes with a lack of readily discernible improvements in service output. Painful and costly lessons have been learnt on the way. In some cases, professionals argue that IT systems increase bureaucracy and paperwork rather than making processes more efficient. This is the situation if numerous paper forms have to be filled in and then entered on to the computer, and this results in huge paper output at a later date.

The UK public sector is littered with costly computer system failures. There have been many such problems documented. The Home Office Immigration and Nationality Directorate computer system has struggled to cope with the practical demands placed upon it, after a serious lack of consultation between the system designers and the users of the system. Such failures included the Post Office Pathfinder IT project that cost £1.2billion, but did not deliver on the specification promised. The Prison Service Directorate reported large scale problems with the implementation of a new system, due to lack of clear agreement about responsibilities at the outset by the Prison Service and the private contractor (OECD 2001a: 162). The implementation of a new air traffic control system at Swanwick was not without incident. Opened in 2002 at a cost of £623 million the system arrived six years late and one third over budget. Air Traffic controllers have complained that the text code produced on computer monitors is too small, causing staff to misread the identity and destination of planes. In one case a plane bound for Glasgow was sent to Cardiff by mistake (*The Week*, 8 June 2002).

Questions continue to be asked about new and emerging contracts. The UK Government made much of its Information for Health campaign (Department of Health 2002), but independent information analysts questioned the efficiency of a decision to spend £91 million on a web based email system for the NHS (*Computer Weekly*, 24 October 2002). In December 2002 a junior government minister in the Foreign Office was forced to concede in Parliament that the future of the foreign office's new Firecrest IT system was in doubt despite an initial investment of £106 million (*Public Finance*, 20 December 2002).

In 2011, the UK Coalition Government established an ICT Strategy to reduce project failure and wastage of public expenditure. It aimed to create a common ICT infrastructure. A review after six months by the National Audit Office (2011) concluded that the strategy needed more specialist employees and more training of existing staff to succeed. In 2013 the UK House of Commons Committee of Public Accounts concluded that better procurement and contracting was part of the solution to avoiding continuing IT failures. The actual purpose of the use of IT should not be assumed to be an automatic evolutionary benefit, but should be carefully considered for its benefits to public services:

> Government still lacks the capability and capacity to commission services, and in the past has acted as if simply buying ICT is a solution in itself. Government is moving away

from thinking first about what ICT is needed, towards delivering a better service and using ICT to support its delivery. This approach should cut costs.

(House of Commons Committee of Public Accounts 2013: 6)

For example, the UK's Universal Credit IT system, designed to simplify welfare benefits and reduce public expenditure as part of the National Coalition Government's austerity program was accused of setting out to spend over £2 billion on a new large scale IT project without any proper plan about how the system was going to work and what it was designed to achieve (Glick 2013).

The UK is not alone in experiencing these difficulties. There is concern about wastage in most countries where the government is attempting to increase computer usage. International reports suggest that there are similar problems in both the public and private sectors, with IT failing to deliver to expectations. An OECD report "The Hidden Threat to E-Government", concludes:

> Governments are not alone in failing. Evidence suggests that private sector companies have similar problems. The Standish Group, for example, estimates that only 28% of IT projects in 2000 in the US, in both government and industry, were successful with regard to budget, functionality and timeliness. 23% were cancelled and the remainder succeeded only partially, failing on at least one of the three counts.
>
> (OECD 2001b: 1)

Because of a history that is characterized by the triumph of hope over experience the UK New Labour Government after 1997 set up a number of bodies to try and modernize the approach to IT implementation in public services. A report from the Office for Government Commerce (2001b) states the need for a change of culture: "a change of approach is needed. Rather than think of IT projects, the public sector needs to think in terms of projects to change the way Government works."

There is still a strong commitment at many levels to trying to utilize an "added value" of IT in public sector processes, even if it is now more likely to be acknowledged that IT can bring as many new challenges about ways of working as it does answers. This is because IT seeks to simplify standard processes to make them administratively easy to carry out, when the complexity of the underlying tasks is often ignored, resulting in large scale problems when the new IT system is implemented. By the time an IT system is implemented there is a mismatch between the reality of practice and the IT administrative system available. In addition, some problems result from technical incompetence, where IT systems and their programmers are simply not able to deliver to complex and large scale system designs. Systems arrive with missing attributes and bugs that cause the system to crash and this takes time and extra money to put right.

The remainder of this chapter looks at some of the particular difficulties with the managerial narrative of IT that has grown in the public sector in the last decade. As an alternative account the chapter also examines professional narratives of public organizations and their process and what this might mean for the use of IT by professionals.

Professional perceptions and involvement in IT projects

The account of new public managerialism explained at the beginning of this book has been linked to a subhypothesis about the growth of managerialism being used to reduce professional powers of discretion, status and judgment in the public service context. Public managerialism is at worst a project to simplify professional working, a project to reduce professional complexity to simple components, in a manner that reduces effectiveness and flexible service response in the name of economy and efficiency. Exworthy and Halford have edited an important work that explores this hypothesis. In their volume they write of the distinction between public managers and professionals. The distinction is described as:

> professionals depend on cultural assets acquired through education and characterised by personal expertise in a given body of practice, while managers depend on organisational assets, acquired through the experience of working in particular contexts and characterised by knowledge of organisationally specific rules, practices and policies.
>
> (Exworthy and Halford 1999: 133)

As stated in Chapter 1, professionals have been reluctant to embrace the idea of competencies and core skills, preferring instead to emphasize the complexity of their changing knowledge basis. They stress the "art and craft" of deciding what is relevant to use from their wide knowledge basis when applying skills that are highly contextual and which need to focus on the individual circumstances of the people they are helping. This is consistent with working in a complex indeterminate environment.

For these reasons, public service professionals have often been cautious about embracing IT in their work, suspicious that it may be a method for undermining their art and judgment, replacing personal dedication with a standardization process and forcing them to replace reflective and human skills with technical skills that involve them in competency based training.

The implementation of care management in social care services for older people as a method for the standardized application of eligibility criteria for public welfare support is one such example. Managers may argue that computerization ensures equity when older people are assessed, but professionals note the indeterminate context, such as psychological disposition and the strength of relationships with family, that cannot be entered into the computer based assessment and calculation. The computer record does not give account of the psychological stress experienced by the family or by the person experiencing a new form of disability. This type of computerization can appear to be removing professional value, rather than adding value. Professionals then see technology as deskilling and dehumanizing.

Professionals who have already served a long period of training before the days when IT was pervasive in organizational life may be reluctant to agree to retraining unless they can see clear evidence of a pay back in their professional domain and experience. A debate results about what minimum level of IT skills is really needed by all educational professionals and how much is discipline specific? Academic teachers prefer IT training that takes account of their subject specific needs and they are more likely to be motivated for retraining if these specific and contextual needs can be taken into account.

Table 5.1 summarizes the key differences between managerial and professional narratives of IT use and each is then discussed in turn.

The approach of professionals to IT systems can be clearly contrasted with the managerial vision of using IT as a method to reduce complexity and simplify administrative systems. Can such managerial simplifications and controls really be achieved? Managerial approaches make bold claims about the immediate value of using IT. "IT supports changes such as reengineering that translate to strategic advantage. For example, IT allows efficient decentralisation by providing speedy communication" (Turban, McLean and Wetherbe 2002: 85).

Table 5.1 Managerial and professional narratives of IT use in public services

Issue	Managerialism	Professionalism
Approach to IT	Solution to cope with complexity and simplify it	IT can expand process complexity … be cautious
Processes that use IT	Processes that use IT can be standardized and then cut costs	Creates inflexibilities and adverse selection
Value of IT in output terms	Precise understanding via Information Management Efficient processes result	Increases the availability of complex knowledge and its ease of use
Information management	Growing information capacity is directed by a hierarchy of process that meets objectives	Chaotic information processes need careful and specialist classification and use
Information use	Efficiency of resources Effective use of resources Financial management systems	Knowledge growth Effective knowledge use
Training and education	Standardized IT competencies	Application of IT skills to professional context
Method of analysis	Reductionist, scientific, separation of means and ends	Synthesize, contextual, experiential, inductive, incremental

The use of IT is seen as an imperative and a relatively straightforward strategy for increasing efficiency. But Taylor (1999: 59) says: "The technological determinism at the core of these visions is at odds with the confusions, sub-optimisations, contradictions and even the systems disasters that characterise the empirical world."

Professionals are often much more cautious in their approach. They fear that the implementation of IT systems can create additional problems, such as:

- the loss of important "value added" information (because current paper systems and human reflection are rejected);
- the system cannot cope with the demands placed upon it, resulting in all information systems being unavailable at certain key times, this creates periodic inefficiency;
- the designers of the IT system do not properly consult with professionals, resulting in a system that ignores important areas of information and gives too much emphasis to some tasks over others; and
- the introduction of IT systems reduces the opportunities for professionals to make their complex reflective judgments and instead leads to erroneous decisions being made on the basis of limited or incorrect standardized information.

Professionals are unlikely to agree that an IT system reduces complexity, rather they will see it as enhancing complexity and they will want to feel confident that an IT system is able to embrace complexity, rather than to deny it. If it offers a standard and robust method for managing complex information and is able, nevertheless, to permit the relatively easy searching and taking of information from the system, then they may be more willing to embrace it. Professionals want an IT system that really works in the context of their experience and gives them quick and easy access to the complex information that they need. One associated difficulty is that many information systems are only as good as the information inputted and staff may have to be convinced that time should be invested for inputting information, before the system is able to pay back the outputs required.

Standardization versus inflexibility

Managers see IT systems as offering standardization in complex areas of working. This offers opportunities for acquiring clear information on performance and by implication offers a route to cost cutting with more efficient outputs and outcomes resulting. Alongside this is the temptation of control and the false promise that IT will bring managers more control over the hard information and associated activities of workers in their organization.

Professionals are often sceptical about the use of IT to provide standard controls over processes. They suspect that this will result in adverse selection processes, because assessment and bureaucratic procedures are over-simplified as a result. This might lead at worst to the wrong people getting the wrong services and miscarriages of administrative justice. Hence computer standardization reduces the chances for human reflection from a professional and experienced member of staff. The fear of the professional is that IT standardization will result in inflexibilities that fail to respond to client need. An example of this is a university computer system that had not been designed for those wishing to take course units as short courses as learning experiences without assessment. The university computer insisted on reporting these cases as exam failures when they had no intention of submitting for examination. Another example is a local authority leisure center computer system that had two membership groupings, one for the gym area and one for the swimming area. The gym membership was supposed to supersede the swimming, making it free to gym users. However a problem with the system refused to accept that when swimming memberships expired, gym memberships had not necessarily also (in many cases the public had taken out the more expensive gym membership some months after their swimming membership). This resulted in customers being shown as in debt when they were not. Leisure staff had the embarrassment of repeatedly asking gym members to show past receipts, when they knew from experience that the visitors were legitimate.

Value of IT to outputs

Managers hope that IT systems will give them more control over processes, so that they can achieve more productive outputs and outcomes. McLoughlin and Clark (1995: 175) concluded after studying the implementation of IT systems in British Rail, BT and ITV: "it was noted that middle and junior managers are often preoccupied with the pursuit of control objectives when new technology is introduced." Managers see IT as providing them with information that will enable output efficiency to be raised.

Professionals see a value in the growth and storage of information for its own sake, regardless of the initial impact on hard outputs. Hence databases offer the professional an ever growing list of topics like case law, medical histories and children's educational narratives that can be accessed with considerable ease. Professionals' complex knowledge base can be managed more easily and IT access can assist their claim for possessing and understanding a highly complex knowledge specialism. Other examples are the way in which public health professionals have utilized geographical information systems (GIS) to explore public health geographies; medics and health professionals use video links and databases to keep up to date on international treatment developments and new surgery techniques. Academics have found that IT can provide them with huge networks of contacts to develop discussion and debate, and ideas about the latest research and theories. IT provides professionals with a rich resource for managing their specialist knowledge base and therefore it can enhance their professional status and ability to be connected to the latest knowledge and practice. It can provide added connectivity and value in professional networks.

Information management

Managers want to proactively manage information, to make it serve the managerial goals of output and outcome efficiency. Information systems become a key tool for this task and allow them to have a more assertive understanding and mastery of the financial and other data that they need to make decisions. IT systems should assist managers to make better decisions. But this view is based on a rational-scientific approach to information that cites that robust linear models can be generated to fully use the range of historical information available, so that future decisions are made more effective. The problem is that the future does not always take the same path as history dictates. Complexity theory casts some doubt on this, although linear models and historical knowledge will certainly be useful in some circumstances:

> Reductionism is great for quantitative aspects of internal details. In contrast, our current understanding of external large scale effects is mostly descriptive and qualitative, geometric rather than numerical. We can recognise a hurricane from satellite photos, but we can't tell what it is going to do.
>
> (Cohen and Stewart 1994: 442)

Information systems built on historical linear assumptions that the data will continue to create similar linear patterns in the future are not the best method for embracing periods of dramatic and transformational change. Similarly Taleb (2007) and Mandelbrot and Hudson (2008) have noted that models based on the occurrence of normal distributions are often erroneous because they underestimate outliers and more extreme events. Trying to build information systems that take account of non-linear computations and millions of variables and their interactions is very expensive and may only improve short-term forecasting. Such projects may be available to large global financial corporations, but are beyond the reach of most public services. Complexity theorists have also continued to cast doubts on any modelling that bases future decisions on past experience given the emergence and evolution of new forms of order.

Professionals see information management rather differently. They place emphasis on the chaos of exponential information growth, and the difficulty with recording accurately, classifying, and making use of what is available. The management of information represents a formidable challenge to professionals, especially where there are managerial demands to simplify lessons and draw conclusions about best practice. Professionals are concerned about a dumbing down of the information available and are often overwhelmed by the chaotic growth of information in the internet society. They fear that their clients will have ready access to specialist knowledge that is not always of good quality and without the ability to interpret it correctly. This does put pressure on professionals to keep one step ahead of their service users in terms of knowledge storage, classification and use.

Information use

Managerialism is determined to use information and to apply it so as to create models that recommend future courses of action. This can then drive efficient and effective use of resources. Examples are regression analysis to assess component cost functions, and current workload surveys for the allocation of future duties and workload. Public sector applications of this kind are fraught with difficulties. Many models have been developed to allocate resources, but these models are often built on historical linear assumptions that become redundant when major events and phase shifts occur in economies and societies. Sanderson (2000) concludes that rigid use of historical information can be like trying to drive your car along the road in front while looking in your rear view mirror. History gives us some good general principles on which to base decisions, but it cannot give us a detailed estimate of the future. It is not possible to be sure what is around the next corner, although one can make a good guess. Occasionally planners and forecasters will be fundamentally wrong. Everyone remembers the weather forecaster who told us not to worry about a hurricane when one actually occurred, or the economist who told us it was a good time to buy property when it was not.

Professionals are challenged by how best to deal with knowledge growth. For example, what research is influential? Professionals want to use information, but struggle with how best to digest and apply it. The advent of diseases like bird flu, BSE, and HIV provided professionals with great challenges on how to model and interpret data in new and unusual circumstances. Professionals look to IT for some assistance, to widen their knowledge base, but not to make the final decisions on what information should be acted on. Professional judgment remains, despite the increasing availability of data and information and various models and theories developed from that information. There will always be some element of uncertainty, especially in new situations where historical lessons cannot be applied easily. Professionals welcome increased information and quality of information, but acknowledge the responsibility and risk associated with human decision making and action. Information helps them to see and understand the complex and evolving patterns that are constantly forming the dynamic order and disorder that constitute the public sphere.

Training and education

Management tends to focus on the need for all public sector professional workers to gain baseline IT skills, as is currently witnessed in both education and health services. Teachers are to be equipped with baseline IT skills, laptop computers and tablets. The fear is that professional staff will not be functional and efficient if they are not conversant with baseline IT skills and by implication that they will fall behind in their professional application and will not be effective in their judgments.

Professionals are suspicious of a drive to force all their members to develop a competence in baseline IT skills and they put much more emphasis on the application of IT to the context of professional work and what skills are actually needed to perform their professional role. Professionals sometimes object to spending time learning generic IT skills that they do not perceive to be advantageous to the development of their professional standing. They want to see that IT skills are specifically related to their job and their need to acquire information and use it. A maths teacher sent on a course to learn Microsoft Excel was perplexed to find that all the examples were from business and seemed irrelevant to her needs as a primary classroom maths teacher.

Method of analysis

Finally it is necessary to comment on the different methodology used by managers and professionals to analyze the implementation of IT in public organizations. Managers are often driven by a classical Fordist and Taylorist approach that sees a separation of means and ends, and process and outcome. IT is viewed as an attractive method for streamlining and controlling processes so that outcomes can be enhanced and made more effective. The methodology is reductionist, scientific and based on linear causality.

Professionals use a different methodology to understand the relevance of IT. Rather than separating IT implementation into a cause and effect on outputs and outcomes they are concerned to take an overview and synthesis of IT development, to discern overall trends and developments in the sector and to consider how new technologies might be relevant to their domain. This more cautious and generalized approach leads to a focus on experimentation and inductive approaches to learning. Incremental adjustment is favored over large scale changes, so that large scale mistakes and disruptive errors are avoided. Information systems add to the quantity of network connections, but not necessarily their quality. IT should be a servant to public values and benefits rather than the master.

Complex adaptive systems and the use of IT in public services

This discussion of IT use in public services has been presented as a dichotomy between management and the professional. While in one sense this dichotomy is real and conflict about the implementation of IT systems into public service work is evident, there is also scope for collaboration and negotiated change. Exworthy and Halford (1999) have raised important questions about the existence of a management versus professional dichotomy and indicated the large number of professionals who become managers and experience the conflict of roles for themselves. Indeed the complex adaptive system approach to public sector change would stress the need for IT based change to be mediated and negotiated. The ideal is for all parties to feel that there is a win–win strategy.

Sources of the conflict between managerial and professional narratives

It is argued that the sources of conflict that can result when managers and professionals are engaged in the public sector IT systems and their implementation are derived from their different value systems and associated narratives. As identified in Chapter 1 the managerial narrative focuses on outputs and outcomes while the professional sees complex and adaptive processes as inevitable given the human subject matter. Professionals are more hesitant to separate process from outcome, preferring to see the two as entangled and characterized by feedback and interaction.

Structure

Public managerialism traditionally sees organizational structure as hierarchical and a dominant method for organizing and determining the control of workflows. There is a tendency to seek a perfected hierarchical hard structure, with clear divisions for functions and specialisms. This reflects the classical Taylorist principles in much public sector managerialism.

Professionalism puts less emphasis on organizational structure as determining workflow but focuses on the indeterminacy of front line activities and tasks such as teaching, counselling, and community work (Howe 1986). Managerialism tries to reduce these abstract activities to prescribed competencies and detectable outcomes. For professionals, organizational structure needs to build strength around small collegiate groups. This strengthens and reinforces the professional role as they reflect on and reconstruct indeterminate professional knowledge. Hence the social work team, the school teaching staff group, etc.; these are communities of practice (Wenger 1998). In the context of softer organizational structures, professionals reflect on their judgment of unique and complex problems and help each other to evolve their indeterminate practice. Professional development emphasizes the importance of the reflective practitioner (Schon 1991) who continues to work with their colleagues to reinforce learning and adjustment, as new knowledge becomes available. In the reflective environment, IT offers an added value as a sophisticated knowledge provider, where the professional has at their finger tips a vast range of information to aid their judgment. IT is used to open up possibilities, rather than to close the number of alternatives down.

Complex Adaptive System (CAS) approaches in public sector organizations that reflect the complexity of the environment stress the limited ability of hard structures to solve "wicked problems" (Carley 1980). These accounts see large scale organizational redesign and hierarchical structure as at best only providing partial answers to problems, and esteem that large scale redesign should be approached with considerable caution. The key issue for CAS is their ability to evolve and adapt in relation to the changing world outside of the host organization. This requires an evolving element of soft structure using methods like task forces, working groups, project groups (as described in Chapter 3). At the same time such organizational soft structures need to be in a dynamic with a small hard core structure, so the organization does not break up and self-destruct into fragmentation and chaos. The attractor here that provides the magnetic pull and provides a link between weak structures is the values and beliefs that construct the culture of the organization. This depends on professional allegiance, collegiality and knowledge development. In addition, the leadership of key individuals is also vital, to prevent the structure being too weak and fragmented. Identified leaders will help workers to clarify their key roles and responsibilities for particular projects, a factor that is vital when developing IT projects (Office for Government Commerce 2001b). Leaders can provide another source of attraction to order.

Information technology can be used to facilitate soft structures. A key example is the use of email to an organization, where email provides an easy and organized way for individuals, groups and sub groups to communicate. Some public service managers are suspicious of the wide use of email, fearing that it presents a loss of control. Other professionals see the widespread benefits that can result, in terms of the rapid sharing of resources and information, although they also fear the consequences of information overload.

Much IT systems work has traditionally focused on Taylorist, rational approaches to design and implementation. The danger is that these approaches can be characterized by a hard systems approach that underestimates the value of existing human resources and their adaptability as part of the solution. Using IT to impose a one-off, hard system solution may only increase the difficulties that a service has in adapting to changing public expectations. A better use of IT is to add adaptability to the organization, so that interaction between members and outsiders becomes relatively easier.

Imposing new IT systems on staff in a stressful environment and a problematic situation may increase the chaos and intractability of a problem rather than bringing instant solutions. Staff need to be carefully consulted and involved in the process to check that the application of IT fits their ground knowledge of what is required. The human centered process becomes a vital constituent of initial systems design. Negotiation and evolution become key aspects. Managers become leaders and diplomats, offering a realistic vision of what is possible. A number of studies and reports emphasize the importance of personal leadership and responsibility, if IT projects are to deliver (Cabinet Office 2000; OECD 2001b).

Culture

Previous attempts to implement IT systems in the public services have focused predominantly on structural work processes and routine project planning, rather than cultural implementation. These approaches follow a traditional project management approach to system design, delivery and implementation. The first stage is to define the existing organizational processes and to decide how these can be computerized. This works from an overview and then breaks into points of detail. The next stage is to convert the identified hierarchical organizational process into a computerized process.

Although such approaches include an element of consultation with front line professionals and future users of the system, they are often under great pressure to move quickly on the basis of contractual obligations, and in large, complex organizations this reduces considerably the scope for professional involvement and consultation. Sometimes cost constraints force a public provider to accept a system that has already been developed for a similar organization, with the promise that it can be adjusted to a slightly different setting.

A cultural approach to IT systems will put less faith in a time limited system that separates system design from implementation. A cultural approach will favor a broad approach to the long-term impact of IT on the working life of the organization, as well as considering the interaction with the values, beliefs and practices within the organization. Technology—like people—should be capable of being adaptable to a new and changing environment, rather than a static system. Technologies that can be incrementally adjusted, updated and added to, will be favored over static one-off products. This implies a different type of contracting with IT providers and programmers. Consortiums of public service IT providers, such as the UK Higher Education Joint Information Systems Committee (JISC) will find themselves more powerful than single users and more able to argue for such contracting arrangements. Purchasers should be wary of one-off deals and apparent "bargains", where there is no ongoing relationship and support from the IT provider.

The cultural approach implies that an organization seeks to see how it can use IT to partner the growth and evolution of the whole organization. Modular systems such as internet and intranet based accounting products, databases, etc. will be purchased and adapted to fit the needs of the organizations, with some IT experts emerging within the organization who can see how best to steer generic products in the service of the professionals and front line workers. Professional and front line access will be characterized by ease of use. Much effort should be put into the presentation of a common portal for the baseline user, perhaps from a standard and familiar web browser. Front line users should experience maximum consultation about the appearance of this general portal. It is as vital as the layout of a workspace, or the décor of a building.

With the cultural approach to IT, the whole emphasis is on how the technology can adjust to serve the culture of the organization and the needs of its clients. As Taylor (1999: 60) says, "new forms of information will, it follows, excite organisational politics"; but he goes on to caution that "organisational politics will tend to push towards the existing ways of doing things rather than new practices". It is here that the professional technological pioneers, that is teachers and other professionals, who can enthuse their peers about the added value of IT become so important. Similarly professionals taking a managerial and leadership role will need to reach an informed sense about how much of the most exciting and pioneering of IT based change to embrace at any one time, or in any one situation. Leaders need to broker realistically against a Luddite stand off that allows no progress to be made.

Detailed project administration models such as PRINCE2 should not be disregarded. PRINCE stands for Projects in Controlled Environments. Such models are often an important guide to the first stages of an IT project. They act as an "aide mémoire" for a project team and their nominated leader. But such project plans need to be regularly reviewed by the team and associated senior managers. Plans need to be adjusted and changed according to the nature of the external environment and internal developments. PRINCE2 divides projects up into manageable stages so that resources can be identified and controlled. The aim is to clearly allocate roles and responsibilities to those involved in the project (Office of Government Commerce 2002b). The OECD has also recommended that large scale projects be broken up into smaller elements, so that they are more manageable in the short term and adjustable in the long term. "A radical approach, increasingly adopted in the private sector, is to avoid large projects altogether, opting for small projects instead. One expert has called this change shift from 'whales to dolphins'" (2001b: 2).

This is described as a cultural shift by the OECD with short-term goals providing the focus. Business and organizational goals drive the project and this requires modest change and technical simplicity if goals are really to be achieved. This can be contrasted with the old model of large scale change projects that were technically complex and not necessarily related to broad organizational goals. PRINCE2 can certainly play its part, but it may become too rigid a method over the longer term, and the model itself needs to be adaptable, if used in fast changing environments. Information technology systems should become like the people in the organizations, able to adapt to new environments and demands. IT systems should not involve the creation of huge dinosaurs that cannot evolve and later become at odds with their environment. This goes with a new realism about IT in public life, or as Taylor (1999: 59.) puts it: "It should lead us to the understanding that the information age can promise little more than incremental changes, or even perversions in electronic form, of what has gone before."

This is too conservative, but careful negotiation and dialogue about the use of IT to manage and deliver change in public services is essential if real progress is to be made.

The project and process—the key to successful IT implementation

Complex accounts of the process of using IT are needed, rather than oversimplified ones. Complex accounts will place emphasis on feedback diagrams, where the unintended consequences of taking various courses of action are carefully considered. Traditional systems analysis is a linear process where organizations have an inputting of information and output result. For example, a higher education student database enters the marks that each student has for each module or unit of study, and this provides an end of year assessment of their overall grade weighting. The police force enters the criminal record for each offender and the outcome is an intelligence database of offender profiles within a local area. A CAS approach is always looking for ways in which the system can learn from the output data and feedback more information as an input. In the higher education system the timetabling and assessment method in a particular module or unit might create an unusual effect in the component part of a final degree mark, perhaps lowering the mark overall. An adapting system will be able to spot this kind of trend. The organization can then learn from it. Similarly the ability to present output information in different ways will allow the IT system to adjust to the needs of exam boards, tutors and heads of departments. A police force criminal records system will be able to spot changing trends over time and match this to the changing profiles of individual offenders in local areas, in terms of crimes that are no longer seen by offenders to pay, or have become unpopular with particular crime groups. This allows for intelligent local policing decisions when resources are deployed efficiently. A good information system is able to adapt to the needs of its users, to change its input scope if required because it is learning from the outputs provided. Taylor (1999: 47) comments that: "Information communication technologies permit reflection upon the organisation into which they are introduced". In short, if IT systems are working efficiently they should be capable of understanding and coping with positive and negative feedback.

The ability of an information system to evolve in this manner in part depends on the ability of human professionals to interact with the system and to get the most from it. A good system will therefore have the maximum involvement of professionals and be seen as fairly simple to use, even though its information structures, inputs and outputs have the potential to be complex. Users need to be familiar with the basic operations of the IT system and confident they can engage with it in a way that enhances their core work (Chua 2009).

This chapter concludes by drawing some general lessons for theory and practice when applying complexity theory to information systems in public service. Complexity is a paradox of simple elements building complex patterns, hence the idea of fractal geometry. This makes one-off large scale responses extremely problematic to deliver, whether it is corporate reorganization design, or the design of a big mainframe computer system. As a result, the public services need IT systems that are built of simple modular structures, but that are able to adapt into highly complex evolving systems (Flyvbjerg and Budzier 2011). An example is the type of web based managed learning environment (MLE) in higher education and tertiary education, where a web based portal offers staff and students access to a range of technologies and has the ability to be integrated with a whole range of software products and external databases. The system can therefore be used in very simple ways, to post messages and files for students, or in much more complex ways, to integrate student records, marks and personal records, alongside the student's day to day need for teaching materials and messages from course tutors. The underlying structure is an electronic backbone through which a whole range of communications can be delivered. New ideas can be added and unhelpful elements taken away.

There is a core of very basic IT skills that all modern public service workers need, but there are dangers with taking this approach too far so that public professionals are forced to spend too much time learning skills that they do not really need in their context and may be redundant. Beyond baseline skills, public service workers need to be facilitated to reflect on and develop the context in which IT adds value to their work.

Professionals will need some IT skills to get the most out of an information technology system, but the basic entry portal should be as simple to use as possible, with the ability for it to be adapted in response to the needs and observations of professionals.

Stacey (2001) has reflected on how knowledge management is highly intangible and difficult to measure with hard data. It essentially can be assessed on the quality of the interactions between professionals within the organization. If maximum benefit is to be gained from the information age then organizations need to find ways of opening up knowledge use and application, via mutual reflection, rather than closing down knowledge application to some predefined categories and algorithms. Information loops need to be permeable and expandable, and this has implications for system design and system use.

Public sector organizations cannot ignore the changes that are occurring in the post-industrial world and they will have to respond to these changes. E-mail, text messaging and mobile phone use are increasingly replacing telephone calls and surface post. For example, one response to a reduction in participation in democratic elections has been to encourage citizens to use these new technologies to vote and this has already had some limited success with increasing voting in local elections in England. Public service users are in many cases using new technology to become better informed. Professionals and managers ignore these trends at their peril and there is an inevitable evolutionary direction to the pervasiveness of information technology in public life. Many will be concerned about the negative results, such as the exclusion of those without access to the technology, but it is likely to be impossible to halt the technological changes. The better way is to reflect on the change and to ensure that it brings with it quality and equitable outcomes.

In the knowledge society, IT is the provider of information and knowledge. The internet allows billions of multi-modal communications to happen simultaneously. It is promoting new forms of network communication that were unthinkable a decade ago. This is a very different resource to anything achieved before. It means that millions of people can potentially interact simultaneously without being in the same geographical place. This is different to the introduction of telephones, which only allow minimal non-geographic interaction, or the introduction of radio and television that are essentially passive forms of information delivery. The information society creates its own external drivers and increasing complexity for the public sector. A society in which the majority of people use computers, where most children learn IT skills at school, where the majority of transactions are carried out by computers and digital technology will create its own pressures and demands on public services to be able to interact in a digital and electronic manner. Professionals have little choice but to embrace the information society. If they reject its presence they will lose social status and their professional power base and social relevance will decline. It is how public service professionals work with the information society that is important.

The CAS explanation of the role of IT in public sector change offers some opportunities for overcoming the dichotomy and conflict of the traditional managerial and professional narratives. A CAS explanation of IT in the public sphere puts an emphasis on the following:

- The entanglement of IT with political and organizational changes in society. This creates difficulty in separating IT issues from social change and should prevent seeing IT systems in isolation. The key point is how information systems interact with other social and organizational changes. The evolution of large scale technological change is inevitable. It has an impact on the whole of society, rather than in isolated places.
- The potential of IT to enhance our ability to have understanding of complex change and complex processes.
- This understanding will, however, always be underdetermined and only partially explained. On balance the ever growing physical capabilities of computers look like providing society and public services with some potentially useful tools and resources in the quest to understand complex knowledge.
- Information technology becomes a tool for managing complexity.
- Even though it is increasingly a part of a complex system, it is a tool for complex knowledge management.
- As a tool for dealing with complexity, it needs to be able to evolve itself and adjust to changing needs and expectations. Technology needs to enable reflexivity on the human condition.

The information society will continue to have an impact on public services. Technology provides the key to the use of mass information. This is reflected in the UK Cabinet Office (2000) publication *e.gov: Electronic Government Services for the 21st Century* that correctly predicted a whole range of online services being delivered within the next decade, including passport and driving licence applications, electronic land registration, and benefit claims and payments. It is the interaction of front line specialists and professionals with technology and information that will determine the usefulness of the information age. Managers will play a key role in facilitating and leading this process. But technology is unlikely to succeed in simplifying and standardizing the public service response to a complex society. As Aidan Lawes, chief executive of the IT Service Management Forum, has said: "We need to radically rethink the role and structure of IT. That means getting the focus on value and not cost, and on process and people not technology. We need to think end to end service" (www.vnunet.com/news, 1 July 2002).

To summarize, there are a number of key issues (Gulla 2012) that public managers must address when considering the use of IT systems and their implementation:

- Avoid entering into short-term legal contracts that provide a one-off solution and leave the supplier with little long-term commitment to help the user adjust the system to future requirements.
- Seek simple technological products that are widely used and have shown themselves to be adaptable to a whole host of environments and situations (for example internet and intranet products that use web technologies).
- Use project management and plans, but with some flexibility. Project management methods should not be used rigidly. They should be tools rather than driving the entire working process.
- Make sure that project management methods are regularly reviewed and adjusted when necessary after consultation with senior managers. Project management should not be used as a punitive tool against which the project team will be held to account, but as a checklist against which to judge current performance and an honest appraisal of where expectations are not being met and rapid change is needed. In the dynamic world of rapid IT change organizations frequently operate on the edge of chaos and some failure is inevitable, but reducing large scale risks and system failures has to be balanced with embracing external change and modernization.
- Ensure that one person has the key managerial responsibility for overseeing and leading an IT development plan, but with a supportive multi-disciplinary team that represents all the professional interests that will be using the system.
- Senior managers must have confidence in, and actively support, the IT project leader. There must be good, regular and open communication between the project leader and the senior management team.
- Ensure that team members are committed to the project and support the project leader from the beginning. The project team should not become too insular and should have good contacts elsewhere in the organization and have an informed view of external developments.
- Make sure that the technical system chosen is acceptable to professional interest groups. Consult as widely as possible before making a contracting decision.
- Link professional interests with implementation of the system, try to ensure that all groups, managers, professionals and administrators feel that they are in a potentially beneficial situation and get some immediate and basic benefit from the new system. Find easy pay back examples of the system's positive use that will build early confidence in it and what can be achieved.
- See the IT system as an evolving part of the organization, like the professionals and teams in the organization. Make sure that professionals, teams and the IT system are able to work and evolve together and are aware of each other's strengths and weaknesses.

- Try to avoid one professional or organizational group dominating the IT system; it is better if all have a fairly equal stake in its success.
- Link the evolution of the IT system to organizational goals and strategy. Do not let the technical experts alone dictate where the system is evolving.
- Involve all professional interest groups in developing a flexible training approach towards using the IT system. The training should put as much emphasis on the professional and administrative context and professional and administrative benefits as possible.
- Seek to learn and collaborate with other public organizations working in similar environments with similar approaches to the use of IT.

Conclusion

This chapter has examined the role of IT in modern public services. IT offers much potential. It offers new resources for managing and facilitating the complex processes that constitute public service work. Good managerial use of IT systems presents some opportunities for constructive network governance that is participative and helps to reintegrate some of the aspects of instability caused by the practices of NPM. As Dunleavy *et al.* concluded when outlining their Digital Era Governance argument:

> It holds out the promise of a potential transition to a more genuinely integrated, agile, holistic government, whose organisational operations are visible in detail both to the personnel operating in the fewer, broader public agencies and to citizens and civil society organisations.
>
> (Dunleavy *et al.* 2005: 489)

Nevertheless, there are dangers if IT is used as a method for simplifying management processes. Many public service processes cannot be easily simplified without a loss of flexibility and loss of value adding. Modern public services need to have flexible structures and working practices, and IT can aid the flows of communication and information in these complex processes. In order for IT to assist the management of complexity, systems need to be built around robust core technologies and networks that can in themselves be constructed on relatively simple, reliable and proven technologies. Examples are the growth of the world wide web and its programming language of html. Such resources allow huge potential for adaptable and bolt on applications. They can allow electronic networks to evolve and develop in reaction to what public services and their users need. Large scale attempts to provide single solution technological answers to complex public policy issues are problematic and the recent history of the public sector suggests that they are fraught with major difficulties, including expensive mistakes.

6 People in public organizations

Introduction

This chapter will argue that complexity theory and its application demonstrate the importance of understanding personal interaction, group dynamics and leadership in public services. The chapter will emphasize the importance of personal qualities and interpersonal communication skills in the public service environment and it examines the integration of leadership, human resource management and professional skills and relates these both to operational management and change management. If managers are going to make good decisions and motivate their workforce they need an informed insight into the workings of their own mind and cognitions, in addition to a sense of humility about the degree of the complexity of their working environment.

The human relations approach

It is argued in this book that the human relations approach is the most important aspect of management and organizational practice in contemporary public organizations. This chapter begins by acknowledging the historical roots of this perspective in literature and identifying its characteristics. It progresses to proposing and arguing for a distinctive human relations approach to management in public organizations that is based on an appreciation of social and organizational complexity and how organizations and managers are best developed to work in such a challenging environment.

The foundations of the human relations approach

The foundations of the human relations approach to management can be traced to the 1920s. As a developing perspective it offered an alternative to the simplistic, classical and scientific approaches of Frederick Taylor in the early nineteenth century. Psychologists and anthropologists increasingly asked searching questions of Taylor's mechanistic and measurement based approaches to manufacturing organizations and production lines. Fordism has its roots in the same time period as Taylorism. It is concerned with the values and practices of mass industrial production, as typified by Henry Ford in his manufacture of US cars. The application of such scientific methods to the public sector explains the preoccupation with organizational design, perfecting business process and achieving instrumental economic efficiency.

The type of management practice developed in the public sector in the last 40 years, the NPM, has often been referred to as a predominantly classical approach (Pollitt 1990). It was largely a Taylorist and Fordist project based on rational scientific principles: applying standardization, measurement and redesign of structures and processes as a method to achieve efficiency of process. Human relations approaches were largely ignored in that public management revolution. There was an assumption that the public policy process could be clearly defined and subjected to routine principles and objectives and that causal factors could be directly linked to their effects and also managed and controlled. An example is the constant reorganization of government departments based on the belief that if the perfect organizational structure can be found, many of the contradictions and tensions in working practices will be eliminated. Yet many professionals complain that such reorganizations are hugely disruptive to working networks, often resulting in costly mistakes and diluting service quality. Large scale organizational redesigns can all too often cause instability and chaos rather than rapid improvements in simplifying processes to deliver efficiency.

The human relations critique of strong management control and hierarchical organizational structure leads to the conclusion that softer, more creative and adaptive forms of communication and organizational behavior are important. The theme is explored in this chapter.

In the apparently controlled and predictable world of Taylorism and Fordism the people working in public services all too often became small cogs in a large machine. It is not surprising that many felt disempowered and frustrated. Much of the new public management project ignored the lessons of the human relations school of some 50 years earlier. In the discussions and debates that followed after the NPM revolution there was a growing realization that valuing and rewarding public service staff should be a priority (Cabinet Office 1999; Audit Commission 2002). One major study of conditions in public and private sector organizations found that public sector workers had significantly lower morale than their private sector counterparts and tended to feel less trusting of senior managers (Watson 2002). Public sector workers were more likely than private workers to feel that their organizations did not care about them.

Key human relations studies

What follows is a summary of the best known early studies that defined the human relations approach.

One historical study is attributed to the development of the human relations approach more than any other. It is well known by students who have studied sociology or business studies. This is Mayo's observation of the Hawthorn Electricity Company in America in the 1920s and 1930s. It concluded that physical inputs such as technology and material components could not be easily adjusted to maximize output, but instead workers' interactions with each other and their employer were important aspects of productivity. The study took place over a long period of time and evolved its method from an initial scientific experiment towards a more open, qualitative and participatory account. As a result, the findings were subject to much criticism from the traditional scientific management community. Over time the conclusions were accepted as substantial and resulted in the rising importance of psychology, sociology and anthropology in management and organizational research during the next two decades.

A second key writer in this field was Maslow in the 1940s. His self-actualization thesis stated the importance of providing for the basic material and psychological needs of people if they are to learn in complex environments and adapt to a higher level of psychological performance. The more that an organization and managers were able to provide material, social and intellectual comforts to their workers, the more return could be expected by the organization.

MacGregor (1960) distinguished between the X and Y manager. The X manager took an autocratic line towards leadership and management, believing that staff do not generally enjoy work and need clear rational rewards and motives if productivity is to rise. The Y manager, on the other hand, saw that staff acquired satisfaction from their involvement in and influence on their work and that by understanding the nature of this satisfaction, managers could better understand productivity in their organization. The Y management task required a more interpersonal approach to leadership when compared to the scientific and functional approach of the X manager. Similarly, Likert (1961) argued that a participative management style which was more sensitive to individual differences and needs produced the most effective results when compared to a style of authoritarian control and limited consultation with the work force. For a more detailed account of these historical studies see Pugh, Hickson and Hinings (1983).

Human systems

Given the rapid growth of industrialized countries, based on technological innovation and global consumerism in the post-war period, there was a rising demand for management science in the 1960s and 1970s. There was a need to integrate traditional mechanistic approaches with a new understanding of human processes and work force development using the psychological developments in human relations management. Many university business schools were established at this time. New attempts were made to define methods for managers that would empower them to design, control and motivate the growing multinational and corporate organizations of the era.

Systems theory emerged as an attempt to bridge the complicated division of people, resources and organizations in the external world, but using a rational method based on identifying boundaries and balances (equilibriums) between people, places and processes. The big idea with systems theory was to find the right balance between these different complicated factors.

While systems theory acknowledged how complicated human organizations were, it still encouraged the simplified and reductionist understanding of these structures, where order, control and the scientific improvement of productivity were achievable aims. This is in contrast to the more recent approach of complexity theory that sees organizational systems as so complex they need leaders and managers who can engage with changing dynamics, rather than to find an equilibrium balance between factors. Complexity argues that organizations have inevitable periods of instability, where the issue for managers is not creating balance, but rather enabling and empowering staff to understand the forces of change, to engage with them and to re-establish places of stability. Change is seen as inevitable and a potential opportunity.

A basic mechanical system has a control unit that seeks to return it to a state of equilibrium. A hot water system has a thermostat to regulate temperature (Meadows 2009). The thermostat controls the system's behavior and prevents extremes. A central bank seeks to control the national economy. Previously central bankers sought to use interest rates to return inflation and unemployment to equilibrium and balanced points. Since the global financial crisis, new monetary stabilizers have been used, such as the practice of Quantitative Easing (QE) where the central bank purchases or sells financial assets to influence long-term interest rates. Some large public organizations used to have a tendency to use financial management as a method to incrementally raise and lower unit budgets so as to orchestrate some overall sense of stability, where no one part of the organization was able to develop much faster than the rest over the longer term.

As Stacey (2000: 65) comments on the traditional systems approach to balance and equilibrium: "It is easy to see how these notions lead ... to an emphasis on clarity of roles and task definition and the equation of management with a controlling role at the boundary."

The mistake here is to confuse the complicated with the complex. Traditional systems theory sees public organizations as complicated, not additionally complex. This is the difference between a jumbo jet and a human organization:

[S]ome systems have a very large number of components and perform sophisticated tasks, but in a way that can be analyzed accurately … Other systems are constituted by such intricate sets of non linear relationships and feedback loops that only certain aspects can be analyzed at a time.

(Cilliers 1998: 3)

The interaction of human beings makes public services a complex system, rather than a complicated one. In such organizations there is no amount of detailed analysis that can create perfect understanding. A team of mechanics can dismantle a jumbo jet and reach a clear theory from the components about how it works. A team of management consultants cannot work in the same way in a public organization. A jumbo jet is highly predictable and can be balanced in its flight by the use of its complicated computer based control system. The public organization, unlike the jumbo jet, has an evolving life of its own, and by the time management consultants have drawn up a theory of the cultures, structures and processes of the organization based on detailed analysis of its people and parts, the wider system will have evolved further in its construction. There is no possibility for returning such an organization to an empirical balanced state but it might be possible to influence change on its ever moving dynamic state. Management consultants will find that their own behavior interacts and changes the organization they are working with, creating an interactive process of feedback that a mechanic does not share with a jumbo jet. Human organization systems are more than complicated, they are complex, and evolve a life of their own. Much of this complexity is to do with the unpredictable behavior of people and the communications and interactions between them. It may be possible to forecast patterns of behavior and activity and to achieve periods of stability, but impossible to predict to a very high degree, attainment and output achievement.

Complexity theory and human relations

Given that human beings are themselves complex systems that are to some extent unpredictable, organizations should certainly be thought of as indeterminate and relatively unstable. Disorder is often a reality, rather than there being any sense of a stable state of equilibrium. The miracle is that organizations do find a sense of order and purpose for much of their working lives. Order is achieved via collaboration and integration (Table 6.1) and both of these stabilizing states are achieved via forms of communication and rewards. Managers play a key part in establishing and maintaining these stabilizing features. In some circumstances managers and organizations may decide to seek instability, to use disintegration, fragmentation and competition to achieve change. However, research in public organizations (MacLean and MacIntosh 2011) implies many of the forces for instability and change come from outside of public organizations, and in the main, managers seek to create a stable place

Table 6.1 Organizational stability and instability

	Stability	*Instability*
Processes	Integration	Disintegration and fragmentation
Motivation	Collaboration Shared benefit	Competition Individualized benefit

to understand and respond to such external changes, rather than adding to instability, but there are sometimes exceptions to this. A key example of external imposed change on a public organization is government inspired political change that requires reorganization of a public policy process and how a service is delivered and experienced.

Complexity interpretations focus on the self-organizing features of organizations rather than the ability of managers to control and determine the path that an organization takes (Teisman, Van Buuren and Gerrits 2009). Managers become facilitators of this self-organizing process. Autocratic styles may be necessary in some limited circumstances, but in the wrong context they can close down the creative possibilities of self-organization and cause resistance to change and unproductive behavior. Most organizations need a few clear central rules and codes of conduct, but at the local level too many detailed rules and procedures can close the system down by causing demotivation and frustrating bureaucracy. Such bureaucracy has in the past been a significant cause of low morale in public services, perhaps more of a concern than low pay rates (Audit Commission 2002). Better to let people decide the day to day detail of their working lives in small teams and partnerships, especially when they have demonstrated that they can cooperate and perform in the public interest. Let them self-organize the areas of work that they know best, but with reference and accountability to a central strategy, mission and core rules.

Management, interpersonal skills and leadership

The task of leading and coordinating a complex system defies a uniform and single model. Leadership, like interpersonal skills, is not always easy to define, but nevertheless such attributes are in high demand. A report by the Association of Graduate Recruiters (2002) put good interpersonal skills at the top of the list of most sought after skills by employers when recruiting graduates from university. An all-round ability to interact with others, to understand one's own behavior and its influence on others, and the potential to lead, are extremely highly valued by employers.

Such skills are difficult to teach and difficult to learn—in part explaining why they are at a premium. This explains the increasing popularity of psychology amongst school leavers in seeking university places in many countries, but psychology degrees alone are not the answer. It is the application of a particular type of psychology, interpersonal behavior, that becomes critical. This is exemplified in the seminal book, *Emotional Intelligence*, by Daniel Goleman, who summarizes people with high emotional intelligence scores as:

> socially poised, outgoing and cheerful, not prone to fearfulness or worried rumination. They have a notable capacity for commitment to people or causes, for taking responsibility, and for having an ethical outlook; they are sympathetic and caring in relationships. Their emotional life is rich, but appropriate; they are comfortable with themselves, others, and the social universe they live in.
>
> (Goleman 1996: 45)

Goleman argues that an understanding of emotions is more critical to a successful career (and personal life) than traditional measures of rational cognitive intelligence. He documents the interaction of the emotions and rational intelligence, showing that those with a high IQ score are often disrupted by interpersonal events because they have a very low level of ability to understand their emotional reactions and emotional history. Goleman discusses the entanglement of emotions and rational thoughts within the individual personality. He proposes that a balance is needed where a person's emotions check their rational thinking and vice versa. Other applied psychologists and occupational psychologists have made similar arguments (Kahneman 2012; Peters 2012).

Peters distinguishes between two aspects of the mind and thinking, a person's inner "chimp", and "computer". The chimp is the part of the brain that is programmed to provide emotive responses often based on physical needs and childhood emotions. It provides rapid first responses based on feelings and first impression and it is designed to meet physical requirements or to provide a quick defence. The computer is the more rational part of the brain that is programmed by experience and reflective learning. It tries to identify facts and uses these to build a true picture of reality. For Peters, the key for success is to master the chimp by understanding its reactions and weaknesses and training its impetuous reactions. He notes that stress, illness and tiredness can lead to "computer malfunctions" and the chimp being let loose.

The language and concepts of complexity theory lead to a slightly different interpretation of Peters and Goleman's theory. The interaction of a manager's emotions and rational thinking is indeed critical, but what is needed is the correct dynamic for a given situation in time and space.

Motivation

Hierarchy of needs

Maslow's hierarchy of needs informs us that a person's motivation and engagement with employment is strongly related to the extent to which employers meets their human needs. The first demand from employees is to secure adequate income to provide food and shelter. In extreme cases and under extreme threat and pressure, in order to survive, a person may suspend other more sophisticated aspects of their value system to ensure physical survival. Poorly paid work that does not provide a living wage will leave workers anxious and worried about their life outside the workplace. Concentration and commitment is likely to be limited and confined to meeting an employer's basic requirements. Once the employee's baseline needs for survival are met, however, the employee will start to look to meet psychological, social and learning needs. Satisfaction from completing tasks and via forming meaningful relationships with colleagues starts to become much more important so that social psychological needs of self-efficacy and self-confidence can be met. In such circumstances, workers seek confirmation of their value systems, and opportunities to reinforce these values to themselves and others through behavioral reinforcement.

Values and motivation

At this point in time, values are more likely to interconnect with workplace behavior. The thought process of all workers is dynamic and subject to some internal debate and dissonance, while a healthy mind also seeks stability and resolution. Values are a key component that people use to resolve such conflicts. Workers also, like organizations, have a hierarchy of values. At the top of this hierarchy are the strongest and most deeply ingrained values that are the least likely to change. As Kernaghan (2000: 102) notes: "Public servants are more likely to comply with the rules that remain and to respect the intent of guidelines if they see the connection between the content of these rules and the guidelines and fundamental public service values."

For individuals, values are less likely to come from the workplace but from personal and historical experience of family, education, religion and community. Such deep values are more static when compared to public organizations where the employees' collective memory and behavior is less stable. But in the public services employees will often bring a strong value component to their work that consists of public and collective values, for example, believing in the importance of care, equality of opportunity, citizenship and human rights (Desmarais 2014). These core values will have been disciplined and reinforced during professional education and training. The public professional employee will look to demonstrate these values in their workplace experiences and behavior (Australian Public Service Commission 2013).

Values and performance

One of the dangers of NPM practices described in Chapter 1 is that they oversimplify the motivation of workers in organizations, assuming a more traditional market driven, profit driven model of motivation, where workers will primarily be motivated by financial and associated target driven rewards.

Of course, there are circumstances where the ideal can happen, and financial and output targets can match the dominant public value system of a public agency and its professionals. An example might be educational attainment improvements in a junior school in a poor neighborhood. There is often a public consensus that understands the benefits of a focused effort to develop core language and mathematics skills at a young age. But at secondary school, this consensus might become more difficult to maintain. As children enter adolescence and early adulthood, their own dynamic interaction with society becomes more complex. Continuous academic improvement will not be appropriate for all. For some, difficult family circumstances such as absent parenting or parental illness, sibling bullying and rivalry, adolescent peer group pressures and the resulting development of early forms of mental ill health, will dictate that schooling must focus more on interpersonal skills, psychological adjustment and resilience. Economic issues, such as the availability of future training and employment start to interact with the interpretation of the value of the final years of schooling and may be the source of conflicts. In this environment the instrumental use of educational targets can become much more contested and subject to different value interpretations. Managers are at the core of these conflicts and have to broker between them and help the organization to find resolutions. This is a difficult and sometimes impossible task because these conflicts inside the organization mirror major conflicts and dissonance in society itself. Performance is likely to be better if some coherent attempt can be made to acknowledge, resolve and prioritize in the midst of such social complexity. The articulation of values, the resetting of value hierarchies, and the resolution of value conflicts, is a key approach to improving shared performance.

Decision making

In Chapter 1 it was identified that a core role and task of managers was to make decisions on behalf of the organization. Good decision making is associated with the interpersonal insights and skills of the manager and their relationships with other employees. But how can managers improve their decision making skills when faced with the challenge of complexity?

Managers make decisions about the allocation of resources, often connected with expenditure, and the allocation of duties and prioritizing of activities. In this way decision making creates an order in organizational activity. They make decisions in an organizational and social context. That is with reference to strategies, policies, procedures and legal statutes and duties. Managers have a responsibility in organizations to make decisions by exercising judgment and authority. This means making choices, sometimes hard choices, that will affect the lives and outcomes of others. It is for this reason that management decision making is interpersonal and relational.

Large and complex organizations with a variety of specialisms frequently get criticized for a failure to make decisions and for allowing overly complex processes of reflection and deliberation (Collinson and Jay 2012). In such situations, it is often said that there is a lack of clarity about who should take a decision, and committees and groups fail to make a decision because they have a tendency to prefer collaboration and agreement and risk avoidance, rather than prioritizing assertive action and responsibility. Collaboration and agreement are worthy outcomes of a process, but must be balanced with the need for an organization to adjust and evolve in relation to the wider social world (Rhodes et al. 2011). An inability to change and make decisions, while avoiding conflict, can ultimately threaten the later survival of an organization because it has failed to evolve and adjust in accordance with an external landscape.

The Nobel prize winner Daniel Kahneman (2012) provides an important understanding of how decisions are made that has implications for managers and their psychological training and preparation. His analysis of the operation of the human mind has some similarities to the observations of Goleman (1996) and Peters (2012) as already discussed. The similarity is that he proposes two overlapping systems at work in human thinking. He argues that the mind has two cognitive operating systems. System 1 is fast, instinctive and more linked to feelings and emotions experienced, while system 2 is rational, deliberative and more conscious, as it slowly processes complex information and alternatives.

In circumstances that demand an immediate response people have to rely on system 1. Examples would be swerving to avoid an oncoming vehicle. Fear of the consequences of hitting the vehicle causes the driver to take evasive action without much further rational assessment. In such circumstances the way that system 1 has been programmed in the early years serves one very well. But this is not always the case. When faced with a new combination of circumstances, where over time system 2 has persuaded someone it is correct to take a new type of action, system 1 may still be giving very different and contradictory messages. An example is the first time that a person undertakes a new extreme sport like an abseiling descent in rock climbing. An abseiling descent is a relatively common leisure activity. It is safer than ascending a rock face (where some upwards movement for more advanced climbers might go above a safety rope connection). Modern equipment, training and equipment for a descent reduces all known risks to a very low level. The almost nil risk is a consequence of so many people having considered safety and thereby eliminating risk during the evolution of the sport through better training standards and equipment development. Having completed the training and safety briefing ready for a first abseiling descent, the novice stands fully equipped and supervised ready to step over a cliff backwards to make their descent. Their rational thinking system 2 tells them all is well and they are ready to proceed, but for many first time abseilers, system 1 thinking is still giving them messages of fear that what they are about to do is extremely dangerous and foolish!

This example illustrates that the human mind, while sophisticated and complex, is not perfect. Different types of information are offered into a context and in part influenced by previous experiences and programming, but an emotive assessment of the past is not always a good guide to the future. Thus, Kahneman and other psychologists working in the field of decision making, provide insights into the limitations of how systems 1 and 2 operate together in a challenging complex world and what can be done about it.

System 1 based decision making can be problematic when a manager responds rapidly to a situation on the basis of an immediate emotional or value based response. Here the system 1 thinking might be inappropriate and based on personal prejudice and inherent bias. System 1, in part, functions by simplifying a complex problem. It uses heuristics or so called "rules of thumb". These rules are based on historical experience. More rational processing steps are skipped to create speed and immediate efficiency of action. This avoids delaying for a slow fine tuning that might give more precision and effectiveness. Fine tuning in system 2 involves internal debate, greater memory recall and relative judgments, but such time for thinking and reflection may not be available. In emergencies, people have little choice but to rely on system 1, but in other situations such as being placed under pressure by others for a decision in non-urgent external circumstances, it may be best to attempt a delay and allow the more rational system 2 thought processing to be used. This, for example, justifies the advice that managers should not rush to answer challenging emails, but at least wait until the next day. System 2 does not work well under immediate pressures and with other distractions. Psychologists have demonstrated this with experiments where subjects are asked to undertake fairly complex calculations while undertaking physical exercise. The findings show that it is difficult for system 2 thinking to make progress with complex calculations while distracted.

How can managers get better at decision making? One important method is to develop more personal insight into how they make decisions. Are decisions made in a reactionary way, for example, on the basis of strong negative historical feelings, or can the manager's value based decision be linked to emotions such as anger or injustice that are evidenced by an underlying robustness of public values?

If managers are working in pressurized circumstances, where they often have to make rapid responses under pressure, rehearsing the typical circumstances likely to be experienced and learning basic and relevant information (like key legal principles or medical first aid) becomes imperative. In this sense, training can improve system 1 functioning, to some extent, and constrain problematic "chimp" behavior.

System 1 decisions are always inevitably based on limited information recall. These may be "binary heuristics" where the mind recalls a few related recent examples. This illustrates that training in public services needs to be ongoing and not a one-off preparation at the beginning of one's career. Refresher training for accident first aid and fire wardens who make first responses with a limited choice of equipment is critical.

Psychologists like Kahneman (2012) have found some general built in biases in our system 2 mind based computer, but by being aware of them, people predisposed to these inbuilt biases can have some insight into the effects on decision making. Some of these are the consequence of the interaction of system 1 and 2, given that they are interactive, interconnected and not mutually exclusive systems.

One major set of errors in decision making is due to "Confirmation Bias". People favor information that confirms their prior values and beliefs. In effect, they are seeking opportunities to confirm their social expectations. Once the mind settles into a routine of dealing with a particular set of circumstances, by recognizing patterns, the tendency is to keep repeating the same decision and it becomes a major exercise of conscious judgment to recognize an exception to the norm, or a more significant tipping point where the underlying circumstances and context are evolving to change.

A similar bias is asymmetrical assessment prior to decision making where either, only positive influences, or alternatively, negative influences, that impact the decision are taken into account. This is where appropriate organizational checks and peer working can be designed to aid better decision making. This is different to building in multiple layers and checks that prevent or postpone important decision making (Collinson and Jay 2012). One simple mechanism is "pairing", where two managers sign off certain decisions, rather than taking it to a meeting or committee. The extent of such checks needs to reflect the actual degree of organizational risk and they may need in themselves to be reviewed and changed as external circumstances bring new challenges and threats to the organization. But while complex evolutions can lead to organizational inertia (Collinson and Jay 2012), two minds are better than one, and as Kahneman (2012: 417–18) concludes: "Organisations are better than individuals when it comes to avoiding errors because they naturally think more slowly and have the power to impose orderly procedures."

Research shows that people do not intuitively make good assessments of probability, proportionality or relativity, although they can be helped if they have a relevant mathematical tool of reference and enough time to use it. Managers have a natural tendency to be loss averse. As a result if they perceive they are losing they are reluctant to give up fighting the difficult circumstances, even if the loss gets worse. Conversely, if managers perceive that a situation is stable and the organization functioning reasonably well they will be less inclined to take any risks. If managers have an exceptional success, they may become over-confident assuming an outlier event is a new average. The problem here is a cognitive amplification of the present state and a reinforcement of feedback, rather than a balancing. This is similar to what Kahneman (2012) describes as "regression to the mean", where current performance has to be assessed against averages and normal distributions over a considerable period of time before too many immediate conclusions are drawn. The human mind has a tendency to only draw on a limited range of recent experiences.

Advertisers use inbuilt biases, such as the desire to avoid losses, to win customers. The supermarket aisle offers three packets of biscuits for the price of two. Against this offer the single packet of biscuits looks expensive and customers do not want to make a loss, so are hooked into the bulk saving. Later, the decision may feel less rational if the customer either over eats or throws the extra food away. But such critical reflection requires major system 2 engagement with the issue. Many have experienced a phone call from a salesman offering a ridiculous offer that is then explained as an offer that is so good the person is a loser if they reject it. The benefits are never as good as presented and the perverse truth is often if they accept the offer for something they actually did not need they end up losing and are worse off. The ethics of public service management suggests that managers should not deliberately use such strategies of psychological manipulation to change an employee's behavior, but they should use the knowledge that people feel vulnerable to losing and being perceived as a loser, and that staff may do irrational things when under such pressures. It is important to try and present change as an opportunity for contributions and personal development, rather than allowing employees to perceive changes as a loss of personal impact and values.

Managers not only face the challenge of the complexity of the organizations they are employed by, but also have to find a better understanding of the workings of their own mind. They must reconcile their behavior and decision making with their own public service values, and guide others in this craft of matching values with action. This is how they make sense of complexity.

Leadership and managing

There is much suggestion in literature that managers need good interpersonal skills and then it will follow that they will become better leaders, but beyond this the detail of research is ambiguous and debated. Do managers always have to be good leaders? If managers have relatively little direct control over complex organizations and only have indirect influence, what does this imply for the kind of leadership style they should develop?

Bipolar representation of management and leadership

One approach is to see the overlap between good leadership and good management as relatively minimal. Such approaches emphasize the bipolar nature of management and leadership characteristics (Table 6.2). Managers may not always be the best people to lead (Lynch 1993).

This type of bipolar presentation of management and leadership aspects might help to explain why in some situations a person who is both a leader and manager can find that they are in role conflict.

In reality, dynamic and complex adaptive systems often require individuals to step out of a tightly prescribed role, to take on the skills required for a specific context. It is therefore argued that some employees will need to embrace all three roles, professional, manager and leader at different points in time. This is precisely why public sector managers often feel a sense of conflict within themselves, as well as with their organization and colleagues. They should use this knowledge of different roles with their different perspectives to have empathy and understanding for other employee positions. The key is to allow each role to come to the fore at the appropriate moment and to accept there will also be an overlap between these roles and potential tensions and conflicts that result.

The example below (Table 6.3) looks at a situation when one individual was clearly required to take a central leadership role, over and above their professional and managerial interests.

Academic approaches to leadership

There is considerable debate and frustration amongst academics and consultants about how best to pursue the search for leadership qualities and more importantly, how they can be realized. Some approaches focus on traits and styles.

Key personal traits

Some studies of leadership put the emphasis on the need for leaders to demonstrate key traits in their personality. Such traits include strength of character and self-belief that can deal with periods of criticism and adverse circumstances. This requires a degree of emotional resilience.

Table 6.2 Integrating management and leadership

Managers	Leaders
• Plan to meet current objectives	• Create a long-term vision
• Make the best use of resources	• Set a broad sense of purpose and direction
• Manage today's problems	• Build organizational values and culture
• Focus on making processes work	• Inspire people to share values and vision
• Ensure people work to contract	• Show that values link to outcomes
• Seek improvement through training	• Teach by example and praise
• Establish standard procedures	• Create more effective systems
• Focus on efficiency	• Look to the future
• Look at present	

Source: Adapted from Hudson 1999 and Lynch 1993.

Table 6.3 An example of a management conflict resolution

	General Practice	Hospital Outpatients	Hospital Inpatients
	1 Referral for hospital assessment	2 Manager prioritizes case for assessment from surgeon	
		3 Surgeon decides surgery inappropriate and refers back to General Practice for lifestyle change	
	4 GP refers to specialist rehab program at Hospital Inpatients		5 Occupational Therapy refuse to put patient on rehab program as a priority and put them on the waiting list
Point of role adaptation and service modification	6 GP complains to Hospital Manager about lack of service delivery and waiting, as patient is still seeing them regularly	7 Hospital Manager meets GP commissioning manager to review lower priority cases	8 Occupational Therapy Manager agrees to a collaborative meeting to review user needs and service options
		9 Multi-professional service meeting. Agree there are similar cases, whose needs are not being met.	
		10 Service adapts All parties agree to commit some resource to community based rehab program, to be based in General Practice, but with access to visits out from hospital specialists.	

Emotional resilience is the ability to undertake one's own system 1 or "chimp" behavior to the extent of being able to exercise an appropriate degree of control that ensures collective and organizational benefits at times of instability. There has even been a debate about whether these skills could be taught, or whether they were innate. The literature on emotional intelligence makes a strong case for teaching such personal awareness skills and implies that this will result in better social and working relationships.

Leadership styles

Other leadership literature has emphasized the need for managers and professionals to develop key styles of leadership where certain styles are demanded in response to particular situations. In the complex new public sector Rhodes (2000) has argued for the need for public sector managers working in inter-agency networks and collaborative policy environments to be good at diplomatic leadership and negotiating alliances. In a review of the relevance of complexity theory for leadership in the NHS Plesk and Wilson comment:

> Leadership inspired by complexity theory recognizes that change occurs naturally within the system and that individuals engage in this effort for a variety of reasons. Good practice will spread more quickly within the health care system if leaders acknowledge and respect the patterns reflected in past efforts of others to innovate.
>
> (Plsek and Wilson 2001: 746)

The context approach

Research at the University of Warwick into the role of leadership in the modernization of local government (Hartley and Allison 2000: 37) found that leaders were not always the people at the political and administrative apex of the organization. Often others in more middle hierarchical positions were empowered to develop key creative leadership roles. In this sense leaders were nurturing new developments, rather than pulling management control levers. Often such people had to take a lead role with other agencies in developing a partnership approach to local policy. Leaders were taking a horizontal view of policy where their personal qualities and professional standing were important to making progress. This could be contrasted with the vertical power base of politicians and chief executives who nevertheless at times needed to support new horizontal leaders' creative activity by acting decisively on institutional barriers and bureaucratic hindrances. Leadership created the emergence of new solutions, the substance of which was not always evident at the beginning of activities and projects. Leadership attributes had to be embraced by all players at certain times, although some had to exercise leadership qualities more than others. Leadership was not necessarily more productive than managerialism. The organization needs all the attributes listed in Table 6.2 to be demonstrated at different points of time, depending on the context. This does not support the bipolar approach, but implies that people need to be able to draw on a range of different skills at different points in their career and will need support, training and education if they are to achieve this. Some managers and professionals will need leadership characteristics more than others, depending on the circumstances and context that they find themselves in. Leadership is about being in touch with the organizational context and showing the flexibility to adapt to diverse situations (see the example in Table 6.3). It requires a good understanding of self and one's own system 1 and system 2 thinking processes.

In a seminal journal edition of Leadership Quarterly focusing on the relevance of complexity theory to contemporary leadership, Uhl-Bien, Marion and McKelvey (2007) concluded that the consequences of discovering complexity and understanding its relevance for organizations requires leaders to be more adaptive and enabling, rather than directive. Leadership becomes less about the behavior of key managers, but a more collaborative concept where different people will take on different aspects of leadership according to the context and adapting needs of the organization.

In a recent follow up review of the ongoing research of complexity theory and leadership Hazy and Uhl Bien (2013: 3) propose five leadership functions to assist organizations to manage complexity and the resulting requirement for organizations to adapt. The first is "generative leadership" that promotes the emergence of new ideas and adaptions via entrepreneurial processes and experimentation. The second is "administrative leadership". This has some allegiances with traditional managerial approaches and promotes stability in the face of change. It does this via the refinement of detailed core processes that can continue to provide role clarity, clear demarcation of responsibility and necessary elements of efficiency and performance. The third leadership function is "community building" and develops collaborative culture and values that allow trust, motivation and shared identities despite any challenging periods of organizational change and adaptation. The fourth form of leadership is "information gathering" and provides an important attempt to listen to multiple voices and to make sense of the numerous flows of information with a commitment to using them to develop a reflective and learning culture. The final leadership function is the use of information to confidentially define and communicate where success is occurring and to promote its reproduction via responsible decision making over the deployment of resources, including the recognition of the most important current aspects of competence and expertise. This seminal study nicely illustrates the importance of having a diverse skill set in a large organization and the ability of managers to take on different but complementary roles. It is easy to see that such organizational leadership roles can fall into conflict at certain times, and such conflict might be a necessary creative tension if an organization is to change and adapt for its future survival in a new and different external environment.

A recent (Solace Enterprises 2013) UK based review of senior leadership approaches for chief executives in local government management concluded that while transactional and transformational aspects were important, additional new contextual skills were required. These additional skills relate to the ability to operate in and influence the post-financial crisis environment with all its uncertainties.

The management of change

In an important review of the application of complexity theory to managing change, Kickert discusses the dynamic nature of complex systems and the continuous processes of change that result. This implies much change is emergent, and that there are natural limits to what centrally planned change management programs can achieve: "When change is continuous, the problem is not one of unfreezing. It is a problem of redirecting what is already under way ... the role of the change agent becomes one of managing language, dialogue and identity" (Kickert 2010: 496).

What is needed to reconcile personal, interpersonal and organizational conflicts is a personal contextual approach to human relations management that is honest in its understanding of the inevitability of such tensions. In the complex multi-networked world of the new public sector, some organizational conflicts have to be seen as creative tensions, rather than avoidable negative events. But it is always important to acknowledge in part of the honest assessment that some individuals will be anxious, unhappy and possibly unemployed, as a result of the organizational adaption that complexity creates. Change is inevitable, but not always a positive experience for individual employees.

Plsek and Wilson say that:

> those who seek to change an organisation should harness the natural creativity and organising ability of its staff and stakeholders through such principles as generative relationships, minimum specifications, the positive use of attractors for change, and a constructive approach to variation in areas of practice where there is only moderate certainty and agreement.
>
> (Plsek and Wilson 2001: 746)

The psychology of "Group Think" demonstrates the danger with closed organizational hierarchies that agree internally amongst themselves everything is progressing satisfactorily (Esser 1998). This is a small group that reinforces its own position and self-admiration over time. As a result of over-allegiance to each other, such a group becomes suspicious of outsiders and new members, and refuses to acknowledge any constructive criticisms or out-side threatening events. Such a dangerous isolationism has been a characteristic of certain political governments over the years, but also witnessed in senior management teams at key points in an organization's history. Complexity implies that managers and professionals need an openness that can challenge events and help an organization's critical reflection. This is important to keep up with fast changing events and environments where nothing stands still for very long.

Complexity theory puts great emphasis on acknowledging the different human perceptions that underwrite tensions in an organization and their possible causes. There needs to be an evaluation of different perspectives in a conflict situation. These conflicts and tensions are often at the interface of change, the interaction of the organization with the real world. Unless the organization can evolve through these tensions and learn from them, it cannot adapt towards an optimal dynamic and ensure its survival.

It is leaders who can prevent total fragmentation and assist with the facilitation of conflicts into creative tensions. This facilitates order from disorder and provides a way forward. That is not to say that leadership is charismatic and authoritative. This type of more informed approach is clearly identified in the research into local authority change by Hartley and Allison (2000).

The facilitation of change

As Keene says:

> Leadership in an environment of complexity will be that person who facilitates and creates an environment which makes it possible for the elements within the system to interact and create new forms of reality, guided by the overarching vision and rules. The art of leadership is the ability to release the potential of those within the organisation.
>
> (Keene 2000: 17)

Non-linear processes are a key feature of complex change management where change is viewed as a continuous process rather than a project where there is a beginning and an end point. Instead change is often about cycles, or peaks and troughs, as the leaders and project teams push waves of change through the organization and then allow them to settle alongside existing practice. There will be points of much activity, but also quieter times for reflecting, and then a modified program of change will pick up again, having learnt from the first wave. Each wave should integrate more new learning into the organization and help refine the definition and nature of the change that is needed.

Such change in a complex organization has a number of key features:

- It creates an overall ability of the organization to change;
- It promotes change in many people not just a few;
- Casualties are cared for, where ever possible;
- There will be several ways of moving forward;
- People move to a complex view of the world; and
- Front line employees need to be encouraged to take responsibility and control over the detailed implementation.

Change is about the resolution and management of emerging conflict and tension, in that there are different views and ideas about where the organization and its workers should be heading. While there is no single absolute truth about which way the organization goes, the key point is that the organization must evolve to keep pace with external change, so that it does not become redundant and sub-optimal in a new environment. It is the overall ability of the organization to change rather than the specifics about how it is done that is important. As long as the organization is able to head in the right general direction, there are likely to be lots of variations and possibilities along the way. Sometimes there can be too much debate about the details of change and not enough of an informed overview.

For an organization to make real progress in its relationship with the outside environment, change will be required from many parties and individuals in its membership. Some will change quickly, others more slowly. There will also be a few who find it impossible.

One key principle for negotiating change is an appreciation of the other's positions. Such an attribute is a key component of emotional intelligence (Goleman 1996). This allows tensions and conflicts to be aired and reflected on productively. If issues become linked to overt personal criticism and failure, conflict becomes more deep seated and change more difficult. Scapegoating and shaming is best avoided. Weaknesses and conflicts have to be dealt with head on, but sympathetically and supportively. Given public service organizations have primary values of protecting basic human rights and caring for others, these values have to be upheld within, despite a difficult change process.

The process of reflecting on tensions and conflicts, and the need for change, can be aided if it is acknowledged that there are multiple ways forward—not one perfect way. Keene (2000: 17) calls this "new ways of looking at the same reality". Thus, one of the worst things that senior managers can do is to implement a plan that provides a single and detailed view of the future, without taking any consultation within the organization. Such a plan undermines the value and perspective of other workers and is probably a narrow view! Threats may come from a number of horizons, and some at short notice. There will be several roads to the promised land, not one route only. The first stage is to establish an overall vision and to underpin it with an agreement about what the core values needed are.

Staff and teams need to have a wide view of factors and an ability to think broadly and creatively. Assessments of strengths and weaknesses, threats and opportunities will need to be regularly revised, in the light of changing external events. This can be summarized as people moving to a complex view of the world, rather than a simple one. Short meetings that make regular strategic reviews are better than a full day, such as an annual meeting, which produces rigid and detailed plans (there is more discussion of strategic approaches in Chapter 3).

Stages of change

In order to decide on the best method for implementing change it is necessary to unpack the personal investment that groups of workers have in a given situation, so as to decide when and how to do change. Front line workers need to feel that their ideas have been considered and that they do have some responsibility and control over what is happening. The more responsibility and control workers feel that they have, the more chances there are for successful engagement with change. It is often a good idea to facilitate that front line employees and teams are made to feel that they have created and inspired the change, even if this is not necessarily the case. This can be quite difficult for the catalyst of change to accept, as it means that their own creativity and inspiration may not be fully accepted and acknowledged. Again, such an underplaying of the leader's own ego is a characteristic of emotional intelligence.

In summary a process of change is about negotiating a changing view of the world and encouraging different people to review their own perspectives and actions alongside others.

Senior managers have the responsibility to decide on appropriate decisions and actions and to see that they are implemented. Table 6.4 summarizes the process of change, where tensions are expressed and the self-organizing and coordinating features of the organization realigned to provide a new operational focus.

The process is non-linear, it is impossible to prescribe a periodic pace to the process and different parts of the organization may be at different points in the process at different points of time. It is impossible to make such a process tidy and tightly organized. Most managers who reflect back on periods of change management mention unexpected events and developments.

Motivational interviewing (Miller and Rollnick 2002) can be used by managers to help employees cope with the pressures for change (see Table 6.5). The motivational interviewing approach recognizes that motivation is not a static character trait but rather the dynamic part of a process where the individual's cognition process responds to a changing environment. The individual stages of change mirror the organizational stages of change. In the pre-contemplation stage the person is beginning to experience external pressures to change and its physical and emotional effects, but this has not registered fully into their system 2 computational thinking. Any first reactions tend to be driven by system 1 and they may well be defensive. The manager's task is to try and introduce the employee to more informed and reflective system 2 approaches to possible change. Hopefully this takes the employee into the second stage of contemplation where their system 2 processing begins to debate and reflect on all the current possibilities of change. This leads into the actual changes for the organization and the employee with the aim being to do what is possible to lead the employee into a positive interpretation of change that includes any new role or outcome for them personally.

Complex organizations demand styles of leadership that facilitate an evolving and adaptable system of organizing work. This is built around a core mission and agreement about the key values and purpose. These are the attractor parts of an organization, the themes and functions that keep the parts moving together without fragmenting. Complexity also acknowledges the importance of team working, where teams are dynamic and able to use their mix of skills and adapt

Table 6.4 Stages of change

Stage 1	Operational focus	Settled patterns of behavior	Operational and project focus
Stage 2	Strategy focus	Dissonance developing in organization	Conflicts emerging about current operational issues and need for strategy and change
Stage 3	Facilitation of change	Internal dissonance aired and expressed Conflicts made explicit	Strategic direction proposed. Maximum need for participation and consultation
Stage 4	Support of change	Change negotiated to realign organization Focus moves to acceptance and implementation	Any amendments to strategy decided. Operational decisions made. Project teams and leaders identified
Stage 5	Operational focus	Settled pattern of behavior develops	Realigned work processes allowed to settle

Table 6.5 Motivational stages related to organizational change

Miller's stages	Cognitive stage	Cognitive bias	Event cognition	Staff room account	Restructuring the dialogue
Pre-con-templation	Not con-sciously think-ing about change	System 1 reac-tions likely to prevent system 2 considering change	Immediate peers and col-leagues rein-force that "all is well"	"We know what is best in the office, these new ideas will never work."	There will always be some ways we can improve what we do
Contempla-tion	Considering change	System 2 reflection becoming active	Specific local failure of an aspect of pro-cess, creates complaints, stress and extra work activity	"Much of the proposals will not work, but I agree that the current process is imperfect."	Offer hope as to how the incident can be dealt with differently when the process is reviewed
Change	Informed response	Balance of system 2 evi-dence has moved in favor of change	Presentation of detail of pro-posed changes, with space created for employee con-sideration and reflection	"Given the recent meet-ings and reviews, I can see on balance the proposals might work better."	Encourage full debate, challenge the more extreme views. Facil-itate challenge from com-ments of others
Maintenance	Rehearse responses	Specific events may trigger system 1 his-tories that doubt the continuing validity of change	Local crisis in new process triggers stress and anxiety	"Those com-plaints this morning show these new processes will never work, I always said it was foolish to change."	Reassure, point to examples where the new process has already worked and done better.

Source: Adapted from Miller and Rollnick (2002).

their role and tasks, rather than being defined by static roles of membership. As identified later in this chapter, project based working can provide an important self-organizing element to how a public service profession negotiates change within a public service organization.

Team working

In a team, a weakness can be countered by another's strength, without people constantly being in a competitive struggle about whose skills are most important. A good team will have a matrix of creative tensions that are managed and facilitated so as to allow them to move forward without becoming caught in personal competitions and overtly focused on the team's personal struggles. Team working is a classic example of the creative versus conflict tension demonstrated by complexity theory. Future order and purpose can only result from the paradox of some disorder and conflict in the present.

Key team tensions

Creativity-order

Any team needs to find a dynamic between creativity and conservatism in a given situation. Teams can be over creative, constantly creating new ideas and work based practices that in time create exhaustion and fragmentation for colleagues and clients. Any change needs some time to bed down and for it to be reflected upon. Much change can be a modification of what has happened before, rather than radical new ventures. All team members want some of their creative ideas to be taken up, each will be issuing caution about the ideas of the other:

> We all know that the best teams include difficult people who are talented but difficult. They stretch your leadership skills, but their contribution is invaluable.
>
> (Bichard 2000: 45)

The individuals create and caution together, improving the quality of one idea through discussion and interaction. The ownership of the overall creative process becomes embodied in the team, rather than an individual, as does the cautionary reflection.

Action-reflection

Teams need a changing dynamic between active decisions and more passive reflection. Some teams get into difficulty when they take inappropriate decisions, issuing too many instructions and guidance in the organization, so that other parties become confused and less likely to take note. Conversely teams may go through phases when they are too inactive, due to a lack of confidence and clarity about their organizational role and task. A satisfactory solution has to be found both between the team members themselves and in terms of the group's interaction with outside elements. A team needs to constantly and qualitatively monitor its impact on other stakeholders.

Encouragement-criticism

A team needs a good dynamic between encouragement and criticism. Soon after a team is formed a period of mutual encouragement is often important to build relationships and trust. But in the medium and longer term the team will need to endure constructive criticism of each other's ideas if they are to avoid becoming immersed in a "group think" mentality where they begin to develop an unrealistic view of their own importance, status and authority in the organization. Teams that are unable to be self-critical are in danger of becoming short-term havens for their members, but with little relevance to the remainder of the organization who become displeased at their self-congratulation and increasing irrelevance to the world outside. Such teams get a rude awakening when senior managers suddenly call for an end to their project and funding, and the members frequently express disbelief that the organization is undervaluing them so much. To a large extent, teams have a constant responsibility to remind the organization of why they are needed in the light of changing external circumstances, rather than assuming that because they have always been needed the future will also require their existence.

Team leadership

Can teams be led by one individual, or should they be self-facilitating, based on cooperative methods? There is no simple answer to this question. Public service professional teams are unlikely to benefit from autocratic styles of leadership. All are likely to want to be centrally involved in the deliberations, actions and responsibilities of the team. Good leaders in such circumstances are often facilitators who are able to move to a more supportive role. Some teams may need more of a manager-leader, someone with good administrative and organizational system skills, due to the nature of the work tasks. The dangers with not having a clearly identified manager and leader are that individuals will use this as an excuse for not taking responsibility during hard times and when difficult decisions and priorities have to be made. This might cause a team to stagnate and become redundant. The safest method is probably to have an appointed leader, unless the team is very experienced, some of them have worked together before, and they feel confident and clear about their role and task. "Leaders' effectiveness lies in their ability to make activity meaningful for those they lead. They do this not by changing behaviour, but by giving others a sense of understanding of what they are doing – a coherent viewpoint" (Lissack and Roos 1999: 14).

Project workings

Traditional team working has gone on in the public services environment for years in, for example, the service delivery teams at the front line: subject teachers in schools, Criminal Investigation Departments in the police station, and child protection staff in social work offices. Also, new forms of team are coming into being. Team working progressively finds its form in project management, where a group of people is brought together for a limited period of time to face a particular issue, often one that the organization sees as a priority and an issue that they cannot obviously see any existing structures and teams dealing with. In this sense project team working becomes a creative method for facing change in the outside environment and for helping an organization to evolve. It creates a new grouping, from existing individuals and groupings, perhaps changing some staff roles for only part of their working schedule. The creation of a project team is itself an act of organizational change, it may involve bringing people together from different disciplines, professions and agencies. It can help to challenge conservative self-organization when employees are over defensive of traditional structures and processes.

Such projects are less permanent than the older service provider teams and have to cope with short life spans and perhaps only working together on the project as part of their overall individual job. The danger of such project teams is that their local focus is lost because of the pace of internal and external events, this is particularly likely where membership of the project is part time and professionals involved have other working responsibilities. Similarly, the focus might suddenly shift mid way through their project, because of some external events, and the project fragments because it does not have the experience or commitment from its members to cope. Another danger is that a project develops well in the early and middle stages and gains a good sense of its role and task, but dissemination back into the host organization is weak, leaving it isolated and vulnerable when wider change and events gain pace.

On the other hand, project teams can be ideal for piloting new ways of working and undertaking action based research that leads to the development of new knowledge. If they disseminate well, they can enable a much wider group of staff to feel supported and change their practice. But in these aspects the personal skills and emotional intelligence of group members is critical, given that the majority of employees and professionals may view special projects with suspicion seeing them as taking away important resources and having the ability to avoid some day to day front line responsibilities.

On balance, the strengths outweigh the weaknesses, given that such project work has become increasingly popular across the public sector in the last decade. Projects take a variety of forms, reflecting quite rightly their need to be dynamic and adaptable to the context in which they operate. The best projects are those that have a dynamic range of personal skills where members are sympathetic to each other's experience, strength and weaknesses, leading to growing mutual respect and self belief in what they are doing, without them becoming overzealous. The best projects also remember their allegiance to the organizations that created them and that their co-dependency on the host organization is a critical element. Nevertheless, there is growing evidence that project teams present a clear example of the positive aspects of self organization in a complex world. The strengths and weaknesses of the project approach are summarized in Table 6.6.

Much has been written about project management that denies its human relations element. Such accounts place great emphasis on the role and task definition in project specification. While these accounts can be of importance and of some value, the usefulness of the human relations approach to projects is that it assists the evolving of a project into new and unanticipated circumstances.

Knowledge and staff development

Stacey (2000), one of the leading writers on complexity theory and management, has observed the tendency of older systems based approaches to human action in organizations to be founded on the separation (dualism) of the social and individual.

He argues that complexity approaches to human interaction seek to move beyond this separation, so that individual action and behavior is understood in the context of the changing and challenging social environment.

Training sessions with public service managers that look at financial and budget management often lead to the rapid acknowledgement of something all the group members have in common. Public service budgets have high fixed staff costs, sometimes up to 90% of the budget is constructed by such costs. New public managerialism cited this as a "problem". According to NPM, rigidity in the budget creates inflexibilities and undermined economy

Table 6.6 Strengths and weaknesses of using project teams

Strengths	Weaknesses
• Provides a newly formed team with the space to focus on a specific and changing problem or issue	• Project team may become exclusive and out of touch with some operational front line pressures
• Creates opportunities to bring different disciplines, professionals and specialists together	• The creation of project teams can fragment an organization too much and undermine core operations
• Encourages the organization to create new and adaptable networks, rather than reinforcing old boundaries and work practices	• Potential lack of accountability to senior and core management systems
• Encourages self-organization and local decision making and responsibility	• Project team may suffer from a lack of leadership and project specification, this leading to a lack of decision making, progress and inability to face demanding change
• Facilitates organization reflection on external changes	

and efficiency. These market based approaches to labor in public organizations have led to industrial relations tensions given the push towards privatization and the outsourcing unskilled labor, then introducing more semi-skilled labor and even reducing expensive professional labor. Managers wanted, or were taught to want, more flexible costs—flexible labor costs were rated highly because of the operational flexibility they gave a new public manager. Flexible labor costs would allow managers to hire and fire staff at will, with only short-term contracts offered, and support services outsourced to service companies.

Such approaches to the labor market can come back to haunt the public sector with a recruitment crisis and much disillusionment from those employed in the sector (Audit Commission 2002). The crude classical economics of the 1980s had denied the positive externalities of the public employee, the added values of their commitment to public service values, their loyalty and their education and training attainments, attributes that had a financial worth that was not showing up on the immediate organizational balance sheets.

The undervaluing of public service employees has been a wake up call to the idea of knowledge management in the sector, or how best to value and keep the brain power and creative ideas of employees inside the productive experience and life of the organization. Knowledge management potentially brings human relations to the forefront, because it is recognition of the value of people in an organization. This is also known as the management of the intellectual capital of the public sector. The qualifications, experience and skills of the public service professionals are of high value.

Traditional approaches to knowledge management

The value of knowledge and skills is explicit in any progressive approach to the public sector. There is a large scale drive in many public services to increase the number of qualified and trained workers and to ensure that even the most qualified update their skills. The danger is that this approach to skills maximization is rather simplistic and based on quantification of total knowledge rather than more qualitative and contextual applications of knowledge to the sector.

Traditional approaches to knowledge management are defined as rational attempts to quantify the value of the knowledge held by the workforce at any one point in time. Knowledge is said to be located within individuals and applied as professional practice. Knowledge has become the key capital of modern post-industrial organizations, replacing the plant and machinery of industrial production (Haynes 2005). This is certainly true in the new high tech industries of computer software and biotechnology. Managerial procedures and information systems are required that can categorize, store and retrieve the vast growth of knowledge in modern organizations. Similarly the term intellectual capital refers to new technology, biotech and service type businesses whose market capitalization is much higher than the sum of their fixed assets. The difference is said to be due to the ideas and knowledge implicit in the company's work force.

Knowledge management focuses on a number of elements. The skills base of employees, such as their qualifications and previous experience; the motivation, personal skills and loyalty of staff; and the commercial benefits from knowledge creation, such as the filing of new patents and the successful branding of products, like websites, financial services, consultancy models and training packages. A related idea is the concept of service integration and added value, where intangible knowledge based products are linked to more traditional products and services. They are developed to add value to existing delivery. For example, a supermarket develops financial services and web based marketing. This may require increasing knowledge and skills of a traditional service output workforce, so that they can service the more intangible and new assets of the company.

Complexity approaches to knowledge management

The management complexity writer Stacey (2001) has written an important critique of traditional approaches to knowledge management in the public sector. He has criticized the individualism inherent in traditional approaches to knowledge management. He prefers to put emphasis on knowledge creation and application via the interaction between individuals and organizational teams:

> It becomes meaningless to talk about managing the learning and knowledge creation process ... Instead, attention might be directed at changing organisational actions and policies that disrupt and destroy patterns of relationship between people because these will destroy the learning and knowledge creation process.
>
> (Stacey 2001: 74)

The major issue for Stacey is the collegiality of knowledge creation and application. He implies that knowledge alone is of little use, but rather how it evolves and is applied to the delivery of public services is what is important, in terms of adding value. For this to happen professionals must be allowed a large degree of responsibility and flexibility in how they operate. Knowledge management is about inspiring and facilitating creative use of knowledge. It is not auditing the cross sectional value of knowledge and skills available. Knowledge is not a fixed entity, but a complex series of actions. It cannot be measured or controlled easily. "It is meaningless to ask how tacit knowledge is transformed into explicit knowledge since unconscious and conscious themes organising experience are inseparable aspects of the same process" (Stacey 2001: 189).

There is little doubt that intellectual capital is real, in the sense that many modern industries and services depend more on the creative and highly developed skills of their workforce rather than the productive capacity of property, plant and machinery. The public services face a particular intellectual capital challenge at the present time, in that insufficient thought has been given to rewarding and retaining highly skilled professional workers who form the key ingredient in service provision. The attempt of new public managerialism to reduce the value of this capital and economize by deskilling the work force and using semi-professional staff is a false economy. Long-term investment in the knowledge base of the public sector is needed and an organizational approach that builds the motivation, value base and creative application of professional knowledge so as to add value to the delivery of public services.

The Audit Commission (2002) highlighted that bureaucracy, paperwork and performance targets were the main reason why many public service workers were leaving their jobs prematurely. This could be contrasted with the reasons why people had joined public services in the first place, such as "to make a positive difference" and "to work with people". The motives and commitment of those joining was adding an important value to the organizations they joined, but this was not being managed or developed, leading to inefficiency and wastage.

Boisot (2011), in an important review of knowledge management and complexity theory, sees the two concepts as co-existing. There is a paradox about managers codifying knowledge to simplify and reduce complexity, and this is apparent when there are benefits of allowing knowledge to be used in more complex and diverse ways at the point of service impact.

A value based management

An exploration of the implications of complexity theory for management in public and non-governmental organizations reveals that people, their values, needs, motivations, skills and contributions must be at the core of any meta theory and integrated management practice. Central to this is a value driven approach, as values—rather than profits—should be at the core of public and non-governmental organizations. Values also form the important underpinning method for stability in these organizations, given the way that they act as attractors towards the rule of order in a given system.

A value based approach can be constructed with reference to norms and logics (see Chapter 2), the key components being: values, norms, logics and their application to organizational rules. Values are the inner cognitions that come to be shared by a group of people. In a management situation this will be within the organization of interest, but in the wider public and non-governmental policy environment this might include public values that are shared across several organizations.

Public values

It is important to remember what is meant by values in public organizations (see Chapters 1 and 2). By studying values we make explicit how different forms of human behavior and action are valued and seen as to the benefit (or not) of the individual and society. Individual benefit and collective benefit may be in conflict.

The dynamic interacting of changing values, norms and logics, and their communication, need more research and understanding as a component in the application of complex systems theory to public management. Previous applications of the methodology have tended to focus more on the operational domains of public employees and the organizational context with regard to how work processes can be understood as part of an evolving whole system (Allen, Maguire and McKelvey 2011). Much focus has been on the flow of work activity. An example would be taking a helicopter view of inputs, activities, outputs and outcomes and relating them to the external context and how the various scales and levels in complex situations can better be understood in terms of their interaction with specific activities in the public sphere. In short this might be described as whole systems management (Seddon 2008). Cultural analysis of the workplace has played its part in some of this type of approach, for example in the work of Stacey (2011), but in these approaches the emphasis has been on understanding the cultural values and behavioral impact inside the system rather than the influence of changing contextual values that flow in and out of a specific system. In public administration, the value interface with the wider public and civic world is critical. Attractors in complex systems are widely recognized as value based rules that impose some form of order (Haynes 2012: 10–12), although that order will be dynamic and unpredictable in its specific effects at any one time and place. Attractors can achieve boundaries of stability around outputs and outcomes, with the possible maintenance of certain trajectory patterns going forward. Attractors linked to value based rules, expressed as norms and logics, are not deterministic in cause and effect, but result in likely patterns of behavior and action.

Values and complexity

While values are a source of order in complex systems, major value conflicts can also be a source of disorder and instability. Values, like most other phenomena, in complex systems are constantly evolving. Values are established in the human mindset as beliefs that underpin cognition. Some are attached to strong emotions, driven by longstanding family, educational and communal experiences. These values can drive system 1 responses (Kahneman 2012). Other values are subject to more ongoing rational considerations and thereby enter the rational logics that drive considerations in system 2 thinking (op. cit.). These are more likely to be values learned in secondary and tertiary education and professional training, and they are of particular relevance therefore to public services.

Behavior reinforces values. Childhood stories may reinforce accounts of what values are important, but if more recent observed and experienced behavior does not reinforce such values, their impact will be less over time. Nevertheless, certain environmental events can retrigger them and bring them back to the forefront of system 1. So given environmental stimuli, they can still return to influence actual behavior.

There are some considerable changes in public value systems in recent decades. In many countries managerialism has been accompanied by increased marketization and financial devolution with financial measurements being applied at a more micro and local level and used to make judgments of comparative efficiency. In addition, attempts have been made to give service users the ability to behave as customers with a choice where possible. These changes were discussed extensively in the first chapter. It was noted that many public service professional groups had found aspects of these changes difficult and had experienced value tensions with the management regimes that resulted. One key way that professionals express these value conflicts is through collective activity with their professional bodies and trade unions. At times they may attempt to resist managerial changes on the basis that the value tensions are too conflicting and they feel a need to preserve particular aspects of their own values and beliefs about what is of primary importance to the public.

A key thing about these value conflicts is that they are dynamic and not static or bi-polar over time. They are also multi-dimensional. This is best illustrated by the problem that public professionals have when not cooperating with political and managerial driven changes. Even though resistance may start from the basis that conflict is necessary to protect what the professional sees as the primary public values, the agenda and debate can change rapidly. In the main this is because the dynamic situation of conflict results in some instability and in this instability individuals and groups find that their relative value systems may move in relation to their working environment as they choose to prioritize one value over another.

An example of this is the strong value of care that public service professionals bring to their work, and that is one of the most primary values. As a result when industrial action starts, or is suggested, the majority of professionals are reluctant to withdraw their labor or aspects of their labor that might harm their service users. While decisions have to weigh up and rationalize different values, they can be placed in different relative orders of influence depending on the context of the decision and the evidence drawn down to make that particular decision. We can explain this relative movement of the influence of values with reference to hierarchies of dynamic operational values, as demonstrated in Table 6.7.

Values and norms

It is the underpinning values of public service (as taught to all public professionals in their training, and very often a key part of their motivation in seeking training) that provide added value to public services. As indicated in Chapter 2, internalized cognitive values are converted to behavioral norms by a process of interaction. So in personal relationships, values about the importance of loyalty and commitment to long-term partners, are manifest in the

Table 6.7 Hierarchies of dynamic operational values

Value	Society	Organizational	Personal
Care	Human rights	Legal duties to service user	Ethic of care Collective social responsibility
Self-determination	Individualism Liberty	Choice for the individual service user	Respect and empathy for individual
Efficient use of resources	Austerity, limiting taxation and public expenditure to preserve individual wealth creation	Management obligations (directives, measurements and controls)	Meeting own and immediate family, partner's needs
Effectiveness of interventions	Value for money Political accountability	Collective social and organizational purpose	Ethics of the relational

behavior where individuals commit to each other for their long-term shared benefit. This might be joint ownership of resources like the purchase of a house or financial savings. The behavioral norm being acted out by this belief in the value is the reality of long-term relationships and shared living. These values are formalized in social institutions like marriage and civil partnerships. Governments recognize such institutions and reinforce them with supportive policies, so the behavior becomes normalized and social norms are created, with expectations that others will behave in similar ways. Nevertheless, in long-term relationships, it is ultimately only the long-term mutually reinforcing behavior of shared care that maintains the value of the specific relationship over time and thereby the cognitive presence of the value in the person's own hierarchy of values.

Table 6.8 shows a simplified structure of values and norms exhibited by a public service worker, alongside a mutual inclusive personal value and norm. Here in most contexts there is not likely to be much conflict between personal and professional values and norms unless there is a particular dynamic such as the employee's own older parent falling seriously ill and they needing to take significant time away from work to care for them. In that context their value of care to their own immediate relative will take preference over their value of care to their professional clients. This effects their behavior and ability to commit to employment time.

Managers have a role in reinforcing the primary values and norms of professional public service workers. These values provide an underpinning stability for public services and allow quality daily services to be provided regardless of what other instabilities are created by changes in the rationality of an organization. Allowing public professionals to achieve such values in the manifestation of norms of professional behavior is likely to be associated with a high degree of motivation. In the day to day management, such reinforcement is achieved by drawing attention to good practice and outcomes where service users celebrate what is achieved. Such management approaches provide reinforcing feedback for behavior that improve public services.

Similarly management intervention to correct behavior that does not achieve high standards is a form of balancing feedback. Here managers have to battle with some expressions of conservative self-organization from public service workers that is resistant to any change, but can be confronted for its inability to meet core values in a satisfactory way.

If public professionals are encouraged to build on core values and norms in this way, innovation and the beneficial evolution of services can be achieved by the emergence of new

Table 6.8 Simplified structure of values and norms for professional employees

Professional		Personal	
Value	Norm	Value	Norm
Duty of care	Always puts care of the service users as the primary aim of activity	Care of family as duty Care as a reciprocal social obligation	Regular visits to family Financial support to family
Self-determination	Promote user and carer decisions and facilitate choices that encourage this	Need to respect other's individual dignity and personal space. Relationships are interdependent	Reciprocal exchanges over time
Efficient use of resources	Deploy staff and spend money where they will maximize the benefits for the collective public good	Part of looking after myself and others is the best use of resources to achieve personal and family goals	Plan and prioritize income and expenditure, in communication with partner and family
Effectiveness of interventions	Understand longer term outcomes, such as quality of life and happiness and that these may be more important than immediate service outputs	Life experience and education are of value when deciding what will affect my future	Trial and error decisions, these reviewed with partner and family

forms of order as demonstrated in dissipative self-organization. The key is to embed dissipative self-organization in primary public service values.

Conclusion

Emotional intelligence and system 2 reflection need to be at the core of the post-industrial approach to human relations in organizations. It moves thinking away from the rationalist managerialism of post-Taylorism where the manager must address key tasks and be sure of their role. Emotional intelligence and system 2 decision making shift the focus to maximizing the psychological and personal skills of the manager and leader, seeing this as central to the success of any organization.

This overview of emotional intelligence and system 2 decision making needs to influence management training and personal development and become embedded in the professional education and training of public service workers. The need for personal insight to underpin leadership, team work and good communication with outsiders are aspects that will add value to professional work in any context. These skills are particularly necessary in a new policy environment where structures, cultures and values are rapidly evolving in a global context. There is a growing danger that individuals can feel vulnerable, exposed and threatened by new networks, and global persistence of NPM in the face of economic austerity. This vulnerability requires a supportive environment where public service values, insights and skills are fully recognized and developed. The type of reflective and collaborative thinking needed, if complexity is to be understood and managed appropriately, and optimal decisions made, is summarized in Table 6.9.

Table 6.9 Influences on management cognitions in decision making

Routes to decision making and action		
	Strong (checking with system 2)	*Weak (overreliance on system 1)*
My perceptions of others	I judge what to do on the basis of previous evidence of staff behavior and behavioral outcomes.	I judge what to do on the basis of what my staff say about themselves, or their own perceptions of situations.
Emotional insights, checking them out	I try and take time to consider alternatives and to check out my peer's opinions.	I have a good instinct about people, my first gut instincts are good.
Performance: general	All staff have both strengths and weakness; it is unusual for one staff member to have only strengths, or to be very weak. Over time I get to understand this by observing staff performance on different tasks.	Staff are either "good" or "bad" and my first impressions normally allow me to know which type they are.
Specific performance on a key task or specialist area	What is the person's average performance on a key task over time?	They did exceptionally well (or badly) when I observed them.
Use of management statistics	I consider statistical information carefully and see it as an important source of information.	Statistics rarely tell me much about anything, my instinct is a better guide to what the most important issues are.
Service user information	If, over time, I am hearing the same feedback from different service user sources I need to investigate it closely.	I rarely give weight to individual service user accounts, they have their own bias and very personal circumstances.
Complaints	It is important to consider the balance of evidence available and any repeating patterns over time. Formal complaints processes are difficult and resource intensive, but it is important to try and deal with them by way of sound quasi legal principles and practices.	Complaints reflect the unrealistic pressure on public organizations, and defy any rational legal explanation. They tell us more about a minority of people's bias and distorted perceptions than much else.
Use of management team and management peers	I like to share ideas with my close management peers before making a decision, it increases the evidence available and checks my own biases and perceptions.	I do not like to rely too much on my immediate peers, as I have to take responsibility and provide leadership. They look to me for direction and I must give it.
Management training and coaching	Management training is important to rehearse problems and to put my experience into a wider context and to consider research and information about areas of practice.	Management training is often a waste of time, the best approach is to build self-confidence, based on your own experience, and to learn from your own experiences of handling previous problems.

There is a need for a renaissance of the human relations approach in the public service environment. The previous functional ideas of the new managerialism were far from new and had their roots in early classical scientific approaches to management and organizations that underplayed the value of the human input. Public services should never have allowed their managerial and administrative cultures to move so far away from placing an emphasis on the high value of human input and the strengths that personal service and a commitment to the public and community can bring. Such values were high on the list of attributes in the early days of the emerging public services at the end of the nineteenth century. A new public service ethos needs to strengthen the value base of public service in a world where market and public sector have become entangled. Given the recent collapse of public trust in the economics of finance and business accounting methods after the 2007–08 financial crisis, the private sector also needs to share with the public sector some restatement of the public values of honesty, integrity, social commitment and trust. At the core of this is the value base of money and credit creation and how banking plays its part in society (Ryan-Collins et al. 2012). Even money itself is not "value free", but in large part an unrecognized form of public benefit that has been privatized for commercial benefit.

The value of a human approach to public service professional work cannot be under-estimated. There is a tension in a government policy that asks public service workers to be innovative and enterprising while at the same time increases regulation and imposes potentially narrow definitions of performance. Those who bring commitment demand a major stake in the organization and the application of professional knowledge and humanitarian values to public service delivery. Public service organizations should evolve in a way that makes maximum benefit of this commitment and creativity. Systems of organization that make the most efficient use of knowledge and value based skills will benefit from good team work and project based systems. This will also require management, leadership and the facilitation of coordination and change. The value based management approach as a new method for public service management is summarized in Table 6.10.

Table 6.10 The value based management method

Principle	Management	Examples
Strengthen commitment to core values.	Make values explicit and link them directly to behavior and behavior outputs and outcomes.	Public Health—as defined by "collective responsibilities" and "shared benefits". My behavior may be unhealthy for others. Productive profit and advantage should not have negative effect on the health of customers.
Ensure core values are consistently defined.	At times of change and external threats find opportunities to explicitly reinforce strong shared values, in specific aspects of delivery.	Link the spread of new unhealthy behaviors (like increased obesity) to corporate, social and political economic changes, rather than individual pathology.

Principle	Management	Examples
Ensure core values are demonstrated in operational delivery and behavioral activities.	Make sure the behavioral outcomes of core values are appropriately rewarded and are understood by the organization and reinforced in training.	Work with manufacturers to change food production and labelling. Fiscal system of purchase tax and fines reinforces socially beneficial changes. Promote collective benefits of spaces like public transport and parks and link to shared benefits.
Challenge activities that are weak on protecting core values. Minimize their impact.	Are instrumental activities, like costings, assessing, categorizing, etc. becoming dehumanizing and creating harmful dysfunctional characteristics?	Pressures on acute health care costs and waiting lists seek to reduce services to smokers and overweight patients, thus are punitive and a denial of public ethos and values.
Seek and design value added activities that enhance core values. Ensure explicit linking of core values to service activities, outputs and outcomes.	Where processes have become instrumental because of output efficiency and measurement, add relational and immediate impacts that are directly related to core values.	Collective shared "public" responses: community walks, dances, neighborhood vegetable gardens and allotments, subsidized transport, corporate and work place support to add value to such schemes.

7   Conclusion

Complexity theory demonstrates the indeterminate nature of societies, social organizations and relationships. Managers and leaders have to accept that while they have influence and responsibility their actions will never determine the precise outcome of their domain and at worst, they may sometimes fail in their management task through no immediate fault of their own. But this is being unnecessarily pessimistic. Managers, leaders and politicians have influence and powers of persuasion and the potential to exercise leverage on the future. Streatfield concluded that:

> managers find that they have to live with the paradox of being "in control" and "not in control" simultaneously. It is this capacity to live with paradox, the courage to continue to participate creatively in spite of "not being in control" that constitutes effective management.
>
> (Streatfield 2001: 140)

Etzioni (2014) talks of the need for humble decision making, with managers starting with an honest appraisal of the local and macro limitations and restrictions on their efforts that they face. Ormerod puts this in the context of the policy environment in which public service managers are engaged:

> Structures, rules, regulations, incentives are put in place in the belief that a desired outcome can be achieved … As the financial crisis from 2007 onwards illustrates only too well, this view of the world is ill suited to creating systems which are resilient when unexpected shocks occur … The focus of polity needs to shift away from prediction and control … Instead, we need systems which exhibit resilience and robustness, which can respond well to unpredictable future events, which can recover through strengths of positive linking.
>
> (Ormerod 2012: 287)

Managers also need to understand the complexity of their own mind and cognitions. They need a degree of psychological insight into their own biases and limitations and what can be done about them. This means that they cannot work in isolation but need some close support and a peer group. This support should avoid simply being composed of likeminded people who reinforce a certain bias and create an inability to take a self critical perspective. Better that a support group and peer group is diverse and critically reflective. Organizations should beware of appointing too many senior staff in the image of those appointing them, although some retention and succession of core values could be welcome, there should be diversity in the gender, age and broad outlook of those appointments. As Kahneman (2012: 417) concludes: "Organisations are better than individuals when it comes to avoiding errors, because they naturally think more slowly and have the power to impose orderly procedures." Nevertheless, this premise goes too far if organizations become clustered with overly bureaucratic risk avoidance processes (Collinson and Jay 2012). Better to seek strong values that drive appropriate behavior and decision making, rather than to rely on complex bureaucratic processes. At best, strongly held public values should program system 1 management thinking rather than immediate management decisions being based on individual personal histories and the emotive responses they generate. For as Kahneman (2012: 81) says, "System 1 is gullible" and biased towards believing, while "System 2 is in charge of doubting and unbelieving, but System 2 is sometimes busy, and often lazy". Public services should expect high standards of managerial emotional intelligence and self awareness. They should invest in developing these skills and promote ways of thinking linked to public values rather than old style "value free" NPM rationalism. The latter has been shown to prejudice market values.

Public service managers are sailors navigating an ocean with a mix of unstable and stable weather. The operating environment is notable for its multi-dimensional challenges, and the contradictions and tensions that result when trying to simplify management objectives and performance targets. It is easy for a fragmentation of activities to follow with a resulting lack of direction and strategic purpose. Decision making becomes difficult and unclear. The policy environment strays into periodic instability and chaos. The flux between stability and instability is real. Sometimes the dynamic change is harmful and unproductive, but also it can provide an opportunity to take a new overview of the policy environment, the re-evaluation of the operation of specific institutions and policies. Instability can provide an opportunity to take new courses of action. In some circumstances, out of disorder emerges a new form of order. This does not happen by mystery or magic, but by human action and purpose. Rarely is such change initiated by one manager or leader, but involves a group of people often with a shared leadership element and their own distinctive style. This needs a shared value driven approach. This active group is the catalyst for a much larger group of people, allowing them to potentially take on board the action of change, bringing them to a point where ideally they feel able to embrace some change, where they see the need to reorganize their part in the working process to include a change agenda.

The more that a process of change is absorbed and accepted into the depths of an organization, the more subject it becomes to a self organized evolution and reinterpretation. Finally, it takes on a life and energy of its own rather, independent of the activities of the managers and leaders who initiated it. The most influential leaders often make themselves redundant because their ideas and arguments about society and its values become absorbed in the community and reworked into the self organization of people's everyday life. As a result, the agenda continues to move and their individual approach can be replaced by others.

Management of complexity in the policy environment is rarely about autocratic approaches. Sometimes people have to be told what to do and when: deadlines have to be set, roles and jobs specified, project and planning targets prescribed, but an autocratic approach can feel counterproductive, because many public service workers are professionals with a relatively high degree of autonomy and an ability to influence the policy process in their own individual way (Lipsky 1980). The most powerful change processes are those that find their way into the values and practices of daily workers and professionals, so that they are self organized and reinterpreted into the front line of service operations. Nevertheless, conservative self organization can be a defensive reaction to change that does not retain the best aspects of previous value based approaches and interests of service users. Similarly, innovative dissipative self organization needs to be built on firm public service values. Good examples are local NGO activity that seeks to meet unmet need: for example local currencies and loans supplied via community banks, and green energy companies that promote shared micro investment into renewable solar power.

Large scale policies and processes that are overly centralized are vulnerable to errors, disruption and negative events. Examples are specially written computer programs that are not well integrated with existing standard hardware and software. If the supplying company that designed them goes bust, or they fail to deliver on their ambitious claims for a large public service, the consequences can be grave, not least a large waste of public money. "Anti fragile" prefers small scale, bottom up behaviors and activities that are seen to have normative collective values that can be copied and reproduced by others, achieved through applying common principles of design and application in different settings and context. Anti fragile sub systems and behavior is actually human action that adapts rapidly to ensure survival, and in part, its ability to do this is its preconceived state, including reference to its value base and stock of shared resources.

Such evolving practices are likely to include a strong element of local resourcing and local resource management, so that they are more resilient, and only at risk of an isolated local failure rather than a catastrophic national failure. Such resilience could be a computer system designed around already commonly available hardware and software, but connected to the local context, while some aspects are shared with other localities. These approaches are context driven, with some elements copied, rather than the whole approach being top down and idealized. Similarly resilient policies and management models take the best elements of what already works elsewhere, being careful to apply them as context specific. Piloting new policies in local areas and learning from them is often a better approach than a sudden national roll out of a major new initiative.

Values are at the core of public services and concepts of public intervention. They are the attractors in this complex system that provides the necessary attraction to order and stability. History has evolved public services to protect the weak and vulnerable, to ensure collective survival, to prevent society becoming chaotic and unstable in a way that reproduces the worst aspects of competitive human behavior, where people are only focused on their own survival and ignoring the needs of others. There is a long history of public values being related to defining and protecting basic human rights, the implementation of law and order to deliver fundamental rights, to prevent violence and abuse, and ensuring health and education are available to all, not only to the most powerful and wealthy. These values are anti-fragile and attract social stability and order.

It is the interactions between people in modern public organizations that define its activities, outputs and eventually outcomes. Relational aspects are central to public service management. These interactions follow particular patterns through formal and informal networks. Managers are often key connector hubs in these networks and have pivotal ability to influence via communication and message passing. General definitions of management have long recognized the importance of general managers in sharing information. Good communication is a key component of a successful organization. Similarly good management collaboration and peer support is another route to anti fragility and resilience. All too often managers are isolated in hierarchical power structures and exposed to an individualized, competitive sub culture. Perhaps this is why middle managers in public service organizations often describe their combined roles as impossible to deliver on. Public service values should dictate that they collaborate horizontally with their organizational peers.

Kahneman's (2012) Nobel prize winning work on the limits of rationality in human communications shows the numerous dysfunctional effects on organizational behavior including activities, transactions and outputs. Managers' powers are limited, in part due to their own personal history and bias, but they can develop some skills to do better at learning from past mistakes and enabling an organization to improve.

Organizations often have unrealistic expectations for recruiting senior managers and leaders. They look for an outstanding breadth of skills and often over commit themselves to finding an ideal person. Even if such a person can be found, they are burdened with very high expectations and an unrealistic range of responsibilities are passed to them.

The reality is that such management and leadership responsibilities are often better shared by small teams at each level in the organizations, so that a single person does not face unrealistic pressures, undue stress and an impossible workload. It is also more likely that a mix of general management skills will be coming from a small mix of senior staff rather than one person.

If an exceptional individual is able to succeed in a general role, this generates succession issues, as it becomes difficult to replace exceptional individuals. Considering the establishment of small team approaches to leadership and management also makes succession planning possible, because it becomes easier to cover vacancies and to think about rebalancing a team with the right mix of experience and strengths. To create clarity in a small team approach, it is common to have one more senior person, supported by a small number of others, who have similar, but more detailed responsibilities, or different functional specialisms. They can meet and communicate regularly together and share generic responsibilities and offer a reflective and considered position on key decisions going forward. Kahneman's (2012) work puts emphasis on the limitations and weaknesses of individual managers rather than their strengths and so it is important to find ways of connecting them into shared organizational patterns of responsibility and decision making, rather than isolating them, and putting them under pressure to compete as individuals. For example, when individual managers are busy and multi-tasking, Kahneman (2012: 41) notes, "system 1 has more influence on behaviour when system 2 is busy", and so the manager is then more likely to rely on emotional, historical and intuitive judgments. He gives a similar example where people needing to make a complex system 2 mathematics decision, find it more difficult when they are mildly physically active, rather than sitting down. General managers are prone to mistakes and poor judgments when isolated and under multiple pressures.

To ensure some stability, focus and continuity, all public organizations need a minimal core senior management element. No organization can exist without some element of core, because it would no longer be organized into a coherent entity and would be in a continuous state of instability and chaos. The core and its elements attract order, by setting base line rules and regulations; these should be based on recognizable and acceptable values. But they allow for a flexibility of practice around the core. The core is often defined by place and time. Key buildings are owned and used by the organizations; key activities take place there at certain times. The definition of the working day (for example, 8am to 4pm) provides periodic and temporal attraction to order and patterns of activities. The softer structures and cultures of the organization are defined in relation to this hard core. Every organization has to have some minimal organizational structure even though management writers and consultants frequently caution against seeing this structure and its design as any kind of solution or purpose in itself (Hudson 1999). The physical core provides an attractor state that sets the starting point for organizing the people and work practices within the organization. A building and series of timed organizational events draw people in a predictable but not static manner. The social and cultural identity, mission and operating principles of the core organization provide a dynamic attractor state that will have common influences on all workers, but also a creative element of individuality and diversity will remain on the periphery. Each individual will be pulled and attracted to elements of this cultural core but will interpret them in their own unique way. Here, there is a complex and creative dialogue between the attractor conformity structure of the organization and the individuality of the human agents that work there.

Communication and interaction are vital in the modern public service. If the best practices and outcomes are to emerge in the process of self organization, good lines of communication and interaction are needed. One of the best known writers on complexity theory and management in recent years, Ralph Stacey, found this to be such a truism that he developed an interest in psychological group processes and analysis. For him the value of the knowledge in a modern organization is not in the static recorded value of that knowledge, but in the living processes of analysis, synthesis and interaction about that knowledge, as the workers in the organization communicate their knowledge and work with it in the way that a potter works with clay or an artist with paper and paint. The use of knowledge is a creative process; it cannot easily be closed down to simple competencies or stored in static computer hardware. If such closure is attempted, losses in creative production are likely. The key to maximizing production and output becomes installing a collaborative approach to communication and interaction where ideas are shared and jointly developed rather than seen as the territory of individuals and the subject of fierce conflict and argument. Similarly, the wrong approach to audit might undermine creative organization and development, giving the message that no risks should be taken and suggesting a minimalist approach to action. Professionals need spaces and opportunities to come together to collaborate, share practices and influence the relationship between work activities, outputs and outcomes. If such groups are conservative in their self organizing, and resisting responsibilities, it is important to inject different human dynamics and to enable them to share areas of organizational responsibility. If all else fails, and such a conservative group cannot take responsibility for any aspect of the organization, and negative performance considerations result, managers may have no choice but to intervene wholeheartedly. When such difficult intervention is needed, it should be supported and sustained, as it is unlikely to be achieved by one person alone as they will be seen as a threat and unsupportive. It is therefore vital that they are not isolated in this difficult role. Such "balancing managerial feedback" requires organizational commitment and support.

The dominant logics of the classical approaches to management and economics evident in the 1980s had the effect of placing great emphasis on outcomes over process. This continued to evolve in the 1990s and into the new century with a strong focus on performance outcomes. This book has discussed the performance agenda in some detail, in particular in Chapter 4. A key argument was the need to re-engage process with outcome, to see process as part of the outcome agenda, not separate from it. Any process has a form of outcome and any outcome is the result of a process. A medical diagnosis may make a person feel better, and, because some activity is taking place, it can start to contribute to healing. A social work assessment is an opportunity to engage with a person, to offer some psychological intervention that may enable them to re-assess their own life and feel better about themselves. These process outcomes may not be immediately obvious to classical performance models, but processes that create spontaneous outcomes, both positive and negative, often unintended, are all around us. Teaching activity and lessons are no guarantee of learning, but some kind of outcome is guaranteed the moment a child or student walks into the classroom; their thinking and behavior will change because of that process. Will they become bored, day dream, or be inspired by some new knowledge? What is being argued here is a holistic and opening up approach to the relationship between process and outcome that moves away from the reductionist and rather negative discourse of conventional and classical performance management. Public service processes should be viewed as positive opportunities to add value and drive some initial output. If nothing else, they are relational, and relationships are at the core of human existence and how human beings define themselves. It is argued that the separation of professional processes and managerial outcomes is a dualism, a false dichotomy. Instead, this book has argued that professional and managerial conflicts and tensions are constantly being expressed and explored, with attempts made to resolve them, often because these tensions exist within the experience of individual people working with both manager and professional tasks.

Public service processes can have multiple outcomes, and the ability to understand the interaction of feedback between public policy processes and the public is vital to understand if the relationship between process and outcome is ever to be properly understood and maximized. In particular, the mechanics of feedback teaches that in some circumstances reinforcing feedback grows rapidly. In some circumstances reinforcing feedback loops occur where a maximum effort and action is needed to break a cycle of reinforcement that has a negative normative impact on collective public values: examples are exponential increases in specific local crimes, or rapidly rising housing costs that make housing unaffordable to below average wage earners. Assertive political leadership is likely to be particularly important in these circumstances, as it requires standing up for public values and working against a strong tide of anti-social reinforcement. An inability to stand against the negative social consequences of such reinforcing feedback might not just be political, but also a management responsibility.

The process of political democracy also provides a check on system behavior; it represents a democratic buffer against continuous political reinforcement of certain values and ideologies. The right to vote and any similar revelations of public confidence are far from perfect rational responses, but they provide a key element in the self organizing and self correcting society, in the same way that buying and selling trends and changing taxes and tax rates allow adjustment in the economy. Both democracy and markets have a key part to play in the complex society where disorder and instability can create edge of chaos experiences and tipping points, from which come new organizational forms and ideas.

The management, leadership and professional development of public employees also have a major part to play in developing creative and productive processes and outcomes. The ability of the public service worker to act, with a value driven courage, and conviction, and based on a public service ethos is important. This is different—but perhaps complementary—to producing a standardized manager who has achieved a set of uniform skill competencies.

The clear overlap between public service professionalism and managerial systems can be identified as a value based mind-set that is a willingness to embrace complexity, to attempt to deal with it because of serving the community and the public interest. Public service managers will not want to be only identified with the implementation of output based objectives. They need to be viewed as the creative managers of the numerous tensions in the public policy process. The state and government have placed them in this difficult context, it has a duty to allow them to face contradictions with integrity, rather than suggesting that the answers are always singular, simple and straightforward. Social and economic tensions can lead to destructive instability, but public service managers should offer important chances to turn the resulting disorder back into creative order. It is a responsibility that must be shared with democracy, via politicians and the wider community.

Bibliography

Alford, J. and Hughes, O. (2008) Public Value Pragmatism as the Next Phase of Public Management. *The American Review of Public Administration* 38: 130–148.

Alford, J. and O'Flynn, J. (2009) Making Sense of Public Value: Concepts, Critiques and Emergent Meanings. *International Journal of Public Administration* 32(3–4): 171–191.

Allen, P., Maguire, S. and McKelvey, B. (eds) (2011) *The Sage Handbook of Complexity and Management.* London: Sage.

Allen, P., Clark, N. and Perez-Trejo, F. (1992) Strategic Planning of Complex Economic Systems. *Review of Political Economy* 4(3): 275–290.

Am, O. (1996) *The Simple and the Complex: The Patterns of Life.* London: The Local Government Management Board.

Andrews, R. and Entwistle, T. (2014) *Public Service Efficiency: Reforming the Debate.* London: Routledge.

Association of Graduate Recruiters (2002) Members Want their New Recruits to Carry on Learning. *Association of Graduate Recruiters News.* www.agr.org.uk.

Attwood, M., Pedler, M., Pritchard, S. and Wilkinson, D. (2003) *Leading Change: A Guide to Whole Systems Working.* Bristol: The Policy Press.

Auditor General (2000) *Supporting Innovation: Managing Risk in Government Departments.* HC 864. London: The Stationery Office.

Audit Commission (1986) *Making a Reality of Community Care.* London: HMSO.

Audit Commission (1995) *In the Line of Fire: Value for Money in the Fire Service – the National Picture.* London: HMSO.

Audit Commission (2002) *Recruitment and Retention: A Public Service Workforce for the Twenty-first Century.* London: Audit Commission.

Australian Public Service Commission (2013) *Strengthening a Values Based Culture: A Plan for Integrating the APS Values into the Way we Work.* Canberra: Australian Government. http://goo.gl/ZUnaH.

Bar-Yam, Y., Read, R. and Taleb, N. (2014) The Precautionary Principle. www.fooledbyrandomness.com/pp2.pdf.

Barnes, M. (2012) *Care in Everyday Life: An Ethic of Care Practice.* Bristol: Policy Press.

Barnes, M., Matka, E. and Sullivan, H. (2003) Evidence, Understanding and Complexity: Evaluation in Non-linear Systems. *Evaluation* 9(3): 265–284.

Battram, A. (1996) *The Complexion: A Lexicon of Complexity.* London: The Local Government Management Board.

Battram, A. (1998) *Navigating Complexity: The Essential Guide to Complexity Theory in Business and Management.* London: The Industrial Society.

Beautement, P. and Broenner, C. (2011) *Complexity Demystified: A Guide for Practitioners.* Axminster: Triarchy Press.

Bellamy, C. (1999) Information Technology. In S. Farnham and D. Horton. *Public Service Management.* London: Macmillan.

Benington, J. and Moore, M.H. (eds) (2011) *Public Value: Theory and Practice.* London: Palgrave.

Bevan, G. and Hood, C. (2006) What's Measured is what Matters: Targets and Gaming in the English Public Health Care System. *Public Administration* 84(3): 517–538.

Blackman, T. (2001) Complexity Theory and the New Public Management. *Social Issues* 1(2). www.whb.co.uk/socialissues.

Bichard, M. (2000) Creativity, Leadership and Change. *Public Money and Management* 20(2): 41–46.

Boisot, M. (2011) Knowledge Management and Complexity. In P. Allen, S. Maguire and B. McKelvey *The Sage Handbook of Complexity and Management*. London: Sage.

Boons, F., van Buuren, A., Gerrits, L. and Teisman, G. (2009) Towards an Approach of Evolutionary Public Management. In G. Teisman., A. van Buuren and L. Gerrits (eds) *Managing Complex Governance Systems: Dynamics, Self Organisation and Coevolution in Public Investments*. London: Routledge.

Bottle, R. (1997) *The Death of Inflation*. London: Nicholas Brearley.

Bouckaert, G., Peters, G. and Verhoest, K. (2010) *The Coordination of Public Sector Organisations*. Basingstoke: Palgrave Macmillan.

Bourdieu, P. (1977) *Outline of Theory of Practice*. Cambridge: Cambridge University Press.

Boyne, G. (2002) Concepts and Indicators of Local Authority Peformance: An Evaluation of the Statutory Frameworks in England and Wales. *Public Money and Management* 22(2): 7–24.

Brewer, C. and Lait, J. (1980) *Can Social Work Survive?* London: Temple Smith.

Bryson, J.M. and Roering, W.D. (1988) Applying Private Sector Strategic Planning in the Public Sector. In J.M. Bryson. and R.C. Einsweiler (eds) *Strategic Planning*. San Francisco, CA: Jossey Bass.

Buchanan, M. (2004) Power Laws and the New Science of Complexity Management. *Strategy and Business* 34: 2–10. www.strategy-business.com/article/04107.

Byrne, D. (1998) *Complexity Theory and the Social Sciences: An Introduction*. London: Routledge.

Byrne, D. (2001) Complexity Science and Transformations in Social Policy. *Social Issues* 1(2). www.whb.co.uk/socialissues.

Byrne, D. (2011a) *Applying Social Science: The Role of Social Research in Politics, Policy and Practice*. Bristol: The Policy Press.

Byrne, D. (2011b) Exploring Organisational Effectiveness. In P. Allen, S. Maguire and B. McKelvey (eds) (2011) *The Sage Handbook of Complexity and Management*. London: Sage.

Byrne, D. and Callaghan, G. (2013) *Complexity Theory and the Social Sciences: The State of the Art*. London: Routledge.

Byrne, D. and Rogers, T. (1996) Divided Spaces – Divides School: An Exploration of the Spatial Relations of Social Division. *Sociological Research Online* 1(2). www.socresonline.org.uk.

Cabinet Office (1999) *Modernising Government*. Cm4310. London: TSO.

Cabinet Office Performance and Innovation Unit (2000) *e.gov: Electronic Government Services for the 21st Century*. London: Cabinet Office.

Cabinet Office Strategy Unit (2002) *Electronic Networks: Challenges for the Next Decade*. London: Cabinet Office.

Cairney, P. (2012) Complexity Theory in Political Science and Public Policy. *Political Studies Review* 10 (3): 346–358.

Campbell, J. (1993) *Edward Heath: A Biography*. London: Jonathan Cape.

Carley, M. (1980) *Rational Techniques in Policy Analysis*. London: Heinemann.

Castellani, B. and Hafferty, F. (2009) *Sociology and Complexity Science: A New Area of Inquiry*. Germany: Springer.

Causer, G. and Exworthy, M. (1999) Professionals as Managers across the Public Sector. In M. Exworthy and S. Halford. *Professionals and the New Managerialism in the Public Sector*. London: Open University Press.

Chapman, T. and Hough, M. (1998) *Evidence Based Practice: A Guide to Effective Practice*. HM Inspectorate of Probation, London: Home Office.

Chua, A. (2009) Exhuming IT Projects from their Graves: An Analysis of Eight Failure Cases and their Risk Factors. *Journal of Computer Information Systems* 49 (3): 31–39.

Cilliers, P. (1998) *Complexity and Postmodernism: Understanding Complex Systems*. London: Routledge.

Cilliers, P. (2011) Complexity, Poststructuralism and Organisation. In P. Allen, S. Maguire and B. McKelvey (eds) *The Sage Handbook of Complexity and Management*. London: Sage.

Clarke, J. and Newman, H. (1997) *The Managerial State*. London: Sage.

Cohen, J. and Stewart, I. (1994) *The Collapse of Chaos: Discovering Simplicity in a Complex World*. London: Viking.

Collinson, S. and Jay, M. (2012) *From Complexity to Simplicity*. London: Palgrave Macmillan.

Commission on Public Private Partnerships (2001) *The Final Report of the Commission on Public Private Partnerships*. London: Institute for Public Policy Research.

Conway, D. (1993) What do Managers do? *Community Care*. 19 August.

Corrigan, P. and Leonard, P. (1978) *Social Work Practice under Capitalism: A Marxist Approach*. London: Macmillan.

Coveney, P. and Highfield, P. (1995) *Frontiers of Complexity: The Search for Order in a Chaotic World*. London: Faber and Faber.

Cullen, Lord. (2001) *The Ladbroke Grove Rail Public Inquiry Reports*, 1 and 2. London: Health and Safety Executive. www.hse.gov.uk.

Cutler, T. and Waine, B. (2003) Advancing Public Accountability? The Social Services "Star" Ratings. *Public Money and Management* 23(2): 125–128.

Day, P. and Klein, R. (1987) *Accountabilities. Five Public Services*. London: Tavistock.

Department of Health (2001a) *Building Capacity and Partnership in Care: An Agreement between the Statutory and Independent Social Care, Health Care and Housing Sectors*. London: Department of Health.

Department of Health. (2001b) *NHS Performance Indicators: A Consultation*. London: Department of Health.

Department of Health (2002) *Information for Health*. London: Department of Health.

Desmarais, C. (2014) All Motivated by Public Service? The Links between Hierarchical Position and Public Service Motivation. *International Review of Administrative Sciences* 80(1): 131–150.

Dewson, S., Eccles, J., Tackey, N.D. and Jackson, A. (2000) *Measuring Soft Outcomes and Distance Travelled: A Review of Current Practice*. Brighton: Institute of Employment Studies. www.employment-studies.co.uk.

Drucker, P. (1964) *Managing for Results*. New York: Harper and Row.

Dunleavy, P. and Hood, C. (1994) From Old Public Administration to New Public Management. *Public Money and Management* 14(3): 9–16.

Dunleavy, P., Margetts, H., Bastow, S. and Tinkler, J. (2005) New Public Management is Dead – Long Live Digital-Era Governance. *Journal of Public Administration Research and Theory* 16: 467–494.

Eisenhardt, K. and Piezunka, H. (2011) Complexity Theory and Corporate Strategy. In P. Allen, S. Maguire and B. McKelvey (eds) *The Sage Handbook of Complexity and Management*. London: Sage.

Esser, J.K. (1998) Alive and Well after 25 Years: A Review of Groupthink Research. *Organisational Behavior and Human Decision Process* 73(2–3): 116–141.

Etzioni, A. (1967) Mixed Scanning: A Third Approach to Decision Making. *Public Administration Review* 27: 385–398.

Etzioni, A. (2014) Humble Decision Making. *Public Management Review* 16(5): 611–619.

Eve, R.A., Horsfall, S. and Lee, M.E. (eds) (1997) *Chaos, Complexity, and Sociology: Myths, Models and Theories*. Thousand Oaks, CA: Sage.

Exworthy, M. and Halford, S. (eds) (1999) *Professionals and the New Managerialism in the Public Sector*. Buckingham: Open University Press.

Farnham, D. and Horton, S. (eds) (1996) *Managing the Public Services*. 2nd edition. London: Macmillan.

Fenton, C. and Langley, A. (2011) Strategy as Practice and the Narrative Turn. *Organisational Studies* 32 (9): 1171–1196.

Financial Crisis Inquiry Commission (2011) *The Financial Crisis Inquiry Report*. New York: Public Affairs.

Flyvbjerg, B. and Budzier, A. (2011) Why Your IT Project May be Riskier Than You Think. *Harvard Business Review Idea Watch* 1271: 23–25.

Geyer, R. and Rihani, S. (2010) *Complexity and Public Policy: A New Approach to 21st Century Politics, Policy and Society*. London: Routledge.

Giddens, A. (1998) *The Third Way: The Renewal of Social Democracy*. Cambridge: Policy Press.

Giddens, A. (2000) *Critics of the Third Way*. Cambridge: Policy Press.

Gladwell, M. (2001) *The Tipping Point: How Little Things Can Make a Big Difference*. London: Abacus.

Glick, B. (2013) DWP Writes Off Millions of Pounds on Universal Credit IT, Damning NAO Report Reveals. *Computer Weekly*. 5 September. www.computerweekly.com/news/2240204715.

Goleman, D. (1996) *Emotional Intelligence: Why It Can Matter More than IQ*. London: Bloomsbury.

Gulla, J. (2012) Seven Reasons IT Projects Fail. *IT Today*. February. www.ibmsystemsmag.com.

Hamel, G. and Prahalad, C.K. (1994) *Competing for the Future*. Boston, MA: Harvard Business Press.

Handy, C. (1990) *Understanding Organisations*. London: Penguin.

Harmon, P. (2007) *Business Process Change: A Guide for Business Managers and BPM and Six Sigma Professionals*. 2nd edition. San Francisco, CA: Morgan Kaufmann.

Hartley, J. and Allison, M. (2000) The Role of Leadership in the Modernisation and Improvement of Public Services. *Public Money and Management* 20(2): 35–40.

Haynes, P. (1999) *Complex Policy Planning. The Government Strategic Management of the Social Care Market*. Aldershot: Ashgate.

Haynes, P. (2005) New Development: The Demystification of Knowledge Management for Public Services. *Public Money and Management* 25(2): 131–135.

Haynes, P. (2007) Chaos, Complexity and Transformations in Social Care Policy in England. *Public Money and Management* 27(3): 199–206.

Haynes, P. (2012) *Public Policy beyond the Financial Crisis: An International Comparative Study*. London: Routledge.

Haynes, P., et al. (2011) *Brighton Systems and Complex Systems Toolkit Framework*. Brighton: University of Brighton. www.brighton.ac.uk/sass/complex-systems/ToolkitFramework.pdf.

Hazy, J. and Uhl-Bien, M. (2013) Towards Operationalizing Complexity Leadership: How Generative, Administrative and Community-building Leadership Practices Enact Organizational Outcomes. *Leadership* 1–26. http://digitalcommons.unl.edu/managementfacpub/108.

Healey, P. (1997) *Collaborative Planning*. London: Routledge.

Hennessy, P. (2000) *The Prime Minister: The Office and its Holders since 1945*. London: Penguin.

Hill, M. (1997) *The Policy Process in the Modern State*. 3rd edition. London: Prentice Hill.

Hill, M. and Hupe, P. (2002) *Implementing Public Policy: Governance in Theory and Practice*. London: Sage.

Hirst, J. (2003) Trouble Ahead? *Public Finance*. 17 January.

Holloway, J. (1999) Managing Performance. In A. Rose and A. Lawton, (eds) *Public Services Management*. London: Prentice Hall.

Hood, C. (1991) A Public Management for All Seasons? *Public Administration* 69(1): 3–19.

Hood, C. (1995) The "New Public Management" in the 1980s: Variations on a Theme. *Accounting, Organization and Society* 20(2–3): 93–109.

Horton, S. and Farnham, S. (1999) *Public Management in Britain*. London: Macmillan.

House of Commons Committee of Public Accounts (2013) *Cabinet Office: Improving Government Procurement and the Impact of Government's ICT Savings Initiatives. Sixth Report of Session 2013–2014*. London: House of Commons.

House of Commons Committee of Public Accounts (2014) *BBC Digital Media Initiative. Fifty-second Report of Session 2013–2014*. London: House of Commons.

Howe, D. (1986) *Social Workers, Their Professional Role and Tasks*. Aldershot: Avebury.

Hudson, M. (1999) *Managing without Profit: The Art of Managing Third-sector Organisations*. 2nd edition. London: Penguin.

Hughes, O. (1998) *Public Management and Administration: An Introduction*. 2nd edition. London: Macmillan.

Hughes, O. (2012) *Public Management and Administration: An Introduction*. 4th edition. London: Macmillan.

Illich, I. (1973) *Celebration of Awareness*. London: Penguin.

Iszatt-White, M. (2010) Strategic Leadership: The Accomplishment of Strategy as a Perennially Unfinished Project. *Leadership* 6(4): 409–424.

Jeffrey, B. (1997) Creating Participatory Structures in Local Government. *Local Government Policy Making*, 23(4): 25–31.

Joyce, P. (1999) *Strategic Management for the Public Services*. Buckingham: Open University Press.

Kahneman, D. (2012) *Thinking, Fast and Slow*. London: Penguin.

Kakabadse, A. (1982) *Culture of the Social Services*. Aldershot: Gower.

Kauffman, S. (1995) *At Home in the Universe: The Search for Laws of Self organization and Complexity*. London. Viking.

Keene, A. (2000) Complexity Theory: The Changing Role of Leadership. *Industrial and Commercial Training* 32(1): 15–18.

Kernaghan, K. (2000) The Post-Bureaucratic Organisation and Public Service Values. *International Review of Administrative Sciences* 66(1): 91–104.

Kernick, D. (2004) Allocating Limited Health Care Resources. In D. Kernick (ed.) *Complexity and Healthcare Organization: A View from the Street*. Oxford: Radcliffe Medical Press.

Kickert, W. (2010) Managing Emergent and Complex Change: The Case of Dutch Agencification. *International Review of Administrative Sciences* 76(3): 489–515.

Kiel, D.L. (1994) *Managing Chaos and Complexity in Government*. San Francisco, CA: Jossey Bass.

Kiel, L.D. and Elliott, E. (1997) *Chaos Theory in the Social Sciences: Foundations and Applications*. Ann Arbor: University of Michigan Press.

Klijn, E. (1997) *Managing Complex Networks: Strategies for the Public Sector*. London: Sage.

Klijn, E. and Koppenjan, F. (2000) Public Management and Policy Networks: Foundations of a Network Approach to Governance. *Public Management Review* 2(2): 135–158.

Kontopoulos, K. (1993) *The Logics of Social Structure*. Cambridge: Cambridge University Press.

Lawton, A. (1998) *Ethical Management for the Public Services*. Buckingham: Open University Press.

Leach, S., Stewart, and Walsh, K. (1994) *The Changing Organisation and Management of Local Government*. London: Macmillan.

Lee, C. and Zachary, R. (2013) Democracy's New Discipline: Public Deliberation as Organisational Strategy. *Organisational Studies* 34 (5–6): 733–753.

Likert, R. (1961) *New Patterns of Management*. New York: McGraw-Hill.

Lindbolm, C.E. (1959) The Science of Muddling Through. *Public Administration Review* 19(2): 79–88.

Lipnack, J. and Stamps, J. (1994) *The Age of the Network: Organizing Principles for the 21st Century*. East Junction: Oliver Wright.

Lipsky, M. (1980) *Street Level Bureaucracy*. New York: Russell Sage Foundation.

Lissack, M. and Roos, J. (1999) *The Next Common Sense: The E-managers Guide to Mastering Complexity*. London: Nicholas Brealey.

Luhmann, N. (1995) *Social Systems*. Stanford, CA: Stanford University Press.

Luthans, F., Hodgetts, R.M. and Rosenkrantz, S.A. (1988) *Real Managers*. Cambridge, MA: Ballinger.

Lynch, R. (1993) *Lead! How Public and Nonprofit Managers Can Bring out the Best in Themselves and their Organizations*. San Francisco, CA: Jossey Bass.

MacGregor, D. (1960) *The Human Side of Enterprise*. New York: McGraw-Hill.

MacLean, D. and MacIntosh, R. (2011) Organizing at the Edge of Chaos: Insights from Action Research. In: P. Allen, S. Maguire and B. McKelvey (eds) *The Sage Handbook of Complexity and Management*. London: Sage, pp. 423–458.

Mance, H. (2013) Why Big IT Projects Crash. *The Financial Times*. 18 September. www.ft.com.

Mandelbrot, B. and Hudson, R. (2008) *The Misbehaviour of Markets: A Fractal View of Risk, Ruin and Reward*. London: Profile Books.

Marmot, M. (2010) *Fair Society, Healthy Lives. The Marmot Review: Executive Summary. Strategic Review of Health Inequalities in England post 2010*. London: The Marmot Review. www.ucl.ac.uk/marmotreview.

Marion, R. and Uhl-Bien, M. (2007) Introduction to the Special Issue on Leadership and Complexity. *The Leadership Quarterly* 18(4): 293–296.

Marsh, D. (ed.) (1992) *Implementing Thatcherite Policies: Audit of an Era*. Buckingham: Open University Press.

Marsh, D. (ed.) (1998) *Comparing Policy Networks*. Buckingham: Open University Press.

Mazzucato, M. (2011) *The Entrepreneurial State*. London: Demos.

McGuire, M. and Agranoff, R. (2011) The Limitations of Public Management Networks. *Public Administration* 89(2): 265–284.

McLoughlin, I. and Clark, J. (1995) Technological Change at Work. In N. Heap, R. Thomas, G. Einon, R. Mason, and H. MacKay. *Information Technology and Society*. London: Sage.

Meadows, D. (2009) *Thinking in Systems: A Primer*. London: Earthscan.

Medd, W. (2001) Complexity and the Policy Process. *Social Issues* 1(2). www.whb.co.uk/socialissues.

Merali, Y. and Allen, P. (2011) Complexity and Systems Thinking. In P. Allen, S. Maguire and B. McKelvey (eds) *The Sage Handbook of Complexity and Management*. London: Sage.

Merrington, S. and Hine, J. (2001) *A Handbook for Evaluating Probation Work with Offenders*. London: Home Office.

Meynhardt, T. (2009) Public Value Inside: What is Public Value Creation. *International Journal of Public Administration* 32(3–4): 192–219.

Miller, W.R. and Rollnick, S. (2002) *Motivational Interviewing: Preparing People to Change*. 2nd edition. New York: Guilford Press.

Minogue, M., Polidano, C. and Hulme, D. (1998) *Beyond the New Public Management. Changing Ideas and Practice in Governance*. London: Edward Elgar.

Mintzberg, H. (1973) *The Nature of Managerial Work*. New York: Harper and Row.

Mintzberg, H. (1994) *The Rise and Fall of Strategic Planning*. London: Prentice Hall.

Morin, E. (2006) Restricted Complexity, General Complexity. Presented at the Colloquium Intelligence de la complexité: épistémologie et pragmatique. Cerisy-La-Salle, France. 26 June 2005. Trans. Carlos Gershenson. http://cogprints.org/5217/1/Morin.pdf.

Morris, S. (1998) *The Handbook of Management Fads*. London: Thorogood.

Mullins, L. (1996) *Management and Organisational Behaviour*. 4th edition. London: Pitman Publishing.

Mwita, J.I. (2000) Performance Management Model: A Systems-based Approach to Public Service Quality. *The International Journal of Public Sector Management* 13(1): 19–37.

National Audit Office (2011) *The Cabinet Office: Implementing the Government ICT Strategy: Six Month Review of Progress*. House of Commons 1594 Session 2010–2012. London: National Audit Office.

Newman, J. (2001) *Modernising Governance: New Labour, Policy and Society*. London: Sage.

Oakeshott, M. (1994) Rationalism in Politics. In D. McKevitt, and A. Lawton. *Public Sector Management: Theory, Critique and Practice*. London: Sage.

OECD (2001a) *Management of Large Public IT Projects: Case Studies*. Public Management Service. Paris: OECD Publishing. www.oecd.org/puma/.

OECD (2001b) The Hidden Threat to E-government: Avoiding Large Government IT Failures. *PUMA Policy Brief* No 8. Paris: OECD Publishing. www.oecd.org/puma/.

OECD (2007) *OECD Reviews of Human Resource Management in Government*. Paris: OECD Publishing.

OECD (2012) *PISA 2012 Results: What Students Know and Can Do: Student Performance in Mathematics, Reading and Science* (Volume I). Paris: OECD Publishing. www.oecd.org/pisa/keyfindings/pisa -2012-results-volume-i.htm.

Office for Government Commerce (2001a) *Draft Guidelines for Managing Risk*. London: Cabinet Office.

Office for Government Commerce (2001b) *Successful IT: Modernising Government in Action*. London: Cabinet Office.

Office for Government Commerce (2002a) *Managing Risk*. London: Cabinet Office.

Office for Government Commerce (2002b) *Introduction to PRINCE2 – Management Overview*. www.ogc. gov.uk/prince.

Office of the Deputy Prime Minister (2001) *Strong Local Leadership – Quality Public Services*. London: TSO.

Ormerod, P. (1998) *Butterfly Economics*. London: Faber.

Ormerod, P. (2005) *Why Most Things Fail: Evolution, Extinction and Economics*. London: Faber and Faber.

Ormerod, P. (2012) *Positive Linking: How Networks are Revolutionising Your World*. London: Faber and Faber.

Oropeza, J. and Perron, M. (2013) *Citizenship Participation in Latin America: Innovations to Strengthen Governance. Evidence and Lessons From Latin America (ELLA)*. London: Department of International Development and Fundar. http://ella.practicalaction.org/sites/default/files/130516_CitPar_GOV_GUIDE.pdf.

Osborne, D.E. and Gaebler, T. (1992) *Reinventing Government. How the Entrepreneurial Spirit is Transforming the Public Sector*. Reading, MA: Addison-Wesley.

Osborne, S., Radnor, Z. and Nasi, G. (2013) A New Theory for Public Service Management? Toward a (Public) Service-Dominant Approach. *The American Review of Public Administration* 43(2): 135–158.

Osborne, S., Radnor, Z., Vidal, I. and Kinder, T. (2014) A Sustainable Business Model for the Public Services Organisations? *Public Management Review* 16(2): 165–172.

Pal, L.A. (2012) *Frontiers of Governance: The OECD and Global Public Management Reform*. Basingstoke: Palgrave Macmillan.

Parker, D. and Stacey, R. (1994) *Chaos, Management and Economics: The Implications of Non Linear Thinking*. London. Institute of Economic Affairs (IEA).

Peters, S. (2012) *The Chimp Paradox: The Mind Management Programme for Confidence, Success and Happiness*. London: Vermilion.

Pierpaolo, A. and McKelvey, B. (2011) From Skew Distributions to Power-Law Science. In P. Allen, S. Maguire and B. McKelvey. *The Sage Handbook of Complexity and Management*. London. Sage.

Plsek, P.E. and Wilson, T. (2001) Complexity, Leadership, and Management in Healthcare Organizations. *BMJ* 323(7315): 746–749.

Pollitt, C. (1984) *Manipulating the Machine: Changing Patterns of Ministerial Departments 1960–1983*. London: George Allen and Unwin.

Pollitt, C. (1990) *Managerialism and the Public Services: The Anglo-American Experience*. Oxford: Basil Blackwell.

Pollitt, C. (2009) Complexity Theory and Evolutionary Public Administration: A Sceptical Afterword. In G. Teisman., A. van Buuren and L. Gerrits (eds) *Managing Complex Governance Systems: Dynamics, Self Organisation and Coevolution in Public Investments*. London: Routledge.

Pollitt, C. (2013) 40 Years of Public Management Reform in UK Central Government – Promises, Promises … *Politics and Policy* 41(4): 465–480.

Pollitt, C. and Bouckaert, G. (2004) *Public Management Reform: A Comparative Analysis*. 2nd edition. Oxford: Oxford University Press.

Porter, M.E. (1980) *Competitive Strategy. Techniques for Analyzing Industries and Competitors*. London: Macmillan.

Pugh, D.S., Hickson, D.J. and Hinings, C.R. (1983) *Writers on Organisations*. 3rd edition. London: Penguin.

Radnor, Z. and Osborne, S. (2013) Lean: A Failed Theory for Public Services? *Public Management Review* 15(2): 265–287.

Radnor, Z., Osborne, S., Kinder, T. and Mutton, J. (2014) Operationalizing Co-Production in Public Services Delivery: The Contribution of Service Blueprinting. *Public Management Review* 16(3): 402–423.

Rhodes, M., Murphy, J., Muir, J. and Murray, J. (2011) *Public Management and Complexity Theory: Richer Decision-Making in Public Services*. London: Routledge.

Rhodes, R.A.W. (1997) *Understanding Governance: Policy Networks, Governance, Reflexivity and Accountability*. Buckingham: Open University.

Rhodes, R.A.W. (2000) *From Government to Governance*. London: Public Policy and Management Association.

Ricaurte-Quijano, C. (2013) *Self-Organisation in Tourism Planning: Complex Dynamics of Planning, Policy Making, and Tourism Governance in Santa Elena, Ecuador*. Ph.D. Thesis. University of Brighton, UK.

Room, G. (2011) *Complexity, Institutions and Public Policy. Agile Decision Making in a Turbulent World*. Cheltenham: Edward Elgar.

Rouse, J. (1999) Performance Management, Quality Management and Contracts. In S. Horton and D. Farnham (eds) *Public Management in Britain*. London: Macmillan.

Ryan-Collins, J., Greenham, T., Werner, R. and Jackson, A. (2012) *Where Does Money Come From? A Guide to the UK Monetary and Banking System*. London: NEF.

Sanderson, I. (2000) Evaluation in Complex Policy Systems. *Evaluation* 6(4): 433–454.

Sardar, Z. and Abrams, I. (1999) *Introducing Chaos*. London: Icon Books.

Schon, D. (1991) *The Reflective Practitioner*. Aldershot: Avebury.

Seddon, J. (2008) *Systems Thinking in the Public Sector*. Axminster: Triarchy Press.

Self, P. (1993) *Government by the Market? The Politics of Public Choice*. London: Macmillan.

Simon, H. (1957) *Administrative Behaviour*. 2nd edition. New York: Macmillan.

Smith, P. (1995) On the Unintended Consequences of Publishing Performance Data in the Public Sector. *International Journal of Public Administration* 18(2): 277–310.

Snowden, D. and Boone, M. (2007) A Leader's Framework for Decision Making. *Harvard Business Review* November: 69–77.

Solace Enterprises (2013) *Asking the Right Questions: The Need for Transformational and New Contextual Leadership Skills for Local Authority Chief Executives*. London: Solace Enterprises. www.solace.org.uk/knowledge/reports_guides/SOLACE_leadership_skills_screen.pdf.

Stacey, R.D. (1995) The Science of Complexity: An Alternative Perspective for Strategic Change Processes. *Strategic Management Journal* 16: 477–495.

Stacey, R.D. (2000) *Strategic Management and Organisational Dynamics: The Challenge of Complexity*. London: Prentice Hall.

Stacey, R.D. (2001) *Complex Responsive Processes in Organisations*. London: Routledge.

Stacey, R.D. (2011) *Strategic Management and Organisational Dynamics: The Challenge of Complexity*. 6th edition. London: FT Press.

Sterman, J. (2012) Sustaining Sustainability: Creating a Systems Science in a Fragmented Academy and Polarised World. In M. Weinstein and R. Turner (eds) *Sustainability Science: The Emerging Paradigm and the Urban Environment*. New York: Springer.

Stewart, I. (1995) *Nature's Numbers*. London: Weidenfeld and Nicholson.

Stewart, J. and Ranson, S. (1994) Management in the Public Domain. In D. McKevitt and A. Lawton. *Public Sector Management: Theory, Critique and Practice*. London: Sage.

Stiglitz, J.E., Sen, A. and Fitoussi, J.P. (2010) *Mis-measuring our Lives: Why GDP Doesn't Add Up. The Report by the Commission on the Measurement of Economic Performance and Social Progress*. London: The New Press.

Strange, S. (1972) The Dollar Crisis 1971. *International Affairs* 48(2): 191–216.

Streatfield, P.J. (2001) *The Paradox of Control in Organizations*. London: Routledge.

Talbot, C. (2009) Public Value – The Next "Big Thing" in Public Management. *International Journal of Public Administration* 32(3–4): 167–170.

Taleb, N. (2007) *The Black Swan. The Impact of the Highly Improbable*. London: Penguin.

Taleb, N. (2012) *Antifragile: Things that Gain from Disorder*. London: Penguin.

Taylor, J. (1999) New Technologies and Public Management: Issues for the Information Age. In A. Rose. and A. Lawton (eds) *Public Services Management*. London: Prentice Hall.

Teisman, G., van Buuren, A. and Gerrits, L. (eds) (2009) *Managing Complex Governance Systems: Dynamics, Self Organisation and Coevolution in Public Investments*. London: Routledge.

Thompson, G., Frances, J., Levacic, R. and Mitchell, J. (eds) (1991) *Networks, Markets and Hierarchies: The Coordination of Social Life*. London: Sage.

Tullock, G. (1976) *The Vote Motive*. London: The Institute for Economic Affairs.

Turban, E., McLean, E. and Wetherbe, J. (2002) *Information Technology for Management: Transforming Business in the Digital Economy*. 3rd edition. New York: Wiley.

Uhl-Bien, M., Marion, R. and McKelvey, B. (2007) Complexity Leadership Theory: Shifting Leadership from the Industrial Age to the Knowledge Era. *The Leadership Quarterly* 18(4): 298–318.

Urry, J. (2003) *Global Complexity*. Cambridge: Polity Press.

Van Dooren, W., Bouckaert, G. and Halligan, J. (2010) *Performance Management in the Public Sector.* London: Routledge.

Verheijen, T. and Dobrolyubova, Y. (2007) Performance Management in the Baltic States and Russia: Success against the Odds? *International Review of Administrative Sciences* 73(2): 205–215.

Walker, A. (1984) *Social Planning: A Strategy for Socialist Welfare.* Oxford: Basil Blackwell.

Walker, R., Brewer, G., Bozeman, B., Moon, M. and Wu, J. (2013) An Experimental Assessment of Public Ownership and Performance: Comparing Perceptions in East Asia and the United States. *Public Management Review* 15(8): 1208–1228.

Walsh, K. (1995) *Public Services and Market Mechanisms. Competition, Contracting and the New Public Management.* London: Macmillan.

Warner, M. (2008) Reversing Privatization, Rebalancing Government Reform: Markets, Deliberation and Planning. *Policy and Society* 27: 163–174.

Watson, B. (2002) Management Problems in the Public Sector. *Public Management and Money* 22(3): 5–7.

Wenger, E. (1998) *Communities of Practice: Learning, Meaning, and Identity.* Cambridge: Cambridge University Press.

Whiddet, S. and Kandola, B. (2000) Fit for the Job? *People Management.* 25 May.

Whittington, R. (2006) Completing the Practice Turn in Strategy Research. *Organisational Studies* 27(5): 613–634.

Williams, M. (2000) Sokal, Chaos and the Way Forward. *Sociology* 34(2): 341–346.

Wood, R. (2000) *Managing Complexity: How Businesses Can Adapt and Prosper in the Connected Economy.* London: Economist Books.

Woodhead, C. (2002) *Class War London.* London: Little Brown.

World Values Survey (2012) World Values Survey. Stockholm. www.worldvaluessurvey.org/wvs.jsp.

Index